A Teachable Moment

A Facilitator's Guide to Activities for Processing, Debriefing, Reviewing and Reflection

Jim Cain
Michelle Cummings
Jennifer Stanchfield

KENDALL/HUNT PUBLISHING COMPANY
4050 Westmark Drive   Dubuque, Iowa 52002

Photos courtesy of Jim Cain: 1, 2, 3, 5, 17, 18, 22, 23, 24, 25, 28, 36, 37, 38, 40, 50, 78, 79, 104, 105, 143, 147, 153, 183, 184, 186, 189, 190, 267, 251, 252, 253, 256

Photos courtesy of Michelle Cummings: 4, 23, 24, 25, 26, 41, 44, 46, 48, 49, 53, 56, 57, 58, 59, 61, 64, 67, 68, 69, 71, 72, 76, 80, 81, 82, 83, 84, 86, 88, 89, 90, 92, 94, 95, 96, 97, 99, 101, 109, 112, 114, 116, 117, 118, 124, 129, 130, 131, 134, 135, 137, 139, 144, 145, 151, 157, 158, 159, 165, 166, 174, 177, 178, 179, 180, 181, 182, 192, 196, 200, 205, 206, 207, 208, 210, 211, 212, 213, 215, 219, 220, 222, 224, 226, 227, 229, 232, 237, 238, 246, 247, 268, 254, 255

Photos courtesy of Jennifer Stanchfield: 42, 118, 119, 263, 269

Photos courtesy of Photos.com: 46, 51, 55, 56, 66, 77, 106, 107, 110, 111, 118, 123, 126, 132, 133, 136, 139, 148, 154, 155, 156, 160, 162, 167, 168, 170, 172, 179, 193, 194, 199, 214, 225, 228, 236, 246, 248, 249

Photos courtesy of Training Wheels: 219, 230

The back cover photograph was furnished by
The Management Adventure Program (MAP)
of Milan, Italy. *www.mapsrl.com*

Copyright © 2005 by Jim Cain, Michelle Cummings, and Jennifer Stanchfield

ISBN 978-0-7575-1782-2

Printed in the United States of America
10   9   8   7   6   5   4   3   2

Contents

Activity Section

A Brief History

It all began with a single spark.

Jim Cain
Michelle Cummings
Jennifer Stanchfield

While it can be difficult to pin down the start of a significant project to a single point in history, our story is a bit different. In January of 2000, we found ourselves in the same place, at the same time. Jennifer Stanchfield was presenting a workshop on creative debriefing and reflection techniques at the annual Association for Challenge Course Technology (ACCT) conference. The workshop description in the conference program was tremendously understated, as we are sure most of those attending would attest. Simply stated, something wonderful happened. For a few brief hours that morning, we explored a wider variety of reviewing techniques than we had ever thought possible.

Jennifer had brought dozens of interesting props and ideas, and used words like debriefing, reflection, processing and reviewing to describe an unlimited bag of possibilities. The activity she shared with common postcards was magical. Michelle Cummings was there, and brought along some of her truly unique processing props. Who can forget the first time they saw a "body part debriefing bag?" Jim Cain joined us too, and shared his "virtual slideshow" clicker and other ideas.

We discussed topics like debriefing while exploring multiple intelligences, learning styles, MBTI (Myers-Briggs Type Indicators) styles and activities for corporate audiences, youth programs and large and small groups. Some of those attending were looking for new techniques that they could take to wilderness programs with minimal props but maximal effect. One youth group leader mentioned that she had the same group every Tuesday evening for the entire year and needed 52 different way to process.

1

Even with a double session, we ran out of time. The next group was waiting for the room. The conversation spilled out into the hallway. We kept sharing, talking, probing for more information. The conversation lasted into lunchtime. Phone calls. Emails. Co-presenting at other conferences. And finally, a thought. This stuff is great, we need to share it.

And the result of that initial spark is the book you now hold in your hands.

The educational philosopher John Dewey, who is often referred to as the "father of experiential education," believed that in order to truly learn from an experience, there must be time for reflection. Clifford Knapp's book "Lasting Lessons," and his recent writings on the subject of reflection illustrate the importance of this simple but often overlooked component of our educational process. Theorists and practitioners in the field of experiential education and adventure-based and active learning emphasize the value of processing, debriefing and reviewing as one of the philosophical foundations of these fields.

It is our observation that while many practitioners find this subject very beneficial, they also find it challenging to present to their audiences. We wanted to help.

In our roles as experiential educators, corporate trainers, youth workers, challenge course facilitators, leaders and most recently co-authors, we have come to understand that reflection is an integral part of the experience. Challenging yes, but essential, and often the most rewarding component of the programs we create and present. Reflection, processing, debriefing and reviewing bring learning to life!

This is what drives our passion. The following pages present some of the great treasures we have created, shared, researched, traded, borrowed and experienced. Enjoy!

The Value of Reflection

*Experience in itself is neither productive nor unproductive, it is how
you reflect on it that makes it significant or not significant . . .*

Gavin Bolton, 1979
Towards a Theory of Drama in Education

For more than a century, educators, philosophers, facilitators and practitioners have promoted debriefing (and the other prominent expressions for it, such as processing, reviewing and reflection) as an essential part of learning. John Dewey, Bacon (1983), Gass (1993), Nadler and Luckner (1992) and other professionals (Smith, Knapp, Greenaway) have written considerable content on the value of internally processing experience. Yet, even with this level of support and recognition, the practice of reflection is too often discounted or neglected.

In modern society, people are not taught to be reflective learners. Adults are bombarded with endless items on their "to do" lists. Children are programmed in 50 minute increments throughout their school day, followed by structured activities after school and homework in the evening. How often do people just sit down under a tree, and rest, refresh, reflect, think, draw or journal? In this century, we live with a considerable amount of background noise, schedules and other factors that consume nearly all of our waking hours, leaving little time for what we perceive as the luxury of reflection.

Photo courtesy of Jeff Baird, High 5.

The challenge for educational practitioners then, is to swim against the current, to take participants and group members that live in a world without time for reflection, and help them find the time. To help them "make" the time. And not just so that we can check it off our "to do" list. "Yep, I reflected for four minutes today. Time to move on!" The goal then, if we are passionate enough about it is to show the way.

One of the most basic models of our work, the experiential learning cycle (Kolb), proposes that after activity comes reflection, followed by application of the new information we have learned. The complete cycle is required for "learning" to take place. Some "educators" unfortunately interrupt the model after the activity segment, and then are surprised when their "students" fail to retain the information presented.

When John Dewey wrote about experiential education in the last century, he put forth the idea that people do not learn solely from being included in an experience. He believed that there must be some time for reflection in order to truly learn from an experience. Recent information on brain mapping and brain-based learning gives us scientific proof that time for reflection and the use of a variety of reflective techniques facilitate learning.

In Eric Jensen's book "Teaching with the Brain in Mind" he shares research that shows that this type of reflection is not just beneficial but necessary. Jensen shares scientific work in regard to creating the most enriching learning environments. He cites work by William Greenough who, in his research over the past twenty years, has found that two critical ingredients are necessary for an enriched learning environment: challenge and feedback. Challenge and novelty are important according to Greenough who also emphasizes the value of problem solving, critical thinking, relevant projects and complex activities (Jensen, 1998). Maximizing learner feedback is the other integral piece of learning he emphasizes. This scientific evidence for the experiential methods of balancing action and reflection not only supports the whole philosophy of experiential education, but emphasizes the value of creating a variety of ways to help learners reflect on experiences for maximum outcomes.

Processing helps learners make connections between their educational experiences, real life and future learning. It helps learners realize that they can apply the lessons they learn and skills they use in a "contrived environment" such as a classroom or challenge course to real life issues such as resolving a conflict with friends, co-workers or significant others. Processing helps create the purpose, meaning and focus of an activity

as it helps learners take advantage of teachable moments.

So why is the reflective side of experiential education often skipped in educational programming? Why do facilitators share that this is one of the aspects they find most challenging? In writing this book we have shared our experiences struggling with this question. In our observations it seems many are intimidated by processing because they think it is boring, or they do not leave enough time for reviewing. Hands-on practitioners are often so motivated by exciting and engaging group challenges that they do not make the time for what they see as the less engaging "task" of debriefing.

With the writing of this book, we challenge practitioners to think of reflection in a different way. Processing activities can be just as dynamic and engaging as challenge course initiatives or group initiatives, especially with a new frame of mind towards recognizing that reflection is not that "thing" that comes at the end of the activity. It is much more important than that! It is that thing that creates the value and wonder in learning; it is the way ideas come together as a lasting lesson.

There is no one set way to process or one perfect time to process. Using a variety of techniques and using activities that give learners the power to take the lead in reflection are the most engaging and effective ways of viewing processing.

Steve Simpson of the Institute for Experiential Education has coined the term "participant directed processing." In this philosophy of processing, participants decide what meaning is attached to an activity or experience. There may be some guidance from the facilitator initially, but these activities allow for the spontaneity of individual interpretation of experience. You will find that the philosophy of *Participant-Directed Processing* is a philosophical underpinning of this book.

In this orientation towards processing, participants decide what meaning to attach to the activity rather than being involved in a didactic discussion. This view of processing is a departure from the norm in many educational settings. It requires that the facilitator give up some power, giving control of learning directions to the participants, who are the main focus of the experience. The destination might change, but that is the value of what we do—helping individuals and groups create meaningful learning experiences that will enrich their lives.

A Continuum of Processing Techniques

Buzz Bocher, Dan Miller and Steve Simpson

One of the more exciting trends in experiential education is the recent attention given to processing techniques. This book, for example, could not have been written twenty years ago, because there would not have been a sufficient number of innovative processing techniques to fill a book. Today an experiential educator can attend any workshop on processing, and an open discussion among the participants will easily create a list of 10–20 distinct and interesting ways to debrief an experience.

There are, in fact, so many different ways to process that it is important for each experiential educator to carefully think about which activities are most effective for their group at the appropriate time and place in group development. It is not enough to have a grab bag of processing tricks that can be chosen at random just to provide variety in processing; various techniques have unique strengths and weaknesses, and not all techniques are appropriate for all situations. Just as a competent experiential educator has novice, intermediate, and advanced challenges depending on the level of expertise of the group, so should he or she have processing techniques befitting the skill level and the needs of a specific group.

One basic way to organize processing techniques is to arrange them according to the degree to which they direct participants toward pre-determined outcomes. In some instances, there are very specific objectives the facilitator and group are aiming to accomplish, and the processing techniques used blatantly steer participants toward very specific results. In other situations, a facilitator is more interested in letting the participants take the processing in the direction of their choice, and the processing technique reflects that level of autonomy.

Maybe this concept of "situational" processing would be easiest to picture as a continuum (See Figure 1). One extreme on the continuum would be participant-centered and the other extreme facilitator-centered. The participant-centered end would have no facilitator manipulation at all—a total absence of formal processing, either because the experience is so powerful that processing would merely point out the obvious (e.g., why process a spectacular sunset?) or the participants are so cognizant of the experiential education progression that they will process on their own. Many experiential educators know this type of processing by the aptly coined term, *Mountains Speak for Themselves* (MST) (Gass, 1993).

The opposite extreme of the continuum then would be processing in which the facilitator exercises maximum control over the processing. An example of a technique very near this end would be frontloading, whereby facilitators overtly tell participants what they should get out of an activity even before they do it. The purpose of this method, also called the Metaphoric Model (Bacon, 1983), is to have participants think about the primary lesson of the activity while the lesson is taking place. For example, a facilitator may tell a group of people undergoing drug treatment that each step of a difficult hike is like one step toward sobriety. Then when participants complain that the hike is too hard, they know (even without being told) that giving up on the hike is analogous to giving up on their treatment program.

Figure 1

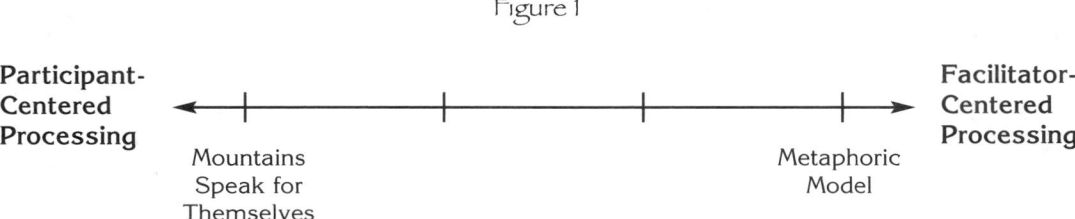

The most common form of processing, a question and answer session immediately following an experience, probably falls to the right of center. Often called OB Plus (OB+), the facilitator guides the direction of reflection by the careful choice of questions for the participants to answer (Priest and Gass, 1997). At its best, OB+ is a form of the Socratic method. The participants discover insights through their responses to questions, but those insights probably would not have been verbalized without the supervision of the facilitator.

Figure 2

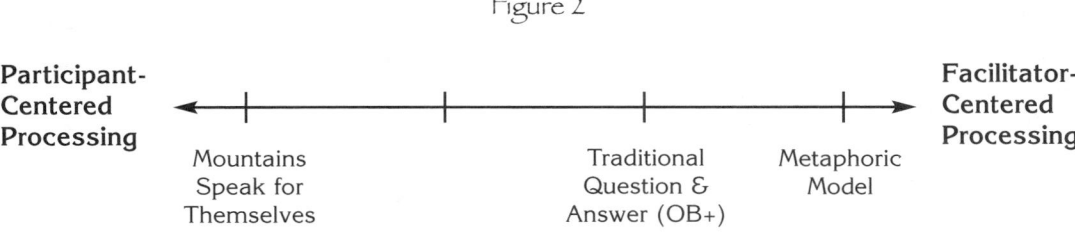

To some extent, these three perspectives (MST, Metaphoric Model, and OB+) dominate processing theory, but as Figure 2 suggests, they leave a fairly big gap between Q & A and no formal processing at all. With processing techniques between OB+ and

Mountains Speak for Themselves, a facilitator either controls the direction of the processing or leaves it up to participants to self-process. Therefore we suggest another category of processing, one called participant-directed processing (See Figure 3). This is processing that incorporates a formal processing technique, with one purpose of the technique being to intentionally shift the responsibility for processing away from the facilitator and put it on the participants. Journaling is an excellent example of this, whereby the facilitator asks participants to go off on their own to write in their journals, and then come back together as a group to share journal entries. The facilitator assigns a specific processing task, sets aside time to process, even serves as gatekeeper for any discussion that may occur, but the themes of the processing are determined by the participants, not the facilitator.

Figure 3   A Continuum of Processing Techniques

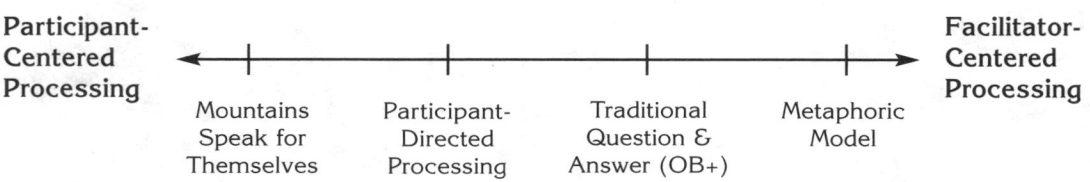

Participant-Centered Processing ← ——————— → **Facilitator-Centered Processing**

Mountains Speak for Themselves   Participant-Directed Processing   Traditional Question & Answer (OB+)   Metaphoric Model

Many processing techniques can be considered participant-directed processing; while the creation of the category may be new, most of the techniques that could be called participant-direct processing are common and well known, and new ones will be presented in this book. Many activities presented here, such as processing cards, reflective partner activities, and artistic expression activities, give participants freedom in their processing, but unlike Mountains Speak for Themselves, they ask the facilitator to provide a framework for the processing to occur. The facilitator still establishes a structure for processing, but then trusts the group to take it from there. To some extent, it is training in the art of processing and will prepare the group to process experiences even when the facilitator is no longer available.

The key point in looking at processing techniques as a continuum is that no type of processing is better than another. Of course, a long-term goal for a particular group is to have its members learn to process on their own, but reaching that point is a progression. Some groups need to be led to the lessons of a program, some groups actually need to be hit over the head with them, and others can discern those lessons on their own. A strong facilitator recognizes the abilities of a group and can use the correct processing technique when it is called for. The activities outlined in this text are designed to give facilitators a variety of tools to help group members in their journey to become reflective learners.

References

Bacon, S. *The Conscious Use of Metaphor in Outward Bound.* Denver, CO: Colorado Outward Bound School, 1983.

Gass, M. A. "The Evolution of Processing Adventure Therapy Experiences." *Adventure Therapy: Therapeutic Applications of Adventure Programming.* Ed. M. A. Gass. Dubuque, IA: Kendall/Hunt Publishing Co., 1993.

Priest, S., and M. A. Gass. *Effective Leadership in Adventure Programming.* Champaign, IL: Human Kinetics, 1997.

Buzz Bocher and Dan Miller are President and Vice President of the Institute for Experiential Education (IEE). IEE created Chiji Processing Cards© and The Pocket Processor©, two tools that are examples of participant-directed processing. Steve Simpson is an associate professor at the University of Wisconsin-La Crosse.

Photo courtesy of Jeff Baird, High 5.

Processing and Multiple Intelligences
Eight Ways of Reviewing

Based upon the groundbreaking work of Howard Gardner, Thomas Armstrong and many others, it is suggested that there are a variety of styles by which individuals come to grasp information, and in fact, learn. At present, eight styles or talents have been identified. These include: *Logical Mathematical, Bodily Kinesthetic, Visual Spatial, Linguistic, Musical, Interpersonal—Knowledge of Others, Intrapersonal—Knowledge of Self* and *Natural Environmental.* Outside the arena of multiple intelligences, some additional styles or talents have also been proposed which include such topics as emotional intelligence, humor, mechanical aptitude, religious influences and spirituality.

Multiple intelligence theory provides a template for creating processing activities that incorporate each intelligence. The books by Thomas Armstrong listed below are highly recommended as a guide for this process. Begin by borrowing these books from your local library, or buying them at your local bookstore. They are worth the price, and more. Read them from cover to cover, and then start reviewing your debriefing techniques and grouping them into the eight categories of multiple intelligences. You can also find a wide variety of multiple intelligence readings on the Internet, in educational books and by visiting the Harvard University Project Zero multiple intelligence website at: www.pzweb.harvard.edu.

Review your present collection of processing techniques to see if you have focused on only a portion of the multiple intelligence methods available. Then identify additional techniques for completing your portfolio of activities in each of the various forms of intelligence. The table below provides examples from each of the eight multiple intelligences.

Intelligence or Talent	Reviewing Technique
Logical-Mathematical	Analysis of group's performance, charting, visual graphical representations, numerically quantifying the performance of the team, investigating the "why did this happen" line of logic, cause and effect discussions.
Bodily-Kinesthetic	Movement during reviewing (Shuffle Left-Shuffle Right),

contact with other members of the group during activities and processing, holding or manipulating objects in the hands while conversing (tactile stimulation or The Processing Cube), skits or active role-playing.

Visual-Spatial	Visualizing multiple solutions, drawing as a form of expression, painting, visual arts, clay formations, sand pictures, using participants in tableau or stop action explanation of the activity, graphically describing the results of the activity, picture debriefs (Chiji Cards).
Linguistic	Talking, listening, dialog, conversation in large and small groups, creative writing and journaling (Team Resume), alphabet games (Alphabet Blocks), word puzzles (seek and find), foreign language words and skills, poetry, haiku, limericks, rap, prose.
Musical	Using rhythm, timing, sounds of nature, creating songs, musical skits, lyrics, melodies, performance art, pipe chimes, sound effects.
Interpersonal— Knowledge of Others	Understanding, empathy, coaching, partner watching, observing the group, working together while paired or connected, active listening, group norms, group contract.
Intrapersonal— Knowledge of Self	Self analysis, relating, journaling, self reflection, understanding your own motivation and actions, goal setting.
Natural-Environmental	Connection to the outdoor setting, exploring nature and the environment, using natural objects in reflection (stones, water, leaves), the five basic Aristotelean elements of earth, fire, wind, water and ether.

Suggested reading:

Multiple Intelligences in the Classroom, 2000, Thomas Armstrong, ASCD Alexandria, VA, USA ISBN 0–87120–376–6. This is an excellent "template" for designing your own curriculum with multiple possibilities for reviewing and learning in different ways.

Seven Kinds of Smart—Identifying and Developing Your Multiple Intelligences, 1999, Thomas Armstrong, Plume, New York, NY USA ISBN 0-452-28137-7.

Reviewing and the Stages of Group Formation

Forming, Storming, Norming, Performing and Transforming in Experiential Learning

Forming	Storming	Norming	Performing	Transforming

The stages of group development presented here come from the research of Tuckman and Jenson. For more information about this work, review the following historical articles:

Tuckman, B., 1965, "Developmental sequence of small groups," *Psychological Bulletin,* Number 63, pages 384–399.

Tuckman, B. & Jenson, M., 1977, "Stages of small group development revisited," *Group and Organizational Studies,* Number 2, pages 419–427.

Tuckman, Bruce W., 2001, Developmental Sequence in Small Groups, *Group Facilitation,* Number 3, Spring, pages 66–81.

You can find additional information related to the stages of group formation and group learning in the Johnson and Johnson book, *Joining Together,* on page 469. See the references at the end of this chapter.

An extended version of this chapter is downloadable in PDF format from the Teamwork & Teamplay website at: www.teamworkandteamplay.com.

Concepts

During a project, your team is likely to encounter most, if not all, of the stages of group formation, commonly referred to as forming, storming, norming, performing and finally, transforming. While entire graduate dissertations, college and management classes and seminars and numerous journal articles have been written on this subject, this brief chapter "opens the door" to explaining and experiencing the stages of group formation, and building some of the skills necessary to successfully navigate each stage. This introduction to the stages of group formation is suitable for a two hour staff training program. Additional resources and references are provided at the end of the chapter for those who are interested in a more detailed explanation of these stages, and techniques for exploring them with your community.

Directions

Consider the five stages of group formation. The following information details how a typical team might progress through these stages, and provides activities for exploring each stage of group formation with the members of a team.

The Forming Stage

This is the polite, opening, get acquainted, icebreaking stage of group formation. This process begins at the moment new team members begin to assemble for the first time. The opening meeting, the general welcome comments from the manager, the facility orientation session and even the informal discussions after the initial gathering are all part of the forming stage. At this point, members of the group are just trying to identify who's who, and possibly where they fit into the plan. This stage includes forming an atmosphere of safety and acceptance, avoiding controversy and is filled with guidance and direction from the facilitator.

Activities for the Forming Stage

Get acquainted and community building activities are used here to form the atmosphere of safety and acceptance. There are a few more activities suggested in this stage because it is important to build a strong foundation if the rest of the stages are to be successfully navigated.

Believe It or Knot

Thanks to Mike Anderson of Learning Works for this excellent get acquainted activity. With the entire group holding a Raccoon Circle (a 15-foot long section of tubular climbing webbing tied with a knot, or, if webbing is not available, a 15-foot long rope knotted to form a circle), the knot is used as a pointer to identify the person talking. Begin by passing the knot to the right around the group. Someone in the group says "Stop!," the knot stops, and the person nearest to it has the opportunity to disclose some interesting fact about themselves, such as, "I can write computer programs in four different languages!" It is now the responsibility of the rest of the participants to decide whether they believe that this information is true or false. After some discussion, the group gives their opinion of the validity or falseness of the disclosure, and the person providing the comment can tell the real story. After the person has revealed the true nature of their comments (true or false), they say "left" or "right" and then "Stop!," and a new person has the opportunity to disclose something interesting or unusual to the group.

The level of disclosure to the group is often a measure of the closeness, unity and respect within the group. For example, a disclosure such as, "I have been with this company for three years," is a lower level of disclosure than "I need to be better at my job for this project to succeed." Depending on the group setting, and the purpose of this activity for your group, different levels of information or disclosure are appropriate. As the group becomes more unified, this activity can bring out greater disclosure between members of the project team ("I'm not sure if I have enough resources to complete my part of the project on time.")

Commonalities

Begin with partners for this activity. This conversational activity has the goal of identifying unique and sometimes unusual events, activities and life experiences that we have in common with other members of our group. The two partners need to identify three unique items that they have in common. Encourage participants to dig deep for these items. For example, they may discover that they both like dogs, but under closer examination, they may also discover that they like the same breed of dog. Additionally, they may discover that they both enjoy reading, but by digging a bit deeper, they may discover that they have read the same book in the past six months or perhaps enjoy the same author.

After identifying three attributes that they have in common, these two partners raise their hands, and find another group of two ready to form a group of four. Now the challenge is to identify two items that they have in common. Again, look deep, and no fair using any of the attributes already identified.

Finally, after this group of four finds out what they have in common, they raise their hands and join another group of four, for a total of eight. The goal for these eight is to find ONE unusual event, interest or activity that they have in common. Have each of these groups of eight tell the other groups what they have in common. Again, the more unique and unusual, the better (or at least the more interesting!)

The Storming Stage

This second stage of group formation introduces conflict and competition into a formerly safe and pleasant environment. In many group settings, this stage typically is encountered around week two. Why week two? Because that is when most team members have had the weekend to think about the resources and requirements of the job ahead. Suddenly those things that did not seem to matter begin to matter, and conflicts arise. Staff behavior ranges from silence to domination in this environment, and a facilitator needs to demonstrate coaching to successfully move through this stage.

Activities for the Storming Stage

While some project team members would rather avoid the conflict of this stage, it is important to build skills and show them how to cope and deal with the storming stage. The activities in this section, therefore, contain just a bit of stress (so that the door may be "opened" to discuss what is really going on). The following activities are very challenging, and need to have a suitable amount of time after each one for discussion within the group.

Cross the Line

This activity requires a single straight line. With half of the group on one side of the line and standing about 6 feet (2 meters) behind the line, and the other half of the team on the other side, the scene is set for a moment of conflict (of "us" versus "them"). Make no mistake, this activity is a bit higher level than most, but it is excellent for setting the stage to talk about conflict, negotiation and win/win, win/lose, and lose/lose scenarios.

Tom Heck calls this activity, "There Ain't No Flies On Me!", and begins this activity by having one side say, "There ain't no flies on me, there ain't no flies on me, there might be flies on you (point to folks on the other side), but there ain't no flies on me!", and then boldly taking a step towards the line (with just the right amount of attitude). The other side now replies, "there ain't no flies on me, there ain't no flies on me, there might be flies on you (pointing at the other folks), but there ain't no flies on me!", and takes a step towards the line. The first side now repeats with twice the attitude, and moves to the line, followed by the second side repeating their lines, and stepping face to face with the other side.

The facilitator now says, "you have three seconds to get the person across the line from you onto your side of the line. GO!"

Typically, this phrasing results in a rather quick tug of war between partners, and usually a physical solution (for one person at least) to the challenge. This provides an excellent opportunity to open the door for discussion on conflict, challenges, attitude, negotiation and how to resolve differences between people. For example, you can ask, "how many partner teams ended up in a win/lose scenario, where one member obtained what they wanted (getting their partner to their side), but the other member did not?" "What about a lose/lose scenario, where both members struggled, but neither one obtained their goal?" And finally, "were there any teams that achieved a win/win solution, where both partners changed sides?" "What is it about our corporate culture that so many members of our team end up in win/lose or lose/lose scenarios, rather than a win/win solution?" "How can we fix this situation?" The next 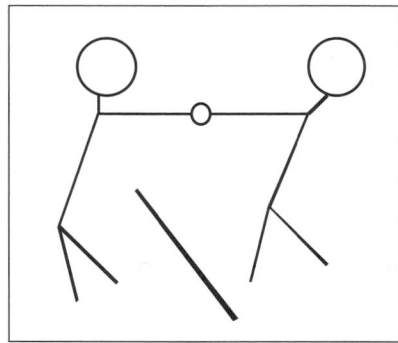 time you are in a "cross the line" situation, what is the first thing you will do to avoid a win/lose or lose/lose scenario?

Blind Square

In a safe environment (large open carpeted room with no obstacles, or perhaps a flat grassy outdoor space) blindfold the entire group, and allow them to search as a group and find a nearby piece of rope (about 100 feet long). After finding the rope, instruct the group that their goal, while still blindfolded, is to create a perfect square with the rope. You might continue and remind the group that a square geometrically consists of a closed shape with four equal length sides, and four 90 degree corners. Participants are allowed to slide along the length of the rope, but cannot let go, change sides or move around another participant.

This simple to explain, but extremely difficult and time consuming to complete, activity works best with a group of about a ten to fifteen participants. You can choose to invite one person to "observe" the group, but not assist them in the completion of their task, and then to share their observations when the group has finished. The storming stage of this activity will be very obvious. Communication breakdowns, leadership abilities, directions, power issues and resource constraints all contribute to team member frustration and often make what appears to be a simple task infinitely more difficult. If establishing realistic scheduling goals is appropriate for this project team, then ask them to estimate a "time to completion" for creating this rope square. If establishing quality standards, or work performance standards is realistic, then ask them to establish (while blindfolded), the performance criteria on how they will measure the outcome of this rope square project. If team members are likely to encounter limitations in technology, wrong or misleading information, or confusion during their project work, consider tying one end of the rope permanently to a tree, fence, car or other non-moving object. Or tie a knot or two in the rope (but not at a distance that is likely to correspond with a corner).

After the group has reached the end (notice, I didn't say "completed" the activity), here are a few ideas to discuss: Was the time estimate reasonable given the task? What was most of the time spent doing? What was the "breakthrough" point in this activity? Were all members of the group equally engaged in the activity? Did some members of the group have more "power" than others? If the group was asked to create another shape blindfolded, do you think you could be more efficient? Quicker? More accurate? This stage of group formation is called the storming stage. What types of team behaviors did you notice during this activity that tell you the group was storming? What skills do you have now that you can use in the workplace when tasks become frustrating or difficult?

The Norming Stage

This third stage of group formation is typically a welcome breath of fresh air after the storming stage. Although the team is not yet at the high performing stage, some of the bugs are beginning to be worked out within the group, and good things are beginning to happen. This stage of group formation includes cohesion, sharing and trust building, creativity and skill acquisition. The facilitator demonstrates support during this stage.

Activities for the Norming Stage

Sharing, trust building, and skill building activities are used in the norming stage.

Inside Out

This is a great initial problem solving activity. Begin with a Raccoon Circle (a 15-foot long rope, tied into a circle) on the floor. Have the entire group step inside the circle. The task now is for the entire group to go from the inside of the circle to the outside, by going underneath the Raccoon Circle, without anyone in the group using their arms, shoulders, or hands.

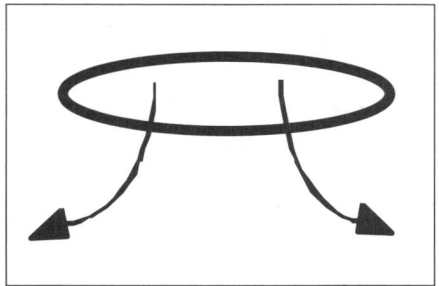

What is important in this activity, is to stress the group problem solving process. In order for other members of the group to assist in the completion of the task, they need to know the plan, and what their part is in the solution.

To this end, encourage the group to "plan their work" and then "work their plan." This means that prior to ANY action, the group will need to plan their approach to solving this problem, and make sure that everyone in the group knows their part of the plan.

After completing the task, debriefing questions include asking the group if they had a plan, and did they change the plan during the completion of the activity, and if so, why? As a second part to this activity, you can also ask the group to go Outside In, again without using their hands, arms or shoulders . . . and see if they "plan their work" before "working their plan."

Finally, Inside Out can be used to explore ethical behavior in the workplace. At a time when corporate responsibility and financial accounting irregularities both make the business headlines, ethical behavior is certainly important. Once the group has returned into the circle, ask if they "followed the rules." Most will likely nod their heads yes. Then ask if anyone used their arms, shoulders or hands to complete the task. For example, to crawl on their hands and knees (see picture). Or to assist another member of their group by holding them up. Suddenly some folks will realize that they interpreted the rules to mean, "not to touch the Raccoon Circle with our arms, shoulders or hands." This is an excellent opportunity to discuss the public's perception of this groups ability to follow rules, corporate guidelines, policies, civil ordinances or federal mandates.

Not Knots

In this activity, which can be accomplished with only a single piece of webbing (in a straight line, without a water knot), a "doodle" is constructed (see example below) and the group is given the choice of whether this doodle will create a KNOT or NOT A KNOT, when the ends of the webbing are pulled.

The object here is to provide the group with some tools to use when

they cannot easily form a consensus. Typically, upon analysis, about half of the group thinks the doodle will form a knot, and the other half a straight line. If this is the case, ask participants to partner with another person that has a different viewpoint (i.e., one partner from the KNOT side, and one partner from the NOT A KNOT side). By learning how to listen to a person with a different viewpoint, group members learn how to cooperate. After this discussion, ask participants to choose sides, with the KNOT decision folks on one side of the knot doodle, and the NOT A KNOT folks on the other side.

At this point, it is likely that there will still not be a complete consensus within the group. Prior to slowly pulling the ends of the knot doodle, let the members of the group know that you will pull the knot doodle slowly, and that they can change sides at any time during the unraveling of the knot doodle (this illustrates the ability to make an initial decision, but still be flexible as more information becomes available). This is also a good time to discuss "risk taking" on the job, and what the risk is of choosing what might be the wrong side.

The Performing Stage

The fourth stage of group formation provides a feeling of unity, group identity, interdependence and independence. It is the most highly productive stage. Leadership from the facilitator comes in the form of delegation. The team has all the skills, resources and talent needed to complete the task.

Activities for the Performing Stage

This stage is best explored using challenging activities that require advanced skills, but which can be successfully accomplished by the group. Activities that build enthusiasm are also helpful here. Large group projects such as tower building (using Tinkertoys©, uncooked spaghetti and marshmallows, newspaper and masking tape or even PVC tubing), and challenge courses (low and high ropes activities) are useful.

Grand Prix Racing

Turn the Raccoon Circle into a complete circle or loop using a water knot, and you are ready for the ultimate in sport racing. Thanks to Tom Heck not only for the idea for this activity, but also for the enthusiasm to lead it effectively. This activity will boost the enthusiasm of your audience, and provide some moderate competition in the process.

Begin by spreading several Raccoon Circles around the available space, in close proximity to each other. Ask participants to join one of the "racing teams," picking their favorite color team in the process. Use approximately five to ten participants per

Raccoon Circle. Have participants hold the Raccoon Circle with both hands in front of them. Then say in your best announcer's voice:

Ladies and Gentlemen! It is summertime, and that means only one thing in this part of the world—Grand Prix Racing! Now I know that you are such die-hard race fans that just the thought of a race makes your heart beat faster. So this race comes in three parts. First, when I say that "we're going to have a race," your response is a loud, "Yahoo!!!!!" Next I'll say, "start your engines!" and I want to hear your best race car sounds (audience practices making race car revving engine, shifting gears and braking sounds).

Finally, with so many cars on the track today, it will be difficult to see just which group finishes their race first, so we'll need a sign indicating when your group is finished. That sign is to raise your hands (and the Raccoon Circle) above your heads and yell, "Yesssssssss!"

Logistically, Grand Prix involves having the group transfer the knot around the group as quickly as possible, using only their hands. This activity can even be performed for a seated audience. To begin, you'll need a "start/finish" line, which can be the person that was born the farthest distance away from the present location. The race begins at this location, and ends when the knot is passed around the circle, and returns to this same location (Yesssssssss!).

Typically in Raccoon Circle Grand Prix racing, there are three qualifying rounds or races. The first race is a single lap race to the right, with the knot traveling once around the inside of the circle to the right (clockwise). The second race is a multi-lap race (two or three laps) to the left (counterclockwise) around the circle. And the final race of the series is a "winner take all" championship race, with one lap to the right (clockwise) followed by one lap to the left (counterclockwise).

Incidentally, after this activity, the group will not only be energized, but perhaps in a slightly competitive mood. From a sequencing standpoint, you can either continue this atmosphere (with more competitive challenges—such as a volleyball game or corporate olympics) or introduce a bit of counterpoint, by following this activity with one that requires the group working together in a collaborative manner.

The Transforming Stage

The final stage of group formation is the other bookend to the initial forming stage. The transforming stage allows the group to regroup, thank the participants and move on at the completion of the project or task. This stage is marked by recognition by the facilitator, conclusion and disengagement by the team members.

Activities for the Transforming Stage

Allow for the completion and conclusion of the group process. Feelings of celebration and affirmation are suitable. Different team members may experience this final stage at different rates. Do not rush for closure. For some team members, this project may have been the highlight of their career to date. The first activity, A Circle of Kindness, involves appropriate contact between team members, and for many teams (nurses, primary care givers, teachers and other "hands-on" professionals) this style is fine. The second activity, Virtual Slideshow, has no physical contact between team members, is largely verbal, and may be used in settings where less contact is desired.

A Circle of Kindness

Form a double circle with all group members, with one partner facing the center of the circle, and their partner behind them (also facing the center, with their hands on the shoulders of the inner circle person). The inner circle is asked to close their eyes, and only reply "thank you" or keep silent. The outer circle is asked to quietly talk into the ear of the inner circle participants, mentioning something important that they learned from them or appreciated about them during the project, or a pleasant memory or any other positive comment. The outer group then moves one person to the right, and continues. When the outer group has completed the circle, they are asked to become the center group, and the process begins again for a second round. See page 73 for greater description

Virtual Slideshow

With all participants seated in a close space, an imaginary slide projector "clicker" is passed around the group. Group members are asked to "show" an imaginary slide or photograph from the project, illustrating a perfect moment, or perhaps a moment from the future, that will be different because that person had the opportunity to work as part of this team. If you would like a non-imaginary virtual slideshow clicker you can order one from Training Wheels at 1-888-553-0147 or www.training-wheels.com. See page 235 for more information.

References and Resources

Teamwork & Teamplay, by Jim Cain and Barry Jolliff, 1998, Kendall/Hunt Publishing Co., Dubuque, IA. Phone (800) 228-0810 ISBN 0-7872-4532-1 417 pages of activities, like those shown in this chapter.

The Book on Raccoon Circles, by Jim Cain and Tom Smith, 2002, Learning Unlimited, Tulsa, OK, USA. Phone (888) 622-4203 www.learningunlimited.com ISBN 0-9646541-6-4 Hundreds of activities for creating community, that you can present with minimal props. 272 pages of ideas.

"Developmental Sequence of Small Groups," by B. Tuckman, 1965, *Psychological Bulletin,* Number 63, pages 384–399. The "original" article on the stages of group formation.

"Stages of Small Group Development Revisited," B. Tuckman and M. Jensen, 1977, *Group and Organizational Studies,* Number 2, pages 419–427. The revised and updated article.

Tuckman, Bruce W., 2001, Developmental Sequence in Small Groups, *Group Facilitation,* Number 3, Spring, pages 66–81. *A look back 25 years after the ground breaking introductory article.*

Exploring the Five Stages of Group Formation Using Adventure-Based Activities, by Jim Cain, 2003, from the Teamwork & Teamplay website at: www.teamworkandteamplay.com

Joining Together: Group Theory and Group Skills by David W. Johnson and Frank P. Johnson, 1994, Allyn and Bacon, Boston, MA ISBN 0-205-15846-3. Although set in the business world, this book is applicable to academic fields, social organizations and camping programs as well.

Props/Materials Needed: Most of the above activities that require rope can be completed with a Raccoon Circle [a 15 foot (4.6 meter) length of tubular climbing webbing].

Where to Find It/How to Make It: Raccoon Circles can be obtained from Adventure Hardware at 1-800-706-0064 or www.adventureharedware.com or Training Wheels at 1-888-553-0147 or www.training-wheels.com.

The Art of Reflection
Facilitator Tips and Style Notes

- Allowing group members to pass during processing discussions empowers participants to have control over their learning and practice reflective feedback at their own pace. Participants can experience valuable reflection even if they do not share it with the group. When participants are given the power to pass, they learn to trust the facilitator and group and often end up offering a great deal to the group at their own pace.

- Creating a safe and positive learning environment is key. It is risky for people to share their ideas, reactions and opinions in any environment where they feel exposed or unsafe. Helping the group create behavioral norms regarding comments and judgments during group activities and discussions increases the amount of sharing and interaction and enhances the depth of reflection.

- Sequence processing activities by beginning with simple conversational prompts, such as one word whips, that lead into more in-depth discussions. Reflection is an art that needs to be practiced by both the learner and the facilitator.

- Allow for some superficial answers/comments during reflection activities. Remember that this is a practice. When people start to reflect they might start with level surface comments and observations—Persevere! Groups will increase their level of sharing and reflection as they develop through continued participation.

- Silences are okay, even necessary. Allow time for group members to think and formulate their ideas.

- Be prepared for the group to take reflection somewhere different than you had in mind—you too might learn something new!

- Mix up your methods. Variety is not only the spice of life, but according to new scientific brain research, novelty and the use of different learning tools and methods also facilitate learning.

- Processing can happen at any time—not just after an activity is over. Sometimes a group will experience a pivotal teachable moment in the middle of a problem solving initiative. Brain-based learning has shown that immediate feedback and reflection can be valuable.

- Treat debriefing activities as an intitiative in itself.

- Take time to reflect yourself. Reflecting on your own practice as a facilitator enhances your learning about what works and what does not in facilitation and help to see the long term benefits of our programs.

- Use your creativity; use activities you already know as reflective tools. Often openers and icebreaking activities can also be used to process an experience.

- Empower participants, do not force your own agenda upon them. Go with the flow—be flexible. Let them take responsibility for their learning and their interpretation of an experience.

- The facilitator does not have to hear it for it to be quality reflection. Try processing activities that do not involve the facilitator by dividing the group into smaller reflection groups, or allow the group to "self-process."

- Allow for both individual reflection and group consensus activities to reach different learning styles and for richer reviewing experiences.

- Take a risk. Experiment. Allow for the chance that an activity might flop. There is always something to be learned. Some effective debriefing tools have been created purely by accident.

- Let participants know why they are reflecting. Talk about the value of reflective practice.

- In group discussions use open ended questions. Summarize or restate what was said, or even better, have a group member restate the discussion.

- Leave time for processing. Be patient.

- Allow closure at the end of the program.

- Keep a facilitator journal of all your groups and your learnings. Process yourself!

What Makes a Good Experiential Educator?

Positive Attitude

Participants really pick up on and respond to a facilitator's attitudes, demeanor and expectations. We often communicate more than we realize in our body language and tone. If we expect the best of group members they will usually perform their best. Our positive attitude as faciltators is contagious. Remember to believe in your participants abilities.

A Willingness to Allow for Struggle

People learn from struggling through problems. Sometimes practitioners have a hard time letting their groups labor through difficult group problems. Often educators want to jump in and solve problems for students. Let them labor. Obviously there is a fine balance between labor and paralyzing frustration—you as an educator have to figure out that appropriate balance along with your participants. Just remember that people learn more when given questions rather than answers. For interesting reading on this subject see Plato's *Theatetus*. In this work Plato uses the metaphor of the teacher as to the "midwife" of ideas. Allow participants to take control of their learning.

Cultural Sensitivity

Keep in mind cultural differences in language and slang terminology. Some of the activity names adventure educators have used can be offensive or hurtful. For example, we have adapted the activity known as "Minefield" to "Cow Pasture" as many of our students from politically volatile regions could find the concept of a minefield frightening.

Flexibility and a Willingness to Try New Things

Sharing and exploring are fundamental components of experiential education. One of the wonderful aspects about the art and science of teaching is that there is no single correct method. There are as many ways to teach and learn as there are teachers and learners. Good teachers recognize they are learners, and successful participants act as teachers in their practice as learners. Remember to experiment. You can learn a lot from activities that do not work quite as you planned. Allow opportunities for your students to teach you a few things.

Style

Successful educators think about their style, develop it and nurture it. It is our strength. Integral to the idea of experiential education is the recognition that people each have their own learning style. Successful facilitators are always reflecting on their style and methods, aiming to meet the diverse needs of learners. Teaching is a dynamic, ever changing and growing process.

Too often we underestimate the power of a touch, a smile,
a kind word, a listening ear, an honest compliment,
or the smallest act of caring, all of
which have the potential to turn a life around.

Leo Buscaglia

Improving Your Reviewing Skills

A Ten-Step Process to Increase
Your Value as a Facilitator

It is no surprise that we become better at those things we practice in our lives. For the adventure-based facilitator, this means that we can improve our facilitation skills, our reviewing skills, and our overall value as an educator and trainer by practicing and growing in our craft. If you are new to this field, or just want to improve your facilitation skills, here are a few suggestions for how you can reach the next level.

1. Read everything you can find on facilitation skills, reviewing activities and the fine art of processing groups. Visit your local library or perform an Internet search on such topics as: reviewing, facilitation, problem solving, coaching, mentoring, debriefing, groupwork and teamwork. Read something new every week. Visit Roger Greenaway's reviewing website and download tons of worthwhile reviewing information from www.reviewing.co.uk. You can also find additional reviewing information at the Training Wheels website, (www.training-wheels.com) The Teamwork and Teamplay website (www.teamworkandteamplay.com), and High 5 Adventure (www.high5adventure.org).

2. Shadow another facilitator or co-facilitate a session with another presenter. Each of these techniques allows you to act and observe another facilitator. When you are finished, ask for feedback on your efforts.

"Oh no! It's time to process!"

3. Volunteer. In every community you will find opportunities for sharing your knowledge of adventure-based learning and debriefing skills with groups. Your local library, after school programs, summer and day camps, church groups, social clubs and professional organizations are all possible audiences for practicing your skills and trying out some of those newer facilitation activities in your repertoire.

4. Share what you know. Join an Internet listserv (such as the AEElist at Princeton University, or the Ropes Listserv) so that you can discuss your adventure-based experiences with other professionals in the field.

5. Join professional societies that promote quality programming. Find out what AEE, ACCT, ACA, AAHPERD, NSEE, ICORE, and AORE stand for, join them and attend their conferences. Better yet, present a workshop at one of these conferences and share your knowledge with others.
6. Find a mentor that you can trust. Form a partnership in learning with someone whose opinions you value. Perhaps a local challenge course professional, an author, a corporate trainer, a teacher, or some other talented member of the adventure-based learning community.
7. Have lunch. Once a month get together with other professionals and discuss your three favorite activities. Bring your best ones and share them. In six months, your group will have dozens of best ideas from each other.
8. Attend trainings, workshops and conferences. Locate opportunities for expanding your learning by attending and presenting workshops at new venues.
9. Create your own training manual. Organize and compile your favorite training techniques, complete with photographs, sketches and illustrations. You can use this as an informational document to share with your clients, and as a ready reference at your fingertips. Do not be surprised someday if this simple manual turns into your first book, Internet e-book, or workshop reference manual.
10. Create a resume of experiences that will make audiences want to enlist your services. Consider what talents, skills and experiences your future clients will want. Identify each of these possibilities, and then make them happen so that your resume will reflect the best of what you are.

*So when you are listening to somebody, completely,
attentively, then you are listening not only to the words,
but also to the feeling of what is being conveyed,
to the whole of it, not part of it.*

Jiddu Krishnamurti

Sequencing

When thinking about processing activities it is beneficial to think about *sequencing* experiences for maximum effectiveness. In adventure education facilitation theory, we often talk about the importance of sequencing activities for best outcomes. This is just as important for facilitators to think about when planning reflective/ processing activities as it is when planning challenge initiatives or adventure activities. Learning to process is itself "a process," people learn to become reflective over  time and with practice. As with many of the activities and challenges common to the experiential education field, starting with introductory level processing and moving along in difficulty makes for more effective reflection. As facilitators it is important for us to start with reflective activities that are appropriate for the group's needs, background or stage in-group development.

Often educators who recognize the value of reflection try to facilitate with a very traditional didactic approach that is not always appropriate for every situation. Traditionally in adventure education, reflection was facilitated when a group was asked to sit down after an activity and discuss it through a question and answer session led by the facilitator. Though this can often be a valuable method, it is frequently the most difficult and potentially intimidating, especially to those new to reflective practice. In many ways this is the most advanced form of processing.

The ideal state would be for the group to get to the point where they process spontaneously on their own, without the facilitator leading discussion. By starting with simple discussion activities like One Word Whip, Dominos or Concentric Circles, then following with metaphoric methods involving props, journaling, or artwork, groups often get to the point where they can become more engaged in a group discussion and spontaneously reflect together during and after activities. The activities outlined in this book can help individuals and groups practice reflection in many different ways and at many different levels, with the outcome being enhanced learning opportunities for everyone involved.

Processing Objectives and Questions

Asking the right questions is sometimes the scariest and hardest part about being an experiential facilitator, and yet it is the most important part of experiential learning. If we can not get the participants and group to transfer the learning from what just happened to what they do every day, then we lose a valuable opportunity. That great activity with rubber chickens and hula hoops will only be a fun game unless we can help the participants see the meaning beyond the activity.

This section is designed to give you some insight into the types of questions there are, and how to know what kind of question to ask.

There are two types of questions, *closed ended* and *open ended*.

Some attributes of closed ended questions are:

- Solicit a "yes" or "no" or other one-word response. For example: "Did you think the group worked well together?", or "Are you satisfied with the group's performance?" Both can be answered with a yes or no answer.
- Use common lead-in words such as who, when, did, which, would, are, can, have, do, is, will and may.
- Aim to limit talking or to control the direction of the conversation.
- They are useful when you want specific information.

Some attributes of open-ended questions are:

- Solicit more than a "yes" or "no" or other one-word response. Open-ended questions are those that require some thought and generally more than two to three words to answer, i.e., "Describe some specific ways the group worked well together," or "What do you think was the turning point in this activity?"
- Use common lead-in words such as what, how and why.
- Aim to encourage conversation.
- They are useful when you want general information.

Here are some great open ended questions that will help your debriefs be more powerful and meaningful. Many of these questions were provided by Clifford Knapp, and are from his book, *Lasting Lessons*. Thanks Clifford, for your great contributions to this field!

Appreciating Self and Others

1. Who generally appreciated themselves and some of the others in the group?
2. Did you express your appreciation to yourself and others? If so, how did you do this? (consider verbal and nonverbal ways)
3. Would anyone like to appreciate some of the members of the group now? If so, do it now.
4. What expressions of appreciation were especially important for you to hear? Why was that true?
5. What appreciations would you have liked to receive?
6. Do you usually ask for the kinds of appreciation you like to hear? Explain.
7. Do you usually give appreciations to yourself and others? Explain.
8. What did you do in the group that deserves appreciation?
9. What personal strengths (talents) do you have that you did not use today? Explain.

Asking for What You Want

1. Did you ask for all you wanted from the group members? Explain.
2. What prevented you from asking for what you wanted?
3. What was the worst thing that could possibly happen if you asked for what you wanted?
4. If everyone in the group asked for what they wanted, how might it affect the completion of the initiative?
5. Do you need anything from the group members now? If so, what?
6. How do you usually feel when you ask for what you want and get refused or rejected? Did that happen today?

Communicating Effectively

1. Can anyone give an example of when you thought you communicated effectively with someone else in the group? (consider verbal and nonverbal communication)
2. How did you know that what you communicated was understood? (consider different types of feedback)
3. Who did not understand someone else's attempt to communicate?
4. What went wrong in the communication attempt?
5. What could the communicator do differently next time to give a clearer message?
6. What could the listener do differently next time to give a clearer message?
7. How many different ways were used to communicate messages?
8. Which ways were most effective? How?
9. What did you learn about communication that will be helpful later?

Cooperating

1. Can you think of specific examples of when the group cooperated in completing the initiative? Explain.
2. How did it feel to cooperate?
3. Do you cooperate in most things you do?
4. How did you learn to cooperate?
5. What are the rewards of cooperating?
6. Are there any problems associated with cooperation?
7. How did cooperative behavior lead to successfully completing the initiative task?
8. How can you cooperate in other areas of your life?
9. Did you think anyone was blocking the group from cooperating? Explain.

Deferring Judgement of Others

1. Is it difficult for you to avoid judging others? Explain.
2. Can you think of examples of when you judged others in the group today? . . . when you didn't judge others?
3. What were some advantages to you by not judging others?
4. What were some advantages to others by you not judging them?
5. How does judging and not judging others affect the completion of the initiative?
6. Were some behaviors of others easy not to judge and other behaviors difficult?
7. Would deferring judgment be of some value in other situations? Explain.
8. Can you think of any disadvantages of not judging others in this situation?

Expressing Appropriate Feelings

1. Can you name a feeling you had at any point in completing the initiative? (consider—mad, glad, sad or scared) Where in your body did you feel it most?
2. What beliefs were responsible for generating that feeling? (What was the main thought behind the feeling?)
3. Is that feeling a common one in your life?
4. Did you express that feeling to others? If not, what did you do with the feeling?
5. Do you usually express feelings or suppress them?
6. Would you like to feel differently in a similar situation? If so, how would you like to feel?
7. What beliefs would you need to have in order to feel differently in a similar situation? Could you believe them?
8. How do you feel about the conflict that may result from expressing certain feelings?
9. What types of feelings are easiest to express? . . . most difficult?
10. Do you find it difficult to be aware of some feelings at times? If so, which ones?

11. Are some feelings not appropriate to express to the group at times? If so, which ones?
12. What feelings were expressed nonverbally in the group?
13. Does expressing appropriate feelings help or hinder completing the initiative?

Leading Others

1. Who assumed leadership roles during the initiative task?
2. What were the behaviors which you described as showing leadership?
3. Can everyone agree that these are traits of leaders?
4. How did the group respond to these leadership behaviors?
5. Who followed the leader even if you were not sure that the idea would work? Why?
6. Did the leadership role shift to other people during the initiative task? Who thought they were taking the leadership role? How did you do it?
7. Was it difficult to assume a leadership role with this group?
8. Why didn't some of you take a leadership role?
9. Is it easier to take a leadership role in other situations or with different group members? Explain.
10. Did anyone try to lead the group, but felt they were unsuccessful? What were some possible reasons for this? How did it feel to be disregarded?

Liking Yourself

1. Did anyone criticize or put themselves down at any time?
2. What did you say to yourself?
3. At what point in the initiative did this happen?
4. Is this something you tell yourself in other situations? When?
5. Do you usually get upset with yourself and put yourself down when you make a mistake or are not perfect?
6. What sentence could you say to yourself to counteract the put down message?
7. Were any others in the group aware that you were critical of yourself?
8. Do others in the group put themselves down in similar ways?
9. Is it possible that when you criticize yourself it could be considered a personal strength in other situations?
10. In what ways did you contribute to the initiative task?
11. Which contribution made you feel the best about yourself?
12. Are you able to feel good about yourself even if you are not able to identify a contribution you made?
13. What are some abilities you have that you didn't use in completing the initiative? Why didn't you use them?

Listening

1. Who made suggestions for completing the initiative task?
2. Were all of these suggestions heard? Explain.
3. Which suggestions were acted upon?
4. Why were the other suggestions ignored?
5. How did it feel to be heard when you made a suggestion?
6. What interfered with your ability to listen to others?
7. How can this interference be overcome?
8. How did you prevent yourself from listening well?
9. Did you listen in the same way today as you generally do? What was different about today?

Making Group Decisions

1. How were group decisions made in completing the initiative?
2. Were you satisfied with the ways of making decisions? Explain.
3. Did the group arrive at any decisions through group consensus? (some didn't get their first choice, but they could "live" with the decision)
4. Were some decisions made by one or several individuals?
5. Did everyone in the group express their opinion when a choice was available? If not, why not?
6. What is the best way for this group to make decisions? Explain.
7. Do you respond in similar ways in other groups?
8. What did you like about how the group made decisions? What didn't you like?

Respecting Human Commonalities

1. How are you like some of the others in the group?
2. Were these commonalities a help to the group in completing their task? Explain.
3. Were these commonalities a hindrance to the group in completing their task? Explain.

Respecting Human Differences

1. How are you different from some of the others in the group?
2. How do these differences strengthen the group as a whole?
3. When do differences in people in a group prevent reaching certain objectives?
4. What would this group be like if there were very few differences in people? How would you feel if this were so?

5. In what instances did being different help or hinder the group from reaching their objectives?
6. Do you usually view group differences as good, bad or neither?
7. Did you become aware of any prejudices that you have toward some people? If so, do you want to change that?

Trusting the Group

1. Can you give examples of when you trusted someone in the group? Explain.
2. Is it easier to trust some people and not others? Explain.
3. Can you think of examples when trusting someone would not have been a good idea?
4. How do you increase your level of trust for someone?
5. On a scale from one to ten, rate how much trust you have in the group as a whole. Can you explain your rating?
6. What did you do today that deserves the trust of others?
7. How does the amount of fear you feel affect your trust of others?

The art of conversation consist as much in listening politely,
as in talking agreeably.

Atwell

The Organization of Activities in This Book

For quick reference all of the reflective activities in the main section of our book are listed alphabetically. In designing this book, we have categorized these processing tools into 5 main types of reflection: Active and Kinesthetic Techniques, Artistic Expression, Alternatives to the Traditional Sharing Circle, Metaphoric Methods and Self Reflective activities. Readers will find many of these areas overlap. All of the methods complement each other.

Facilitators will find using a variety of types of activities will greatly enhance outcomes by matching a variety of learning styles and maximizing teachable moments. The upcoming pages explain the philosophical foundations of each "type" of activity and where to find these activities in our book. The last section of the book not only cross references activities and some of our favorites as well as highlights, but also gives a plethora of resources for those who want to explore this subject further.

Active and Kinesthetic Techniques

Movement is the door to learning.

Dr. Paul Dennison
Author of Brain Gym

For those situations when static reviewing techniques do not suit the needs of your audience, we have included several methods that will keep your group in motion. These activities include movement, activity and opportunities for sensory input that will maintain your audience's focus and attention.

Activities

All My Neighbors Who . . .

Buzz Ring

Clay Sculptures

Concentric Circles

Goals in Motion

Knot Race

Raccoon Circles

Random Ricochet

Shuffle Left, Shuffle Right

For more information related to movement and learning, we encourage you to read the following books:

Sylvester, Roberto. *A Celebration of Neurons: An Educator's Guide to the Human Brain.* Association for Supervision and Curriculum Development. Alexandria, VA. 1995. ISBN 0-87120-243-3 Sylvester suggests that learning does not take place unless the student can pay attention. In order to facilitate this process, some sensory input is needed to activate attention.

Hannaford, Carla. *Smart Moves: Why Learning Is Not All in Your Head.* Arlington, VA: Great Oceans Publishers, 1995. ISBN 0-915556-27-8

Jensen, Eric. *Teaching with the Brain in Mind.* Alexandria, VA: ASCD, 1998. ISBN 0-87120-299-9Chapter nine focuses on movement and learning.

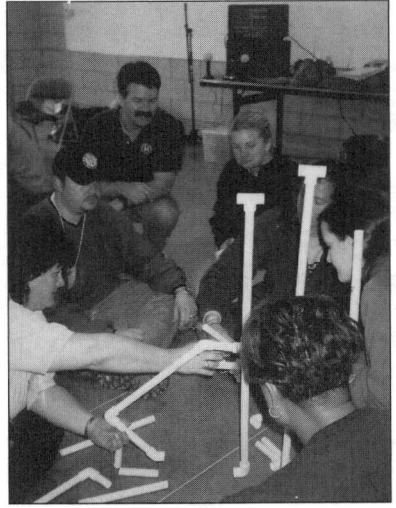

Artistic Expressions:
Creative, Artistic, Musical and Theatrical

All the world's a stage.

William Shakespeare
As You Like It, Act 2, Scene 7

Art has always been one of the most powerful forms of communication. Incorporating artistic expression with active learning can have a great impact on individual and group experience. Some incredibly meaningful processing discussions have come from individual and group art activities.

There is a great deal of power in the creation of symbols to represent feelings and experiences. Humans have been creating symbols since the beginning of time. Creating one's own symbol of experience or collaborating on creation of a group symbol can be incredibly empowering. Creative self-expression activities can range from a drawing that represents a personal or group experience done alone or in collaboration with others to sculpture, performance art, music or a documentary. As long as the emphasis is taken off artistic skill by giving accessible tools such as markers and collage materials

and giving short periods of time in a casual atmosphere, most people readily engage in this kind of creative activity.

The ability to communicate through other mediums than just voice is a wonderful gift. Here is a collection of activities that allow the group to share their thoughts, feelings, inspirations, goals and dreams, using the artistic technique of their choice. And, if you think these techniques are only for children, you might be surprised to know that some of the most creative artwork, stories, songs, rap lyrics, role plays and clay sculptures have come from adults, freed from their traditional boundaries and allowed to set the artists inside themselves free.

Activities:

Balloon Faces	Masks
Group Drawing	Puzzles
Hieroglyphics	Rap Songs
Journaling	Rhythm Processing Experiences
Making Music	Story Bag

For more information about artistic expression, read:

Edwards, Betty. *Drawing on the Right Side of the Brain: A Course in Enhancing Creativity and Artistic Confidence.* Los Angeles, CA: Jeremy P. Tarcher, Inc., 1989. ISBN 0-87477-513-2

*Reflect on your present blessings, of which every man has many;
not on your past misfortunes, of which all men have some.*

Charles Dickens (1812–1870)

*When I'm trusting and being myself . . .
everything in my life reflects this by falling into place easily,
often miraculously.*

Shakti Gawain

*There are two ways of spreading light: to be the candle
or the mirror that reflects it.*

Edith Wharton (1862–1937), Vesalius in Zante

Alternatives to the Traditional Sharing Circle

All my life's a circle.

Harry Chapin
"Circles" from *Greatest Stories Live*

Here are some alternatives for conversation, discussion and verbal expressions for you to share with your next group. Traditional debriefing circle techniques have often placed participants seated in a circle, answering questions posed by the facilitator. Though effective, this technique can be tiresome if it is the only method used; another possible weakness of the more didactic approach is that the facilitator directs the participants interpretation rather than permitting them to explore their own experiences. The traditional sharing circle also borders near the lowest level of reviewing, known as "the tell," where participants review the story of the activity, with little additional insight. The activities shown below provide the opportunity for further immersion into the process, and move past the point of questions and answers into the realm of self-discovery. These variations will "liven up" discussions and give more control of learning to participants.

Activities

All My Neighbors Who . . .
Alphabet Blocks
Answering the Question
Bendy Debrief
Benefits to Society
Buzz Ring
Chiji Processing Dice©

A Circle of Kindness
Clothesline
Concentric Circles
Consensus Cards
Conversation Cards©
Creating Available Space
Crossword Ending

Debriefing Bingo
Debriefing Tic Tac Toe
Dinner Notes
Domino Debrief
Efficiency and Effectiveness
Fear in a Hat
Feelings Cards
Freebie
Friendship Bracelets
Full Court Press
Having My Say
High Five
Index Card Castle
Index Card Debrief
Journaling
Labyrinth Walk
Looking Ahead
A Message for Future Generations
Mood Dudes™
Partner Watch
Playing Cards
Plus Delta
Pocket Medic Debrief
Random Ricochet
Shuffle Left, Shuffle Right

Solo Experience
S.O.S.
Soul of Sole II
Sticks in a Bundle
Stones
Stop 'N Go PRE-brief
Story Bag
SWOT Training
Talking Stick
Team Resume
Thumbs Up
Time Capsule
Timing Is Everything
Tool Cards
Treasure Chest
Treasure Chest-Mini Version
Trigger Bill
Voicemail
Walk a Mile in Your Shoes
Web of Commitment
What I Know, What I Want to Know,
    What I've Learned
Whose Stone Is It?
X-Ray Vision

Metaphoric Methods, or
Symbolic Representations of Experience

*Condense some daily experience into a glowing symbol,
and an audience is electrified.*

Ralph Waldo Emerson

Using objects as symbolic representations of an experience or as personal attributes can be a very effective method of reflection for a variety of learners. These methods provide something tangible upon which participants can attach their thoughts. This helps to give thoughts and ideas substance and shape—often in greater depth than the traditional sharing circle. Because the participants can talk about the card or object rather than about themselves, they sometimes express thoughts that otherwise would be left unsaid. These prop or symbol activities can be especially useful in drawing out introverted members of a group (Simpson, 1997). The strength of these types of activities is that they are not threatening to participants and facilitators and leave the opportunities for creative and meaningful interpretation of an experience wide open.

A visual representation of an activity is something that a person can take away from the activity and be reminded of later in transferring learning from the activity into other situations. When groups agree on an object or symbol that represents their collective experience, this symbol can end up carrying a great deal of power for a group, it can become a kind of mascot representing the group's strengths and achievements, or represent a goal to be reached.

Processing activities that use objects or cards are valuable not only because they are participant directed, but because they are also engaging and can be used in many ways that are appropriate for all age groups.

For more information related to metaphoric methods, we encourage you to read:

The Book of Metaphors, Vol 2, 1995, Michael Gass, Kendall/Hunt Publishing, Dubuque, IA. USA
    ISBN 0-7872-0306-8.

Metaphoric Activities

Bead Ceremony
Body Part Debrief™
Butterfly Life Cycle Debrief
Clay Sculptures
Friendship Bracelets
Gem Story
Group Drawing
Group Juggle Metaphor Drawing
House of Nails
Image Chips
Impression Feet
Jars

Learning Rope
Masks
Message in a Bottle
Metaphoric Cards
    Postcards
    Chiji Cards
    Expression Cards
    Metaphor Cards
Pocket Medic Debrief
Treasure Chest
Treasure Chest-Mini Version
Tool Cards

*If the person you are talking to doesn't appear to be listening, be patient.
It may simply be that he has a small piece of fluff in his ear.*

Pooh's Little Instruction Book, inspired by A. A. Milne

Individual and Self-Reflection

By three methods we may learn wisdom:
First, by reflection, which is noblest;
Second, by imitation, which is easiest;
and third, by experience, which is the bitterest.

—Confucius

Self-Reflection

Great thinkers throughout history, such as Thoreau and Descartes, have written about the benefits of time alone, free from distraction. Time away from the group for individual reflection balances and supports the group process. The benefit of time away gives learners time to reflect on things that might not have come up during a discussion. It gives people an opportunity to explore thoughts that they might not verbalize in a group setting. Journaling and other self-reflective methods can become lifetime skills that help develop insight, one of the hardest but most valuable skills to have in life.

Activities

Affirmation Cards
Group Juggle Metaphor Drawing
Journaling
Labyrinth Walk
Later Letters

Pocket Processor
Reflective Readings
Self Facilitation
Solo Experience
Stones

For additional information about reflection, read:

Knapp, Clifford E. *Lasting Lessons: A Teacher's Guide to Reflecting on Experience.* Clifford E. Knapp, Charleston, WV: ERIC/CRESS Clearinghouse, 1992. ERIC Document Number ED348204.

ACTIVITY SECTION

Activities for Processing, Debriefing, Reviewing and Reflection

Affirmation Cards

Meditation and Self Reflection

Taking a few minutes to reflect on a single word breathes new life into our souls. Affirmation Cards are a simple tool to inspire thoughts and conversation.

Concepts: If you have ever opened a fortune cookie after completing a Chinese dinner, you no doubt pondered the relevance of the fortune to your own life. We strive to make meaning out of such information. Here, the concept is quite simple. Take a minute, prepare yourself, and consider the gift that an angel has brought for you. Perhaps patience will be your word. Or calm. Or truth. Think about it.

Props/Materials Needed: A set of Angel® Cards, Power Thought Affirmation Cards, or your own set of affirming words and messages.

Directions: Here is a powerful self-reflection technique that is ideal for an audience in a quiet and peaceful place.

- After some self-reflection, encourage the group to prepare for an insightful message.
- Present each person with an affirmation card or message, and ask them to read it, and then reflect on the significance of this word or message in their own life. There is no need to have participants share their thoughts, but that is certainly permissible. Some reviewing and reflection techniques are just for individual insight.
- This is a nice closing activity.
- See the activity "Stones" for other suggestions.

Where to Find It/How to Make It: Angel® Cards are available from Music Design, Inc. 4650 North Port Washington Road, Milwaukee, WI 53212–1062 USA.

These cards were originally created as part of a board game by Joy Drake and Kathy Tyler. For more information about The Transformation Game®, Angel® Cards and workshops, contact InnerLinks, P.O. Box 16225, Seattle, WA 98116–0225 USA.

Power Thought Sticky Cards© 2001 by Louise L. Hay are published and distributed by Hay House, Inc. P.O. Box 5100, Carlsbad, CA 92018-5100 Phone: 800-654-5126 www.hayhouse.com.

You can make your own set of Affirmation Cards by writing phrases onto index cards or printing phrases onto cardstock and laminating them.

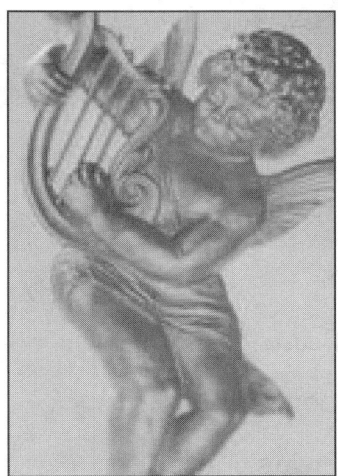

With the gift of listening comes the gift of healing.

Catherine de Hueck

All My Neighbors Who . . .

This activity is a variation of Karl Rohnke's "Have You Ever," Quicksilver, *pg. 224.*

Contributor: Patrick Torrey

Concept: To create a more active processing circle.

Props/Materials Needed: Spot markers, poly spots, carpet squares, plastic squares or index cards.

Directions:

- Have enough spot markers for every participant in the circle and one person in the center. Typically, the facilitator begins the activity in the center position.
- The central person must come up with a phrase that completes the fragment, "All My Neighbors Who . . ." Whatever the person in the middle calls out needs to be something that they have learned or experienced that day.
- Anyone in the group who also learned or experienced what was called out should meet in the center of the circle, to celebrate and give each other a high five.
- Everyone then returns to a different spot marker.
- Whoever ends up in the center position is the next person to state, "All My Neighbors Who . . ."

- Example: "All My Neighbors Who were frustrated at some point today . . ." All those people who had experienced something frustrating would leave their marker, celebrate in the center, and return to a different spot marker. A fun, active way to find out about the learnings of the day.

There was a definite process by which one made people into friends, and it involved talking to them and listening to them for hours at a time.

Rebecca West (1892–1983)

Alphabet Blocks

A "Forced Connection" Activity

While some activities create moments that fill a reviewing session completely, other activities are a bit more subtle. This technique requires participants to reflect, and to create a link between the events they just experienced and the letters or words appearing before them. For example: What word or expression starting with the letter "W" describes how you feel when you see a rainbow? As you can see, these are not direct correlations that jump out at you, but rather ideas that generate multiple answers. They are answers that require a bit more searching and thought to complete.

Concepts: As a participant first identifies words that correspond to the letter they have been given, they are constantly reflecting on the application of that word. With respect to the rainbow example above, a participant may think, "how do I feel when I see a rainbow? Wilted—No. Wet—maybe, if it is raining. Wonderful—yes, that's it!"

If participants are given multiple letters, they can be asked to create a word which communicates their thoughts to the rest of the group. This can be a non-verbal activity, or the facilitator can encourage participants to talk about the work they created.

Vocabulary skills are enhanced by using this activity (great for academics and foreign language skills). Spelling skills are enhanced too.

Most importantly, participants are reflecting on a variety of possibilities, instead of simply moving to an obvious one. Sometimes the connections can be quite unique!

Props/Materials Needed: Letter blocks.

Directions:

- Provide a collection of about a dozen letters, either on cubes (dice) or tiles.

- Toss these out to the group. Those letters facing upward are the only ones available for this activity.

- Next instruct individuals, or the entire group, to create connections between the various letters appearing, or to make a word from as many of the letters as possible.

Where to Find It/How to Make It: Letter blocks can be found in a variety of toy stores, teacher's supply outlets, and game shops. Here are a few possibilities for inexpensive letter sources:

Wooden ABC/123 Blocks from Melissa & Doug Classic Wooden Toys, Westport, CT. Phone 1-800-284-3948 to find a distributor near you.

Scrabble® Brand Crossword Game from the Selchow & Righter Company, Amsterdam, NY. Available in most game stores.

Boggle® Word Game. Also available in most game stores.

Alphabet Dice from Collective Wisdom™, Deltaville, VA. A colonial children's game.

Try taking the alphabet characters from an older computer keyboard. You can also cut letters from magazines or newspaper headlines. Finally, you can make your own set of letters, including foreign alphabet characters, by drawing or woodburning them onto wooden cubes available at most craft stores.

Answering the Question

Insights from *The Book of Answers*

While there are many sources for interesting questions for facilitators, Carol Bolt wrote the first book of answers!

Concepts: Sometimes in life we are just searching for the answers. This can happen even within an adventure-based learning experience. When the answers come, it is our job to make sense of them. Here is an activity that does just that.

Props/Materials Needed: *The Book of Answers,* by Carol Bolt.

Directions:

Photo courtesy of
Jeff Baird, High 5.

- At the completion of a task, the facilitator can innocently ask, "any questions?" When the questions come, they can produce *The Book of Answers,* and allow the group to reflect on the appropriateness of the answers. For example, a participant might ask, "could we have accomplished the task in a different manner?" to which the book offers, "the best solution may not be the obvious one."

Where to Find It/How to Make It: *The Book of Answers,* 1999, Carol Bolt, Hyperion, New York, NY ISBN 0–7868–6566–0

Balloon Blow

This simple prop activity will "stretch" your participants.

Contributor: Mary Ann Loeffler, CTRS, Metro State College of Denver

Props/Materials Needed: One balloon per person.

Concept: To help participants identify changes they experienced during the program.

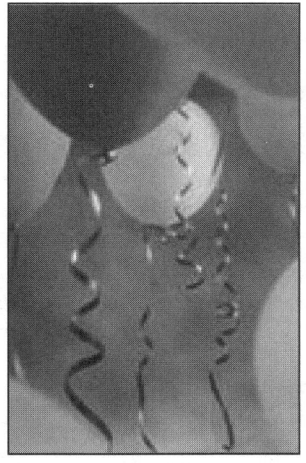

Directions:

- Have your participants stand in a circle.
- Give each person a balloon.
- Instruct them to blow up the balloon and hold onto the end.
- Next, tell them to let the balloon go, retrieve it, and then bring it back to the circle. Have everyone sit and place their balloon in front of them.
- Talk about how after a balloon is inflated, it never goes back to its pre-stretched shape.
- Then, ask questions like, "Where did you stretch yourself today?" "Where did you collapse?" "Where do you find resistance (in your life, school, work)?", "Where do you find energy/breath that helps you flow?"
- Invite each person to share.

Where to Find It/How to Make It: You can buy balloons at most discount or party supply stores.

Balloon Faces

A Creative Drawing Processing Technique

Some conversational forms of processing are difficult for those who are unaccustomed to speaking in public, or who would like additional time to formulate their thoughts into words. Here is an activity that allows both types of participants an opportunity to express themselves in a safe environment.

Concept: This artistic style of reviewing is more individual than group-based. Each participant is given an opportunity to illustrate their own feelings, and to share them with the entire group. It can be interesting to hear how different members of the same team can share totally different experiences from the same activity session.

Props/Materials Needed: Colorful balloons and markers.

Directions:

- Provide a colorful variety of round balloons for each person in the group. It is a good idea to have a few extra, in case anyone bursts their balloons while blowing them up or drawing on them. You may also want to find balloon colors that reflect the skin color of the multicultural group that you are facilitating. You will also need a collection of colorful markers to draw on each balloon.

- Instruct each person to inflate their balloon, and then to draw themselves with the facial expression they now have in regards to today's experience.

- After completing their drawing, participants are encouraged to share their drawing and explain their feelings, thoughts and facial expressions.

Bead Ceremony

Beads and bead ceremonies date back to early times in many cultures around the world. The ceremonies shown here work with all group sizes.

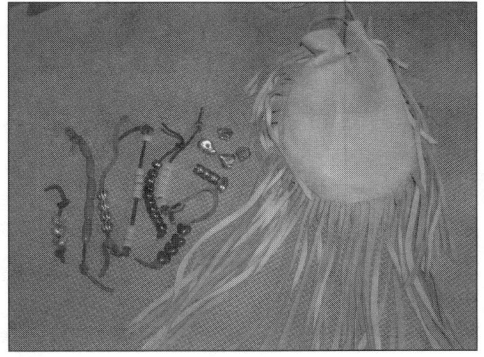

Concept: There are a variety of ways to frame and use beads in processing. The basic concept is to have each bead represent something significant, (i.e., a way you made an impression on me, an element that the group performed well on, something you did really well, a goal met, etc.). The way the beads are passed out, presented, or displayed can be unique to each situation.

Props/Materials Needed: Beads of all sizes, shapes, and colors. Leather strips or shoe laces.

Directions:

- For a multi-day program, a bead ceremony can be a great way to conclude each day. Set the mood for your ceremony in ways that have impact, and create a permanent memory for your participants. Some suggestions include dimming the lights, sitting around a campfire/lantern, or playing background music. Present each participant with a leather necklace (see picture) that has leather fringe on which to place beads. Each time you have a bead ceremony, have everyone sit in a circle. Present each bead separately and tell them the significance of the bead and why they are receiving it. As you are talking, pass the beads around on a leather string and have them pull off one bead and place it somewhere on their leather necklace. After several days, the necklace starts to fill with different colors and shapes of beads. The beads then tell a story of the experiences the group has had together. Participants will be able to state what each bead represents and why they received it. It is a great momento for them to take home, to remind them of their experiences.

- At a conference, invite each participant to pick out ten same-colored beads at registration and put them on a bracelet. Invite them to give away a bead each time someone teaches them something or makes an impression on them. Everyone can have a multi-colored bracelet at the end of the conference.

Where to Find It/How to Make It: You can find pony beads and other shaped beads at craft stores, jewelry stores and many large discount stores. Leather straps and leather pieces can often be found at these same locations. Furniture upholstery shops sometimes donate scraps of leather that they usually throw away. You can buy a special strap tool that will make strips of leather from scraps at craft stores, or visit Tandy Leather (www.tandyleather.com or www.leatherfactory.com).

There are people who, instead of listening to what is being said to them, are already listening to what they are going to say themselves.

Albert Guinon (1863–1923)

Bendy Debrief

This activity was shared by Jason Knott.

Inspired by: Anthony Scott, Camp Eagle Director

Contributor: Jason Knott

Concepts: Using bendable characters to depict feelings experienced. Talking about how body language plays into different emotions.

Props/Materials Needed: Enough bendable characters for each person in the group. The more choices, the better.

Directions:

- Ask each member of the group to choose a bendable character and to mold it to look like a feeling they experienced in the activity/session.

- Have each participant share why they molded their character the way they did. This allows participants to express a body position—not just a facial feature for how they are feeling.

Where to Find It/How to Make It:

You can find bendable characters in most toy stores. You can also find stickers with different expressions on them to put over the smiley face of the bendy figure. Sometimes it is hard to talk about a sad feeling when Mr. Bendy is all smiles.

Benefits to Society

Think Globally—Act Locally

It can be a bit of an eye opener to realize that the skills learned in an adventure-based learning program can be utilized to change the world. This processing activity helps participants consider the greater good of their efforts.

Photo courtesy of Jeff Baird, High 5.

Concepts: Considering who the lessons of today will benefit increases the value of this information. Understanding that I have gained a new skill is one level of understanding, but realizing that this skill can benefit additional folks, some of whom I have yet to meet, brings even more value. A list of individuals and groups to consider is helpful, and assists individual group members in considering all the possible outcomes for the skills learned in today's program.

Props/Materials Needed: Visual models are helpful for this technique. Draw the following titles on paper plates, index cards, or laminated pages.

Me	Our School
My Partner	Our Society
The Whole Team	Our Country
Other Work Groups	Other Countries
My Family	Our Customers
Our Families	The Whole World
Our Community	Future Generations
Our Class	

Directions:

- At the completion of the program or activity, ask the group what skills they have learned during this activity.

- Next ask them how this skill benefits the various individuals and groups listed here.

- Allow participants a few moments each to consider the groups listed. Remember, not all forms of review require verbalization. Even while participants are considering the list, they are reflecting on their experience.

Body Part Debrief™

This activity is one of the most successful debriefing activities available and certainly one of our favorites. It has been used with groups as young as four year olds, and all the way up to senior citizens' groups. Corporate groups respond well to this activity and the balls have an uncanny way of creating a safe environment for people to share.

Created by: Michelle Cummings and Brian Brolin.

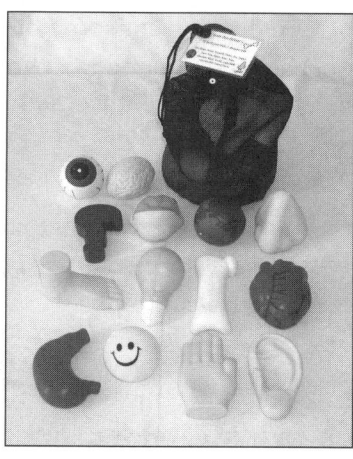

Concept: The Body Part Debrief activity is a great activity for both new and seasoned facilitators. It is simple enough in nature that groups of any age will use it with ease. The body parts have a "coolness" factor to them that fosters a safe environment for people to talk. If you are having a hard time getting your participants to share or reflect, this activity will help solve that problem.

The basic concept for this activity is that you have different balls or objects that are shaped like body parts. Each part can represent a metaphor related to that part. For example:

"Eye" ball

- Could represent something new that you saw in yourself or someone else.
- What vision do you have for yourself or your group?
- What qualities do you see in yourself?
- How did you see yourself perform within the group?

"Stomach" ball

- Could represent something that took guts for you to do.
- What pushed you outside your comfort zone?
- What sick feelings have you felt before?
- Was something hard to stomach for you?

"Brain" ball

- Could represent something new that you learned about yourself, a teammate, or the group.
- What thoughts do you have?
- What did you learn through your experience?

"Heart" ball

- Could represent a feeling that you experienced.
- What things come from the heart?
- What means a lot to you?

"Hand" ball

- In what way did the group support you?
- Could represent someone you would like to applaud for a job well done.
- How did you lend a hand during the activity?

"Ear" Ball

- Could represent something you listened to.
- What was a good idea you heard?
- Could represent something that was hard to hear—did you receive constructive feedback or not-so-constructive feedback?

"Smiley face" ball

- Could represent something that made you smile or laugh.
- What are some of your positive attributes?
- What are some positive attributes of the group?

"Foot" ball

- What direction would you like to see yourself/or your group go?
- Have you ever stuck your foot in your mouth and said something you wished you had not said?

"Lips" ball

- Have you ever said anything that has hurt someone's feelings?
- Give an example of when your actions spoke louder than your words.
- Could represent something that was spoken or whispered.

"Bone" ball

- What strengths do you have?
- Have you ever come close to a breaking point?
- Have you ever felt broken?

"Full body" ball

- Who or what supports you?
- What are you good at, i.e., what uses all of your abilities?

"Spine" ball

- What is the backbone of your company, family or organization?
- What took a lot of backbone to do?

"Nose" ball

- Did you stick your nose into someone else's business?
- What about that performance really stunk? What would you have changed?

Props/Materials Needed: Body part balls. You could also draw body parts on a piece of paper.

Directions:

Here are two different ways you can facilitate this activity.

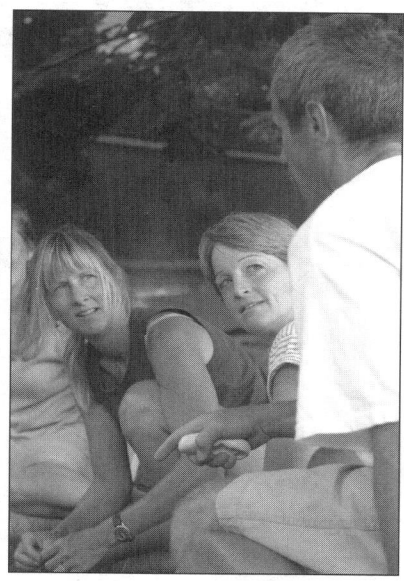

Photo courtesy of Jeff Baird, High 5.

- Present each ball and explain the different metaphors they could talk about when they receive that ball. Frontloading this activity can give the participants an idea of what to do. Once you describe a ball, toss it randomly to someone in the group. Then as you describe the other balls the person who received the first ball will have time to think about what they want to share. Once all of the balls are out in the circle go back to the person to whom you tossed the first ball. Let them share with the group and then have them toss the ball randomly to someone else in the group. Then go to the second person you threw a ball to, etc. You can use as many balls as you would like; however, more than four balls can confuse the order in which people are supposed to talk.

- Another way to set this up is to describe each ball and then leave the balls in the center of the circle. Then a person can choose what they want to share. Have them come forward and pick up a ball that relates to their experience. Depending on the time you have allotted for sharing, you can let participants share as much or as little as they want.

Where to Find It/How to Make It: Michelle Cummings designed a set of soft balls and objects that represent various body parts and sells them at Training Wheels as Body Part Debrief and Body Part Debrief Deluxe. (www.training-wheels.com)

These experiential resource sets are also available at Training Wheels, Grip-It Adventures, Leahy and Associates.

You can also find individual objects such as eyeballs, ears, noses and hearts at science stores, craft stores and novelty shops.

Experiential Moment

Jennifer Fox Marter of Synergo shared a great story about her experience with the body part debrief.

In Portland, Oregon there is an event that happens every spring known as the Rose Festival. Part of the festival is two days of boat races in "Dragon Boats." One Dragon Boat team (Pink Phoenix™ from Portland) is made up of women who are all breast cancer survivors. Pink Phoenix experienced a day of teambuilding on Synergo's course and had such an amazing day, they still have not stopped talking about it! At the end of the day they were wrapping up, all standing in a circle using the body part debrief activity as "talking pieces." It came around to one woman who said that none of these items spoke to her. She reached into her shirt and pulled out her prosthetic breast, threw it into the circle and said "Now that's a talking piece!"

Bucket Full of Ideas

Voting Made Simple

Here is a simple technique for voting within the group that allows participants to voice their ideas without saying a word.

Concepts: For some groups, especially those that are new to each other, speaking up can be difficult for some members of the group. Encouragement by the facilitator is helpful, but in the end, members speak up when they feel safe that their opinions and comments will be accepted and listened to by the other members of the group. The Voting Buckets used here allow each participant to voice their opinion, without having to speak out loud.

Props/Materials Needed: A token, such as a tennis ball, stone, or marble, for each member of the group and enough buckets for the number of choices presented.

Directions:

- At the completion of the challenge, the facilitator invites each member of the group to take one of the tokens available.

- The facilitator presents the buckets that have been identified with the categories the group must choose from. For example, the categories GOOD, BETTER, and BEST can be written on three different buckets.

- The facilitator invites the members of the group to toss their tokens into the bucket of their choice.

- At this point, it should be fairly simple for the group to identify the bucket with the most votes. It is important for the facilitator to create a safe place for those members whose vote falls outside the majority of the group. Rather than saying, "hey, who voted GOOD when the rest of us voted BEST?", the facilitator can ask the group, "can you imagine how someone could vote GOOD for this last activity?" This style of facilitation encourages a sense of empathy and open communication, rather than animosity towards an alternative view.

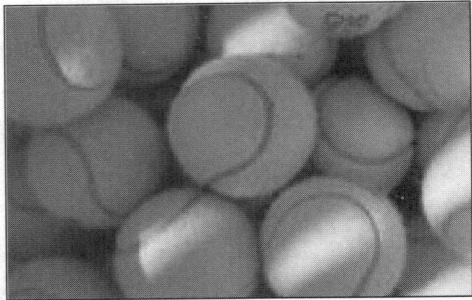

Where to Find It/How to Make It: You can find buckets and unique storage containers and planters at garden supply stores. Choose tokens that can be tossed without breaking.

Free and fair discussion will ever be found the firmest friend to truth.

G. Campbell

Butterfly Life Cycle Debrief

This debriefing tool aids in discussions about change.

Concept: There are four stages to the life cycle of a butterfly: egg, larva, chrysalis, and butterfly. Individuals and groups go through many stages throughout their experiences. Using the stages of the butterfly can aid discussions around the different stages experienced by the group.

This activity is much like the Caterpillar/Butterfly Debrief except it talks about the four stages of the butterfly.

Props/Materials Needed: There are a couple of different props that can aid in the visual and tactile impact of the activity. There is a Caterpillar/Butterfly reversible puppet made by Folkmanis. There is also a set of plastic pieces called the Butterfly Life Cycle stages. There are 4 small plastic pieces to the set that represent the four stages of the butterfly: egg, larva, chrysalis, and butterfly. The pieces are accurate replicas and are large enough to handle nicely. You could also print off pictures of the four stages.

Directions: Demonstrate the miracle of metamorphosis and change with this ingenious reversible caterpillar/butterfly plush tool or the Butterfly Life Cycle set.

- The concept of change is a great concept to talk about with this activity. Any groups or individuals going through some kind of change can make comparisons between themselves and the stages of the butterfly. Pass the tools around the circle as you talk about the different stages and let them look and touch them.

Some things to talk about:

- Change takes time, it does not happen overnight, much like the caterpillar becoming a butterfly.
- Caterpillars come in different shapes and sizes. Some are beautiful and furry, others are bald and deemed ugly.
- Butterflies come in different shapes, sizes, and colors.
- In the caterpillar stage it takes a long time to get from place to place. Once change takes place you can spread your wings and fly.

- For the caterpillar's change to take place, it has to go into a cocoon state, away from others, for his change happen. This process is much like a recovery center or counseling session.
- For the butterfly to develop properly it must struggle out of the cocoon by itself. If it receives any outside help it can cause the butterfly to abnormally develop and/or die.
- A caterpillar is not recognized for what it used to be once it becomes a butterfly.
- For working teams use these four stages of groups in relation to: Forming, Storming, Norming, and Performing.
- For addictions groups use the pieces as representations for the different stages of recovery.
- For Religious groups: Use the stages to talk about personal faith development.
- For kids going through puberty: Ain't change fun?
- For kids advancing to the next grade: How will things be different next year? New teachers, new classes, new friends, etc.

Where to Find It/How to Make It: You can find this reversible puppet at science and nature stores. You can also use clip art or find pictures of the different stages to share with your group. (www.insectlore.com). Also available at Training Wheels (www.training-wheels.com).

Buzz Ring

Talking in Circles

Pat Rastall came up with this activity after visiting a science show and seeing this "whirring ring thing" there. He bought one, took it out to his ropes course and created this activity which he calls the Buzz Ring.

Creator: Pat Rastall

Concept: This great ring will get your participants talking about the "buzz words" in a fun way. Get the rings buzzing and talk about what those buzz words mean.

Props/Materials Needed: One Buzz Ring.

Directions:

- To process with the ring, talk about what the "buzz" words are that your group may encounter during the program. For example, your group may come up with the words: trust, teamwork, communication, respect, and leadership. Each "buzz word" is assigned to one of the small rings.

- Explain to the group that you are going to get the buzz words "buzzing" on the ring. Go ahead and start up your buzz ring!

- The object is to pass the buzz ring around the circle while seeing if the group can keep the rings buzzing the whole time.

- While the group is passing the ring around, you can talk about the buzz words and what they will mean throughout the day in your program. You can also have your group set goals based on some of these words including allowing for mistakes, passing rules, etc. If someone in the group makes the rings stop, you can process it immediately or encourage them to get the rings going again and then process it at the end as a large group.

There are several things to bring up as you process this activity. Here are a few examples:

Was anyone nervous to be the one receiving the ring? Why? Examples they may give may be, not wanting to fail in front of the group, or not wanting to let the group down by making a mistake. This opens up a great opportunity to talk about how those issues might come up throughout the day as the group does initiatives together. It is also good to point out that most people have not played with a buzz ring before, so being willing to try new things in front of the group is important. It is a great way to start the day and then to come back to at the end of the day.

Sometimes if the rings stop in the process, a participant will give a good effort at getting the rings going again but only get three of the five rings buzzing and then continue passing it around. This gives you a good avenue to talk about how difficult it can be to keep all five of the buzz words they came up with (trust, teamwork, communication, respect, cooperation) going at one time. Can we have trust if we do not have respect at the same time? Some good dialogue can develop from this.

Another way to use it is to ask who in the group is good at "multi-tasking." After those people admit (or do not admit!) to the skill, pass the buzzing ring around the circle and ask each participant to tell the group three things about themselves while keeping the rings buzzing. This is difficult even for group members who are great multi-taskers!

Getting the rings started can be tricky and you just need to play with them awhile to figure out which system works best for you. Some place their palm down on the still rings and give them a good spin. Turning the large ring at the same time will get the rings buzzing. Others will slap at the rings and turn the large ring at the same time to get them buzzing. Play with it and see which method works best for you.

Where to Find It/How to Make It: Various novelty and toy shops. Training Wheels. Adventure Hardware. Grip-It Adventures.

Chiji Processing Dice©

The Chiji Dice offer an alternative to straight question-and-answer sessions, and the use of the blue control die adds an element of chance that offers excitement and variety to traditional processing.

Creators: Institute for Experiential Education, Buzz Bocher, Steve Simpson, and Dan Miller

Concept: Chiji Processing Dice are an example of participant-directed processing; they help to shift some of the responsibility for successful processing from the facilitator to the participants. The sequence of fact-finding, analysis of feelings, and transference not only takes participants through a progression for processing a specific event, but also presents an overall lesson on proper processing. In other words, it trains people about processing with the hope that using the dice will enhance participants' ability to self-process.

Props/Materials Needed: One set of Chiji Processing Dice.

Directions: The **question dice** are rolled in sequential order: first red, then orange, then yellow. The roll of each question die is accompanied by the blue **control die.**

- After a group of participants is arranged in a processing circle, the facilitator asks someone in the group to roll the red and blue dice simultaneously. The blue die determines who answers the question and the red die asks the question. For example, a student named Chris tosses the dice. The blue die says, "Roller picks person." And the red die says, "What was your contribution?" This means that Chris, as the roller, picks a person in the group to state his or her contribution to the previous activity.

- The facilitator decides the number of times each question die is used. Two rolls each for the red, orange and yellow dice is most common, although the processing and rolling of the dice may carry on as long as the activity continues to be fun and informative.

- It is recommended to use the dice in this sequence: the red die with the blue die first, then the orange with the blue, and finally the yellow with the blue. The questions on

the red die are fact-finding questions, which are followed by the analysis and feeling questions of the orange die, which are followed by the transference questions of the yellow die. Each die is described in greater detail below:

Red Fact-Finding Die: This is the most basic question die. It asks factual questions or questions that simply summarize the events of the experience. The questions are intentionally easy to answer and set the stage for the other two question dice. Red is the foundation color and represents strength and action.

Orange Analysis Die: The questions on this die elicit feelings from the participants. They also help participants analyze an experience; often participants discuss in detail the same events summarized with the red die. The analysis questions try to find out what went well, what did not go well, and why. Orange is the color of gut feelings and represents vitality.

Yellow Transference Die: This die ties the specific experience to future experiences and to everyday life—after learning from an experience, how can participants apply this knowledge? Yellow is the color of warmth and represents memory, power, and enthusiasm.

Blue Control Die: The blue die determines who answers the questions on the other dice and is always rolled simultaneously with one of the others. Blue is the color of wisdom and represents the opening of communication channels.

Where to Find It/How to Make It: Institute for Experiential Education, www.chiji.com. Training Wheels. High 5 Adventures. Ask your local challenge course vendor.

A Circle of Kindness

I've Always Wanted to Tell You . . .

While some forms of 360 degree feedback encourage brutal honesty, this format is framed in a slightly more benevolent manner. Multiple participants are allowed to quietly express their observations to other group members, and then receive multiple comments in return. This style of feedback can be used as a final closing activity.

Concepts: One benefit of this activity is that it is less threatening for participants to speak to just one person at a time rather than to the whole group. Sometimes participants are more open if they are not speaking to their facilitator, but rather directly to individual members of their group. Remember good processing can happen even if the facilitator is not present to hear it! This is a useful activity not only to process a specific experience, but also as a great closing activity for a session or program day.

Props/Materials Needed: None.

Directions:

- Half of the group forms a circle, facing inward. Participants can be seated in chairs or standing, and are asked to close their eyes.

- The remaining half of the group forms a slightly larger second circle, also facing inward so that a person is standing behind each person in the inner circle. This form of feedback is not intended to be a conversation, but rather a commentary.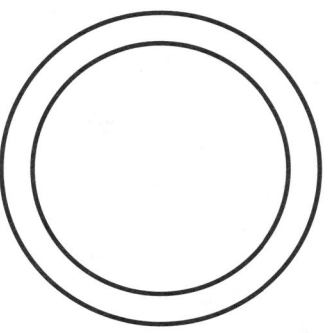

- The most a member of the inner circle can say is, "thank you."

- The outer circle members are invited to whisper into the ear of the person in front of them some personal observations and generally kind comments about their involvement with the group, their personal strengths, or their performance today.

- When finished, outer circle members move to their right, and continue sharing comments with the next inner circle participant. The facilitator may wish to give an example of suitable comments that can be shared in this manner.

Circles of Influence

Understanding Our Place in the Circle

Things happen for a reason, and this visual technique provides some diagnostic clues about the ability of a group to work together successfully.

Concepts: Understanding how our individual contributions link to the entire team's effort as a whole is an important concept. This reviewing technique provides some valuable information about the roles and responsibilities taken on by various members of the group and encourages each of us to consciously think about how we choose the roles we play.

Props/Materials Needed: A sidewalk chalk bull's-eye drawing on pavement, concentric rope circles in the grass, or a flip chart with a bull's-eye target and adhesive notes (with names) to represent each participant.

Directions:

- At the completion of the activity, the facilitator leads the group to a large bull's-eye that has been created.
- Next, the facilitator presents this model, and identifies each of the various circles by name, and explains the significance of each
- The inner circle (or outer circle) represents AUTHORITY, those participants who took the responsibility to "get the job done."
- The next circle represents RESPONSIBILITY, those people who ultimately felt it was their assignment to make sure the job was completed, or that would likely take the blame if it was not completed correctly.
- The next circle represents INFLUENCE, those people whose opinions and comments contributed to the overall result of the group.
- Next comes the KNOWLEDGE circle, those participants whose information was valuable to the group.
- At the next level comes AWARENESS. This is the location for team members who were contributors to the process, but remained out of the loop in the planning stages.

- Finally comes the circle of those who were UNCONNECTED. It is difficult to measure the contribution of these folks, either in positive or negative values.

- At this point, the facilitator invites the members of the group to move to a location within the bull's-eye pattern that they feel illustrates their contribution to the team's efforts in the most recent activity. An additional discussion about how each person found themselves in this location is appropriate. The group can also discuss other members' agreement with each person's position. This is an interesting 360 degree feedback model brought to life.

- An alternative to this activity is for the facilitator to define each segment of the bull's-eye pattern for the group, and then ask participants to draw in each segment the skills, talents or behaviors they would expect from a participant at these levels.

- Next, the group can discuss where each person should stand, followed by a general discussion of each person's placement.

Where to Find It/How to Make It: You can make your own target or bull's-eye pattern with sidewalk chalk or rope, or purchase an archery target from a hunting supply store for indoor use.

Discussion is an exchange of knowledge;
argument an exchange of ignorance.

Robert Quillen

Clay Sculptures

Michelle Cummings utilized this activity at The Saint Francis Academy in Atchison, Kansas, when she worked there as a counselor for at-risk youth.

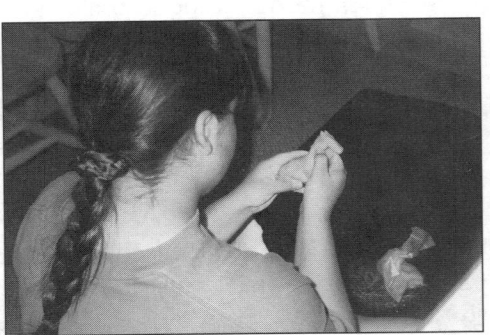

Concept: Providing a therapeutic, hands-on approach to debriefing.

Props/Materials Needed: Molding clay. Plastic mats.

Directions:

- For set up, lay out plastic mats on the floor so each person has their own space to create their sculpture.

- Play instrumental music in the background to set the mood for thinking and creating.

- Give each participant a blob of clay and ask them to make a clay sculpture. Ask them to make it representative of the learnings they have had in the program. Talk about metaphors and how the clay sculpture could be a metaphor representing the issue or learning that each person had.

- After everyone is finished, they can bring their sculpture to a sharing circle and explain what they sculpted and what it represents to them.

- After the sculptures have dried, they can be decorated with paint.

Where to Find It/How to Make It: Craft stores sell several types of molding clay. Quick drying clay is recommended.

Clothesline

This activity is great for a long-term process and review, where envelopes are left up for an extended period and notes can be written each day. At the end of the day, week, month, school year, or when someone needs an emotional boost, they can read the cards deposited in their envelope.

Concept: To allow each participant to provide feedback to their teammates.

Props/Materials Needed: 1 large envelope for each person. A stack of colorful index cards. Pens or pencils. A piece of cord or rope. Clothespins or masking tape.

Directions:

- String up a rope like a clothesline.
- Give each person a large manila envelope to place their name on and to decorate with their own design.
- Use a clothespin or masking tape to attach each envelope to the clothesline.
- Instruct the group that anytime they see someone doing something positive they should write it down on an index card and put it in that person's envelope. This can be done at the beginning of the day and be used repeatedly throughout the day.

- Encourage participants to write a note to everyone in the group.
- At the end of the day, have each person get their envelope and sit in a circle. Go around the circle and have each person share one of the cards that was in their envelope. This is a great way to end the day on a positive note.

Concentric Circles

This activity was adapted by Jennifer Stanchfield from its traditional use as a get-acquainted activity to an engaging processing tool. Variations of this icebreaker have been utilized by many adventure based educational programs. The variation that prompted its use as a reflective activity here was adapted from an activity presented in John Luckner and Reldan Nadler's book: Processing the Experience.

Concepts: This reflective technique is substantially less intimidating for many participants than a general discussion since each person is asked to converse with only one other person at a time. It also creates conversation between participants rather than between the facilitator and participants. Sometimes participants are more open if they are not speaking to their facilitator. Remember: effective processing can occur even when the facilitator is not present to hear it! This activity can be used not only to process a specific experience, but also as an excellent closing activity for a session or program day.

Props/Materials Needed: None.

Directions:

- The group is invited to form two circles with the participants facing each other.
- The participants are asked to greet each other by name and then are asked to participate in an engaging cooperative activity together, such as "finger fencing" or "gotcha" (see the book *Back Pocket Adventure,* by Jim Grout and Karl Rohnke, for creative partner activities).
- After completing the partner activity, participants are asked to share their answers to a reflective question asked by the facilitator concerning the activity or experience the group is processing.
- After a few moments, or when the conversational energy diminishes, the facilitator invites the inner circle to rotate and form new partnerships by having the inner group move three spaces to the left, saying hello to the two people they pass by. The new

partners greet each other and the facilitator provides another cooperative activity and question to discuss.

- The activity continues with alternating movement, activities and questions.

- If you would like more participants to hear some of the insights expressed by others during the activity, before each rotation the facilitator can ask if anyone would like to share their conversation with the group.

- For a closing activity, participants can answer questions such as "Is there a moment from today that stood out for you?" "Were you surprised at yourself any time today?" "Did you see something in another group member that you were especially proud of?"

The art of conversation consist as much in listening politely,
as in talking agreeably.

Atwell

Consensus Cards

Kelly Johnston Smith came up with the concept of Consensus Cards while working with a group of fifth graders. They had a hard time understanding the concept of Consensus Thumbs, the Thumbs Up, Thumbs Down, or Thumbs Sideways system of consensus, so she came up with Consensus Cards. See Consensus Thumbs, page 82.

Creator: Kelly Johnston Smith.

Concept: Consensus cards are a decision-making tool designed for use with participants who need to come to consensus on an issue. Most groups will take a vote and identify majority-rules voting as consensus. Individuals need a way to make their voice heard and the group needs a way to easily check for individual responses. Consensus Cards emerged from this need.

Props/Materials Needed: Consensus cards (see picture).

Directions:

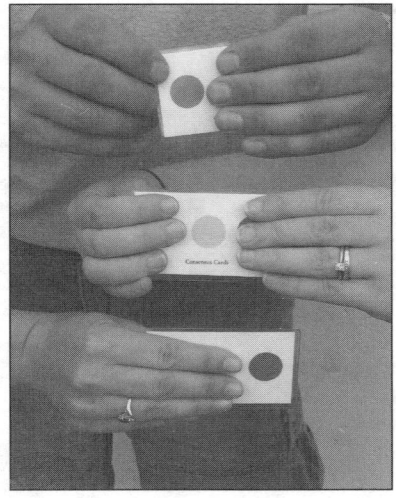

- Consensus cards are palm-sized cards with three colored circles arranged like a stop light on it. The top circle is red, then yellow, followed by green at the bottom. On the back, the definition of each color is printed: red indicates that I do not agree with this plan, yellow indicates that I need more information/I have a question before proceeding, and green indicates that I do agree with this plan.

- Each member of the group receives one consensus card.

- Once a proposal is given to the group, each member votes by holding up his/her card with two of the three colors covered by his/her hand. If everyone is green, the group can go forward with the proposal. If anyone is yellow, the group must respond to the person's need or request before continuing. If anyone is red, the person is given the opportunity to explain his/her resistance and offer a compromise. This visual voting system allows the group to quickly hear from each person and the use of the stoplight colors is familiar to them.

Consensus cards work best when initially introduced as a decision-making tool for a group decision with minimal consequences. For example, you might ask the group to decide how many hits they want as their goal for the activity Moonball, and then introduce the consensus cards for them to use to find out if everyone is in agreement. You can then continue to have the group use the cards throughout the day for increasingly difficult decisions.

Sabotage: If a participant simply answers red to any proposal, in order to delay the group process, the facilitator/teacher needs to intervene appropriately. One way to do this is to require anyone voting red to give the group an alternative suggestion or plan. As is the case with many consensus building tools, consensus cards allow participants to voice their concerns without blocking the progress of the group.

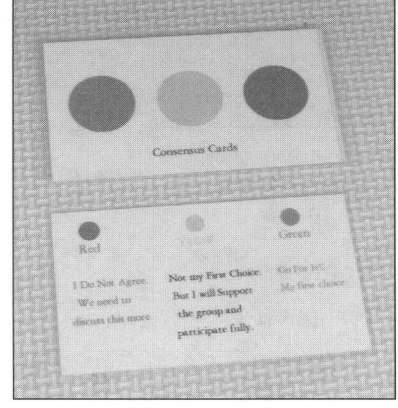

Where to Find It/How to Make It: These cards are very simple to make using clip art. Business card stock is the perfect size, especially for small hands. Print the three-colored circles on one side and the directions for each color on the back. Laminating the cards will give you a tool for a lifetime!

You can find these cards at Adventure Hardware, Grip It Adventures, and Training Wheels.

Consensus Thumbs

Thumbs Up, Thumbs Sideways, Thumbs Down

This facilitator favorite was difficult to credit to a single source, so thanks to everyone who contributed. Have thumb, will process!

Concepts: To aid participants in consensus voting. See Consensus Cards for more consensus activities.

Props/Materials Needed: One thumb per participant.

Directions:

- Define consensus for the group.
- Next, demonstrate the three positions of the thumb and what each position means.

1. Thumbs Up: I agree with the decision.
2. Thumbs Sideways: It wouldn't be my first choice, but I will fully participate and support the group.
3. Thumbs Down: I do not agree. We need to discuss further.

- Help the group understand that consensus is achieved when there are no participants with a thumbs down. If there is one thumbs down you have majority rules, not consensus.

 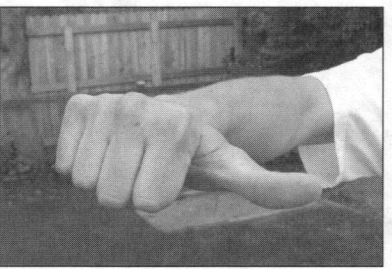 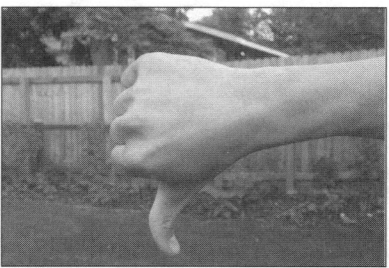

The power of illustrative anecdotes often lies not in how well they present reality, but in how well they reflect the core beliefs of their audience.

Barbara Mikkelson, Snopes.com, 04-10-04

Conversation Cards©

Talk to Me

Facilitators know that one good question is often enough to get a group of people talking, sharing and connecting. Conversation Cards is a tool designed to stimulate conversation, getting to know others on a deeper level, and to explore issues of risk, trust and emotional safety within a group.

Creator: Lisa Blockus

Type of Activity: Self-disclosure and discovery.

Props/Materials Needed: A set of Conversation Cards.

Concept:

- The Conversation Cards concept is simple: a series of thought provoking questions are written on cards and are then divided into categories organized around level of risk and self-disclosure.

- The low risk category includes general questions about likes, dislikes, and other safe topics. This category is high on fun and a great way to get participants better acquainted. An example of a question in this category is, "what is your favorite holiday?"

- Medium risk questions go a bit beyond surface conversation and get people to reveal a little more about themselves. An example of a conversation starter in this category is, "what three words would you most like said about you?"

- The high risk category includes questions that require a fair amount of personal reflection, self-awareness, and a sense of vulnerability with the group to give a genuine response. "What is something that you wish your friends or family better understood about you?" is an example of the kinds of questions included in this category.

Over 200 college students (ages 17–21) around the country—along with professional college personnel administrators, adventure education-facilitators, and counselors—took part in evaluating the questions and sorted them into the three levels of perceived risk. Use has shown that these questions foster great discussion and discovery among high school students as well.

Conversation Cards have proven to be a versatile tool to bring people together. People have used the cards informally around a campfire, over a meal, in the car, and as a break during a business meeting. The cards can also be used as a part of a formal activity with specific outcomes and goals. One structured activity to try is to place the cards in three piles based on the risk level. Each individual takes a turn by drawing a card from ANY pile. The participant then reads the question and shares their answer. Try several rounds of this and watch the risk taking level in the group go up as they become more connected and more willing to share.

Where to Find It: Contact Lisa Blockus, lmb57@cornell.edu. Training Wheels.

It gets you nowhere if the other person's tail is only just in sight for the second half of the conversation.

Pooh's Little Instruction Book, inspired by A. A. Milne

Creating Available Space

The Concept of Available Space

Occasionally, a facilitator may encounter a situation where the time available for a debriefing session is limited. Rather than beginning this session and abruptly interrupting it when time has run out, the concept of available space can be expressed at the beginning of the processing session.

Concepts: While this style of processing severely limits the utility and outcome of the session, it does recreate a typical life situation: limited time. By informing team members of the limited time available, and asking participants to consider the necessity of their comments, group members reflect on their own contributions to the team's progress. Because of the limiting nature of this style of reflection, we suggest that you do not employ this technique more than once in a program.

Props/Materials Needed: Five to ten unique tokens. Such tokens could be polished stones, marbles, tennis balls, index cards, or any other easily identifiable objects.

Directions:

- The facilitator provides a few tokens that are easily within the reach of each group member.

- Each token represents an opportunity for a member of the group to express an opinion during the processing session.

- A few of these items are placed at the center of the reviewing group, and participants are informed of the limited time available for dicusssion.

Photo courtesy of Jeff Baird, High 5.

- Those members who have an urgent need or desire to voice their comments are asked to take a token. When these comments have been voiced, the group moves on.

Creative Questions

The inspiration for this activity came from a set of get-to-know-you questions called Creative Juicers. These cards are no longer in print, so Michelle Cummings developed a new set of questions.

Creator: Michelle Cummings

Concept: Creative Questions is a collection of questions from professionals in the experiential education field. Several of these questions were inspired by Clifford Knapp's book, *Lasting Lessons*. Its purpose is to help facilitators in asking appropriate questions during their debriefing sessions. This enables participants to transfer learning from the experience to real life.

Props/Materials Needed: One deck of Creative Questions. There are 60 laminated question cards that are double sided, 120 processing questions in total. The questions are categorized and alphabetized for quick and easy access. Categories include appreciation, communication, cooperating, feelings, judgement, leadership, liking yourself, listening, self awareness and trust. There are ten or more questions per category.

Directions:

- This is a great back pocket tool for new facilitators who may be less than confident in their own questions. It helps them understand and become familiar with asking open-ended questions that produce more than a yes or no answer.

- Creative questions are great for those groups that have been together for a long time. Group members can ask each other questions and take responsibility for their own processing.

- The variety of questions provided here are a good tool for seasoned facilitators who may be in the habit of repeating the same questions time and time again. Facilitators can retrieve the question cards while the participants are completing their activity and locate questions that pertain to the issues going on within the group. This creates a useful reminder of open-ended questions that can be presented during the debriefing session.

Examples of Questions

Communication

1. Can anyone give an example of when you thought you communicated effectively with someone else in the group?
2. What did you learn about communication that will be helpful later?

Leadership

1. Who assumed leadership roles during the initiative tasks?
2. What were the behaviors which you describe as showing leadership?

Trusting the Group

1. What did you do today that deserves the trust of others?
2. How does the amount of fear you feel affect your trust of others?

Where to Find It/How to Make It: From the processing questions section of this book (on page 29) you can print and laminate your own cards using the questions in the different categories. Laminating your tools preserves your time and effort in putting them together. You can also buy a set from Training Wheels or Adventure Hardware.

Crossword Ending

Thanks to Faith Evans for sharing this great activity.

Concepts: To create a crossword puzzle of what happened during the program.

Props/Materials Needed: A large piece of paper or posterboard, markers.

Directions:

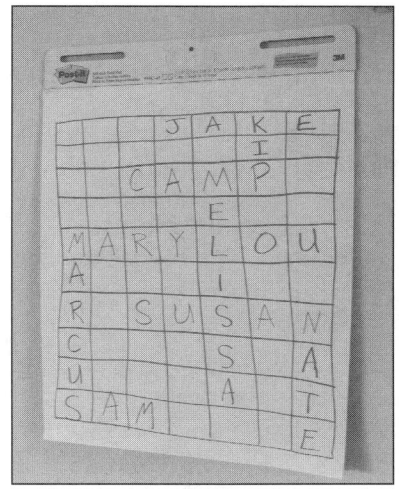

- On a large sheet of paper, write the name of the program or experience in large block letters with a marker. For example, you might write, "CAMP BACKPACK."

- Invite participants to create a crossword puzzle that shows what they think or feel about the experience. Someone might say, "cool," and they would letter the word vertically, using the letter "C" in the word "camp" as the beginning for "cool." Someone else might say, "challenging," and begin that word with the "C" in backpack.

- As people call out their descriptions, others assist in finding a place for each word. Some unusual words may be created in order to accommodate other words—a great example of teamwork, creativity and support!

- Participants may want to add their own names to the crossword as well.

- The chart, posted on a wall, remains as a visible reminder and tangible reinforcement of the experience.

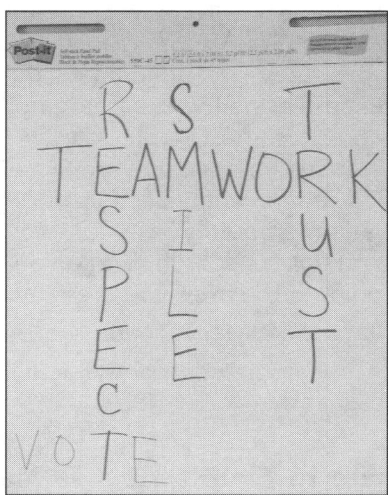

Crystal Clear

This activity is a wonderful opening or closing activity.

Contributor: Mary Ann Loeffler, CTRS, Metro State College of Denver.

Concepts: To help individuals identify or focus on their cognitive state at the beginning of a program and how this may have changed at the end of the program.

Props/Materials Needed: A crystal or amethyst, one that has cloudy sections and clear sections. The bigger the crystal, the better.

Directions:

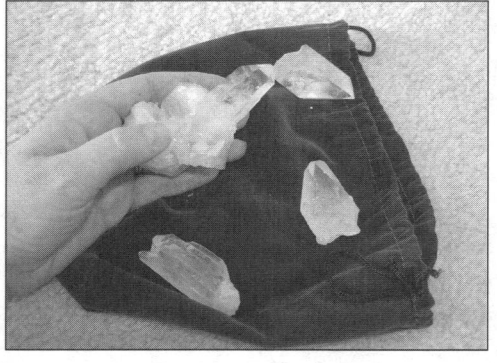

- At the beginning of your program, show a crystal to the group.
- Describe the attributes of the crystal: Part of it is clear, some parts are smooth, it has some rough spots, part of it is cloudy, etc. Use these attributes metaphorically by asking your participants to think about what they are bringing to the group. For example: As the facilitator, hold the crystal and give an example of what is "clear" for yourself, or what you are focusing on. Then talk about what is "cloudy" or unsettling for you. You could choose to share what is going "smoothly" as you point to the smooth part of the crystal or a "rough" situation you are faced with. While you are describing one or two facets, hold the crystal and point to the area you are relating to.
- Pass the crystal around the circle until everyone has a chance to share.
- At the completion of the activity or program, bring the crystal back to the group and repeat this discussion.

Where to Find It/How to Make It: You can find crystals and amethysts at truck stops, novelty stores, museums and jewelry stores.

Debriefing Bingo

Looking for Five in a Row

Here is an activity that encourages participants to look beyond a single answer and also one that promotes additional self-processing.

Concepts: After an adventure-based learning activity, some participants focus on only the dominant skill or talent used during the task. This activity encourages greater self reflection by inviting each member of the group to find five events in a row that they have encountered during the last activity, or throughout the entire program. In some cases, participants find a few blocks that they have experienced, but that do not produce five in a row, and must go looking for another group of five. This processing encourages additional self reflection.

Props/Materials Needed: A debriefing bingo card for each member of the group, or one large card for everyone.

Directions:

- Provide each member with a debriefing bingo card, and the instructions found on the next page. As an alternative, you can ask the group to create their own card, beginning with a five by five grid pattern.

Where to Find It/How to Make It: You can copy the debriefing bingo card shown on the following page, create your own temporary bingo card on a flipchart or more permanently on a piece of whiteboard or plywood.

After reflecting on your experiences, be prepared to discuss the following events by choosing any that create a line of five boxes in a row. For example, you can discuss five separate events during today's experience where you may have listened to someone (tell about it), tried something new (what was this new thing?), considered a different point of view (share it with the group), played outside your comfort zone (what event put you there?), and offered someone encouragement (who were they?).

Laughed	Changed Something	Offered a Suggestion	Developed a New Skill	Listened to Someone
Used My Problem Solving Skills	Said Thank You	Was Glad to Be Part of This Team	Tried Something New	Assisted Someone
Saw Something Amazing	Cheered	Considered a Different Point of View	Made an Improvement	Sacrificed My Personal Goals for the Good of the Group
Tried but Just Couldn't Do It	Moved Outside of My Comfort Zone	Applauded	Learned Something New	Expanded My Personal Boundaries
Offered Someone Encourage-ment	Played a Different Role	Considered a Different Point of View	Felt Challenged	Asked Someone for Help

Debriefing Tic Tac Toe

Three in a Row

The Debriefing Bingo activity found earlier in this book requires a total of five events in a row, which may be too difficult or lengthy for younger audiences. Debriefing Tic Tac Toe requires only three events in a row to complete.

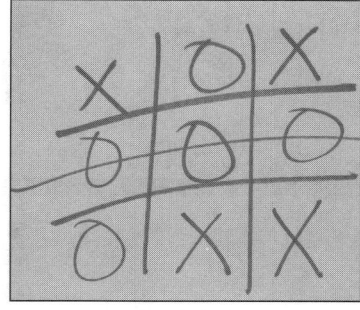

Concepts: A simplified version of Debriefing Bingo that requires participants to find three events in a row that they have experienced in the last challenge, or during the entire program. There are eight possible groupings of three events.

Props/Materials Needed: A Debriefing Tic Tac Toe card for each member of the group, or one large card for everyone.

Directions:

- Provide each member with a debriefing tic tac toe card, and the instructions found on the next page. As an alternative, you can ask the group to create their own card, beginning with a three by three grid pattern.

Where to Find It/How to Make It: You can copy the debriefing tic tac toe card shown on the following page, or create your own temporary card on a flipchart or more permanently on a piece of whiteboard or plywood. You can even draw the grid pattern in the dirt and use index cards for identifying each block.

After reflecting on your experiences, be prepared to discuss the following events by choosing any that create a line of three in a row. For example, you can discuss three separate events during today's experience where you may have listened to someone (tell about it), brainstormed (what was your contribution?), and learned something new (what was it?)

Asked for Help	Really Listened to Someone Else	Tried It a New Way
Partnered with Another Person	Brain-Stormed	Tried It Again
Expanded My Comfort Zone	Learned Something New	Cheered for Another Person

Dinner Notes

This activity was created by Faith Evans at Cheley Colorado Camp, Estes Park, Colorado.

Contributor: Faith Evans, PlayFully Inc.

Concepts: To create a fun atmosphere in which to share impressions and things learned from each other.

Props/Materials Needed: Pencils and small pieces of paper.

Directions: Dinner notes may become a treasured tradition.

- Containers of pens and pencils and small pieces of paper (with your camp logo or other decorations) are placed in the center of each dining table.

- Messengers (participants if possible) volunteer (ahead of time) to deliver the notes from the givers to the receivers.

- During the meal, participants write a brief thank you note, discussing how the receiver has made an impression on you, or something fun (and usually quite simple). The note is signed, folded, addressed on the front with a name (and table number if needed), then waved it in the air to attract a messenger.

- The messenger delivers the note to the intended receiver. If she does not know the receiver, she takes it to a "spotter" table that will identify the receiver or transfer the note to another messenger who knows that participant.

- All participants and staff should be alert to those who have not yet received notes—and be ready to send a few themselves!

- These notes are treasured by participants and find a hallowed home in the back of the dresser drawer at home . . . to be rediscovered later, and read again and again. It is a great activity to keep program memories present!

Domino Debrief

Michelle came up with this activity after using Sam Sike's Onimod activity time and time again. It was a natural progression after using the dominoes as an icebreaker and problem solving tool. Why not as a debriefing tool as well?

Concepts: Using dominoes as a debriefing tool encourages participants to engage in one-on-one processing.

Props/Materials Needed: Dominoes. The jumbo six set of dominoes is the most common set you will find. There are 28 dominoes in the jumbo six set. It is recommended that you use a domino set that is large and easy for your participants to see from at least ten feet away. Smaller wooden dominoes are difficult to see from any distance.

Directions:

- Ask the participants to connect with someone else who has one of the same numbers on their domino. For example, if you have the 4–3, connect with someone with a four or a three on their domino. Have participants create pairs or the occasional threesome if you have an odd numbered group.

- Everyone should be able to connect to at least ten others if you have a group large enough to use all 28 of the dominoes.

- The facilitator asks the group a question and invites them to discuss it with their partner(s). This way, everyone gets a chance to answer the question, as opposed to only one person answering the question at a time.

- Have the group switch partners and find someone else with a similar number on their domino. Then ask another question.

- This activity fosters an environment in which participants can easily share with their partner rather than in a large group.

There are several activities you can do with dominoes. Sam Sikes has an activity called Onimod in his *Executive Marbles* book. It is great for a mixer as well as an interesting problem solving activity.

Where to Find It/How to Make It: To make your own set of large dominoes, buy foam craft sheets (available at craft stores and large discount stores). Draw a line down the center of each sheet with a black permanent marker. Add the dots to complete the set.

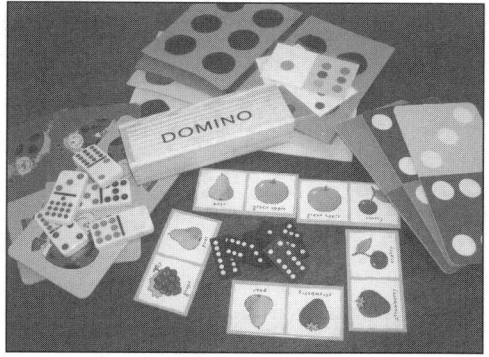

You can also make domino cards with index cards, business cards, or cards that are computer generated, printed, and laminated.

Large foam dominoes and laminated dominoes are available from: Training Wheels, Adventure Hardware, and Grip-It Adventures.

Education begins a gentleman, conversation completes him.

Dr. Thomas Fuller (1654–1734), Gnomologia, 1732

Efficiency and Effectiveness
Two Techniques for Quantifying the Experience

Here is a technique that allows the group to quantify their performance.

Concepts: From a corporate perspective, efficiency and effectiveness are two metrics that help to quantify the performance of an organization. In this case, two simple illustrations are used to present these metrics to the group.

Props/Materials Needed: A simple dial board (see photograph) for each metric, or a paper illustration of a blank dial for each.

Directions:

- At the completion of the challenge, the facilitiator presents the dial boards, labeled with the words "EFFICIENCY" and "EFFECTIVENESS."

- The facilitator may wish to provide a definition for each word. In this case efficiency refers to the ability of the group to complete a task in a timely manner, with minimal "off task" conversation or effort. Effectiveness refers to the outcome of the process. Was the job accomplished successfully, correctly, and without mistakes or errors?

- Group members are then asked to place each indicator dial in the position that reflects the group's performance.

- A discussion about the placement of each dial and whether there is consensus within the group for this location is appropriate.

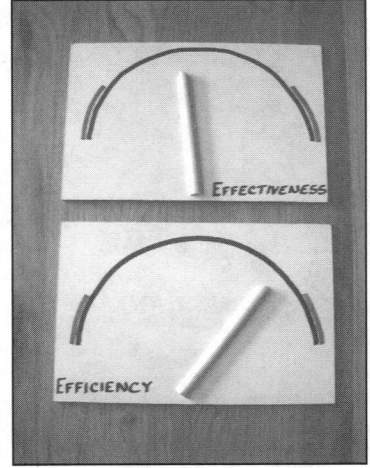

When paper illustrations are provided, group members are asked to individually mark their impression of the correct dial location. A discussion related to the dispersion of dial locations, and the average location, is useful.

Where to Find It/How to Make It: Dial boards can be made from dry erase board materials (available at most larger hardware stores), with a single popsicle stick dial indicator held in place by non-permanent adhesives, magnets or a small nut and bolt. Paper illustrations can be made from the sketches shown here.

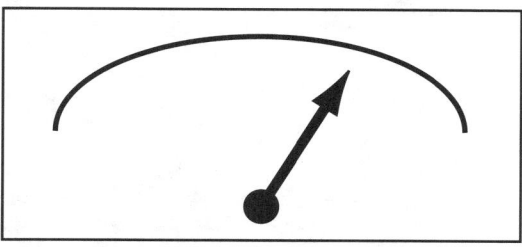

Efficiency

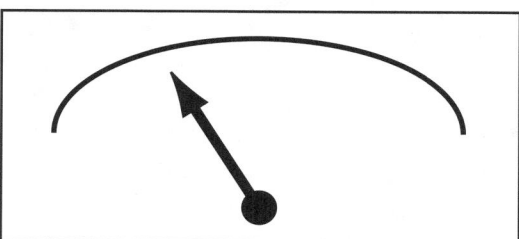

Effectiveness

By three methods we may learn wisdom:
First, by reflection, which is noblest;
Second, by imitation,
which is easiest;
and third by experience,
which is the bitterest.

Confucius (551 BC–479 BC)

Fear in a Hat

Thanks to Faith Evans for this classic debriefing activity.

Inspired by: Outward Bound

Contributed by: Faith Evans, PlayFully Inc.

Concepts: Fear in a Hat is a tool for evaluating where a group is at the start of an activity, and is useful for evaluation at the end to see how far people have come.

Props/Materials Needed: Index cards, writing utensils, hat.

Directions:

- At the beginning of the program or day, pass out index cards to each participant.

- Have participants write anonymously any concerns, fears, or questions they have about the experience they are embarking upon, and drop the cards into a hat.

- The leader (or ideally, the participants themselves) draws a card one at a time and reads the concern out loud and discusses it. It is often appropriate to pass the opportunity for others to respond to members of the group. Use the expertise within the room to build confidence. The idea is to openly address discomfort, and not set one person up (often the leader) to hold all the answers and solve all the problems.

- At the end of the day, read the index cards a second time, and see what happened to their fears and concerns. Were the fears justified? At what point were the answers known? Are they known yet? Are the fears still there? How were they diffused? Take the opportunity for a great discussion around trust and how it is developed, noting and accepting differences in how people respond to the unknown.

- An unusual and memorable hat makes an interesting holding place for the cards.

Feelings Cards

There are a wide variety of commercially available Feelings Cards with expressions, moods and feelings varying in size, color, and content. Some have feelings printed on each card, others have cartoon illustrations of facial expressions.

Concepts: To aid participants in labeling and expressing their feelings and emotions.

Props/Materials Needed: A deck of feelings cards of your choice. A description of several card varieties is presented below.

Directions:
Here are several examples of feelings card activities.

- Use feelings cards if participants are having trouble describing the feelings they are experiencing. Spread the feelings words out and invite participants to choose a word that best describes what they are feeling. Let each person share why they chose the word they did.

- Feelings Cards can be used as part of a sharing circle. Have each participant choose a card and tell the group about a time when they experienced that feeling.

- Use feelings cards as a social skills builder. Invite everyone to select a card face down. Have them place the card to their forehead—word side out—and try to guess what feeling they have on their forehead by everyone else's reaction to them. Participants may say things to each other in order to help them figure out what their word is, but they cannot say the word shown. This is an interesting way to teach verbal and non-verbal social skills and to explore how people react with others when they are in different moods.

Where to Find It/How to Make It: *Mood Swings* book: Creative Therapy, Training Wheels. This book is designed as a free-standing desk display. Choose from the expressions that best fit your mood and display it so that everyone knows! The expressions have a cartoon caricature wildly expressing the different feelings. All of the pages are in full color. To use experientially, you can cut the pages out of the book, laminate them for longevity, and use them as feelings cards. Creative Therapy also produces posters, postcards, and magnets with the same feelings and images. There are 30 images in all. These images match the Mood Dudes, also described in this book.

Feelings Marketplace cards: Project Adventure, (www.pa.org). These cards are 4″ × 6″ and have graphics and the word of the feeling. They have two varieties, one set for children that is printed in blue, and one set for corporate audiences that is printed in black.

Metaphor/Feelings Cards: Training Wheels. This deck of cards is two tools in one. One side of the card is the metaphor card activity while the other side of the card has feelings words. The words are written in different fonts and colors. The deck is laminated and is business card size.

Multicultural Moods: Training Wheels (training-wheels.com). Michelle Cummings has created a unique multicultural deck of feelings cards that depict 30 different feelings through six different ethnicities: African American, Latino, Native American, Asian, Middle Eastern, and Caucasian. Each nationality also separates age and gender by having all 30 feelings for adult male, adult female, male child, and female child. There are close to 750 feelings cards all together. The cartoon faces are lifelike and culturally accurate. Additional activities for exploring diversity come with each deck.

Multicultural Moods

Training Wheels

Action Pak Cue Cards: The Rider Group. Large format 5″ × 8″ inch cards with text and color graphics. (www.ridergroup.com) (ActionPak® Conversation/ Activity Cards © by Craig Rider and Pat Rider, The Rider Group. By permission).

To make your own: Using clip art programs and a variety of available fonts you can make a deck of your own cards very easily. Just figure out what size you want your cards to be and come up with the different feelings words you want to use. Experiment with different fonts and colors and print them onto some type of card stock. You can buy pre-perforated business card stock or post card stock to avoid long hours of cutting. Laminating is recommended to preserve your time and hard work. For a quick set, you could write several of feelings words onto index cards.

The Fine Art of Reviewing

Thoughts and Activities from Roger Greenaway

I hear . . . I forget
I see . . . I remember
I do (plus review) . . . I learn
—Confucius (with additional thoughts from Roger Greenaway)

Roger Greenaway of the United Kingdom is not only one of the most prolific contributors to the field of reviewing, reflection and debriefing activities and techniques; he is also an incredibly nice person. Soft spoken, resourceful and talented in the methods of bringing the most from an adventure-based learning activity, Roger graciously offered to share some of his favorite reviewing activities with us. You are encouraged to visit Roger's extensive reviewing website at: www.reviewing.co.uk.

The Goal Line

Here is a reviewing technique that can be used throughout the day. With everyone standing in a large circle, place a short rope, six feet (two meters) long in front of each participant, with one knot nearest the participant, one approximately at the midpoint and a third knot at the far end. The ropes will appear like the spokes of a wheel.

The knot nearest each participant represents the beginning of the day. The knot at the midpoint of each rope is lunchtime, or the midpoint of the day. The final knot signifies the completion of the program or day.

Participants are invited to share their comments as they journey through their adventure. First, the expectations of the day can be discussed. The phrase "I hope" or "I wish" can be used to start this session. Participants can also be asked to describe where they hope to be at the midpoint and end of the day.

At breakthrough moments, or specific times, the goal lines can be presented and each person allowed to comment on their journey. For example, where they see themselves, how they are approaching the day, updates on their ability to reach their personal goals, and the team goal of having everyone in the middle at the end of the program.

You can find more creative ideas for reviewing with rope at:
www.reviewing.co.uk/articles/ropes.htm.

Rounds

Rounds are a convenient and quick technique for providing a brief opportunity for everyone to voice their opinion. Phrases such as "I wish that . . ." or "I think we should . . ." are used to begin the round, with each participant offering their own ideas to complete each phrase. Additional starter phrases include:

The high point for me was when . . .	I wish I had . . .
I would like the group to tell me . . .	If I had had a camera . . .
I was surprised that . . .	The most difficult part for me was . . .
I am really pleased that . . .	I'd like to compliment . . .
I was helped by . . .	I think we ran off course when . . .

Charting the Path

Charting is a method of visually representing the path of individuals and the entire group throughout the program. With colorful markers, crayons, ropes or tokens (such as polished stones, leaves, marbles, etc.) participants are asked to rank their experience on a scale of +5 to –5 in terms of their feelings, energy level, excitement, and the applicability or utility of each activity. Discussion around what contributed to each ranking can be useful feedback for the entire group. For example, "I thought the second activity was a –2 rating because we really didn't work together to accomplish the task." This technique can also be used to predict the future. "I'd like to see each of us reach a positive value for the next activity." From a multiple intelligence standpoint, participants can observe each other, and then estimate what they think their fellow participants' ratings will be after completing an activity. This observation fits into the "awareness of others" style of multiple intelligence theory.

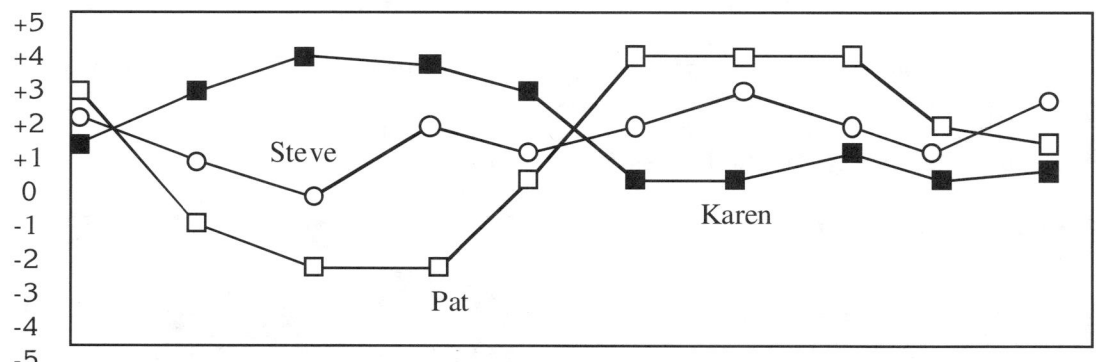

Replay

The most direct form of active reviewing is to do the activity (or part of it) again, but in a different way. This style of reviewing is useful if participants make comments such as, "I wish that I had . . ." or "We should have . . ." This technique can be especially useful for problem solving activities that were not successful during the first attempt. Repeating an activity also provides a new perspective for analyzing what happened during the first attempt by the group.

A second form of replay is similar to the "instant replay" used during professional sporting events. In this technique, several participants recreate the original sequence of actions while other members of the group make verbal comments about what is happening.

Finally, it is possible to take the element of replay a step further, and see inside the thoughts of group members. Like the instant replay method above, a few participants recreate the original sequence of actions, but this time, other group members offer their own thoughts and feelings related to the group's actions. For example, "stop right there . . . this is when I first thought that our plan would not work" or "this was when I started to wonder if I was strong enough to lift myself over that wall." This level of personal disclosure needs to be preceded by a strong sense that the group will listen and respect the individual thoughts of other group members.

Something to Show for It—Bringing the Magic Back

One technique for extending the effectiveness of a program and creating additional self-reviewing moments is for participants to take something back with them from the event—anything from a suntan to a personal souvenir to a certificate of completion. Photographs, a T-shirt with other group members' names written on it, journals or diaries, videos, local newspaper articles, a website address to review photos of the day, a keychain, a patch, a piece of artwork created by the participant, letters to self or a group report can all be elements that participants can take away with them. See Metaphoric Methods or Artistic Expression activities.

Post-Event Coaching, Mentoring and Counseling

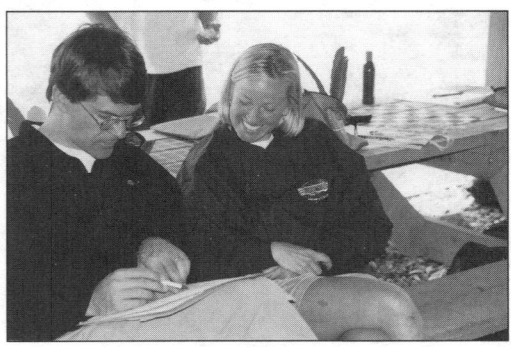

Some programs have a specific goal in mind, such as leadership development, exploring diversity, creative problem solving or exploring improving team effectiveness skills. During the event or program, facilitators can make notes related to the

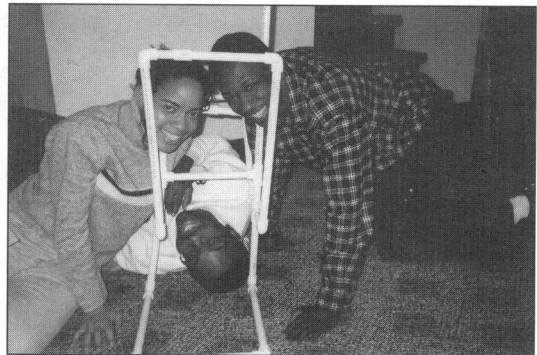

performance of individual team members, and then share these observations with these individuals at their request.

Concepts: For Roger Greenaway, reviewing comes in a variety of styles, techniques and methods. There is "something for everyone," so to speak. As such, Roger suggests that there are five styles of reviewing:

Active:	physical movement and drama-based
Creative:	visual and expressive arts
Feedback:	giving and receiving feedback
Verbal:	group discussions
Individual:	focused on inner thoughts

The above methods are just a sampling of the many additional techniques you can find at Roger's website, and during his extensive facilitator trainings.

References:

Greenaway, Roger. *Playback: A Guide to Reviewing Activities.* Edinburgh, UK: The Duke of Edinburgh's Award with Endeavour Scotland, 1993. ISBN 0-905425-09-X

——. *Reviewing Adventures—Why and How?* Sheffield, UK: National Association for Outdoor Education (NAOE), 1996. UK ISBN 1-898555-01-X

——. *More Than Activities.* Plymouth, UK: Save the Children Fund, 1990. ISBN 1-870322-21-5

You can contact Roger Greenaway at: 9 Drummond Place Lane, Stirling, Scotland FK8 2JF, roger@reviewing.co.uk. Look for information about Roger Greenaway's new publications, workshops and internet resources at: www.reviewing.co.uk.

Five Basic Elements of Reviewing
Debriefing According to Aristotle

While we have learned a great deal about our earth and our environment, there was initially a theory that all matter in the universe was comprised of five basic elements. If that is true, then even items such as teambuilding and reviewing must be made of such elements. According to Aristotle (and others), there are four basic earthly elements: earth, air, fire, and water, and a fifth element, ether, which holds these all together.

Concepts: The five elements presented here offer a framework with which to view the world. When asked to consider the behavior, talents, skills or performance of the group within this framework of four earthly elements and one higher one, most participants can easily identify with these elements.

Props/Materials Needed: This activity can be performed with no props, or the facilitator can provide five word cards or images with each of the elements illustrated: earth, air, fire, water and ether. It is also possible to use tokens to represent each element. A burning candle for fire, a pitcher of water, a cloud or wind for air, rocks and soil for the earth, and a unique elemental symbol or twinkling object for ether.

Directions:

- At the completion of the activity, the facilitator presents the five elements to the group, and gives a brief explanation of each. Present the illustrations or tokens at this time, and give examples of each element in our modern day.

- The facilitator can continue by telling the group that these five elements were thought to make up all that is in the universe.

- Next, participants are asked to analyze their performance in the last activity, and to assess what portions of each element were present. Fire can represent passion in discussion and problem solving. Earth can represent hard work and effort. Ether can represent those difficult to explain events that significantly contributed to the overall success of the project. Water can represent going with the flow. Air can represent rising above differences.

Where to Find It/How to Make It: Check your local public library for more readings from the Greek masters.

Food for Thought

Some of the best conversations occur around the dinner table. Here is an activity that utilizes that sense of sharing.

Creator: Jen Gross Lara, Anne Arundel Community College, Maryland.

Concepts: To engage participants in discussing what is going on in their lives.

Props/Materials Needed: Copies of a place setting, (see next page) or actual utensils.

Directions:

- Pass out a place setting picture to each participant.
- On the plate, list all the things "on your plate" right now.
- On the fork, list what new things you would like to "take a stab at."
- On the napkin, list what things protect you.
- On the knife, list what things are cutting away at you or your time.
- On the spoon, you probably do not want to be spoon fed, list what things you would like help with.
- After everyone is finished, go around and have each person share one or two things on their plate.

Where to Find It/How to Make It: Copy the graphic shown on the following page and pass it out to each participant.

Variation: Present this activity around the dinner table.

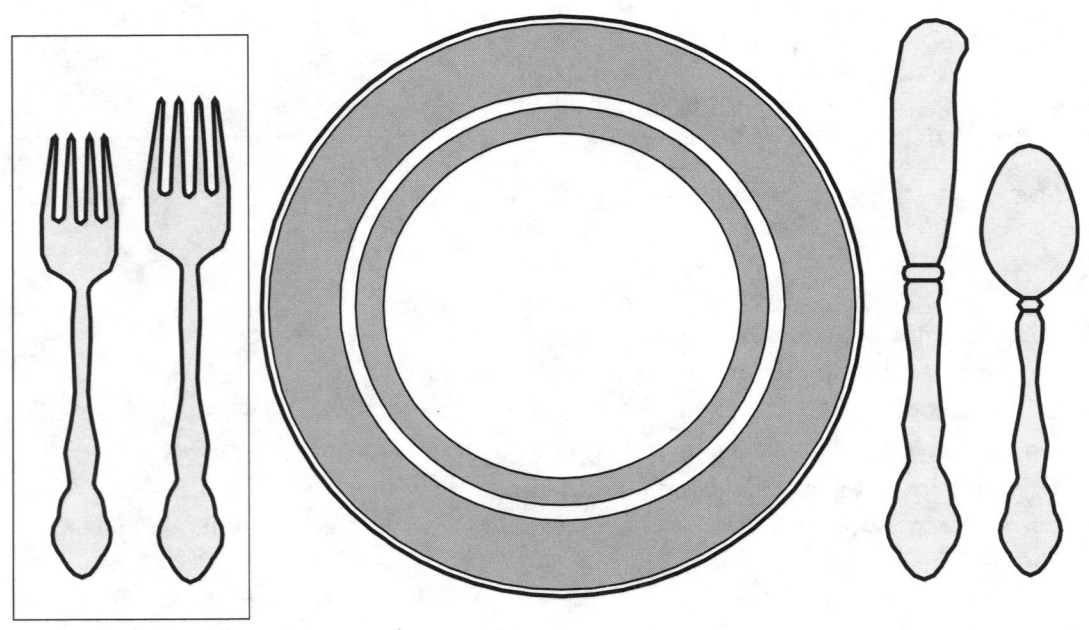

A Teachable Moment

Freebie

Something for Nothing

A Freebie is similar to the "Get Out of Jail Free" card in the popular board game, Momopoly. A tool that allows a team to pass on an activity, to move on, to obtain additional information and to take control of their situation.

The concept of a freebie arose from the experience of one sixth grade group. To say that they were not functioning well together does not adequately describe the enormous conflicts and interpersonal challenges this group had before them. At one point, two of the more volatile (and unfortunately) leaders of the group had stopped all forward movement (literally and figuratively as they were completing a traverse initiative) and were simply arguing with each other. A third student came to the facilitator and asked her to step in and manage the conflict, as the group wanted to get on with the task. The facilitator asked the student what he might do to respond. The student said flat out that there was nothing he could do, so it was suggested that he go and talk with the arguing students. He told the facilitator there was no chance the two would listen to him, and the facilitator again suggested he try. In retrospect, the facilitator realized that the student who had come for help had done exactly the right thing—he had reviewed the resources available and, realizing the group did not have what they needed, he had attempted to outsource the problem to an expert. The Freebie resulted from this experience.

Creator: Kelly Smith Johnston

Concepts: The Freebie provides a group-facilitated conversation on limits, challenge, resolve and ability.

Props/Materials Needed: You can use almost any token to represent the freebie. You could use wooden shapes and paint them with cool colors and graphics. You can also use flying discs. Just make sure the freebie is something tangible that you can give to the group so that they have to "cash it in" when they are ready to use it.

Directions:

- At the beginning of each day, introduce the group to the concept of the freebie.

- Give the group two freebies (if they are given only one, a scarcity mentality arises and the group will seldom use it).

- The freebies can be used at any time throughout the day, to request an answer to a problem, to end an initiative without completing it, or for whatever else they choose (within reason of course). The only stipulation is that the group must come to a consensus on its use. One person cannot come forth and say they would independently like to use the freebie.

- Consensus may need to be explained and taught, as most groups only have experience with the majority rules approach to decision-making (see consensus cards).

Responses to the Freebie

The freebie has been used sucessfully with many groups. By far, the most common result is that the freebie initiates group-facilitated conversation on limits, challenge, resolve and ability. Typically, a frustrated person says to the group, "Come on, let's just use the freebie and do something else." (This is a common response to· frustration and challenge.) Someone else in the group says that they do not think that the freebie is necessary because the group is able to do the challenge. A conversation that ensues concerning what is frustrating, the value for the group in stopping and the value in continuing. More often than not, the group recognizes the increased value in continuing, and not using the freebie becomes a rallying cry for using all of their abilities to complete the challenge. Throughout these conversations, the mere existence of the freebie is usually enough of a catalyst for the group to talk through their issues without specific intervention or guidance from the facilitator.

Where to Find It/How to Make It: Wooden Shapes and other interesting objects are available at craft and discount stores.

Friendship Bracelets

Kids young and old enjoy friendship bracelets. This activity makes them even more meaningful.

Contributor: Faith Evans, PlayFully Inc.

Concepts: For participants to give colored strands of embroidery floss to each other and to make a bracelet to wear. The bracelet can represent the learnings of the program or of positive attributes of each individual.

Props/Materials Needed: Colorful cotton embroidery floss.

Directions: Cut 12 inch (30 cm) lengths of cotton embroidery floss. Discuss the significance of each color.

    red = high energy, intense

    blue = calm, friendly

    green = natural, good resource

    yellow = sunny, positive

Participants select several strands of floss and give them to each other. They should tell group members why they chose each color. These gifted strands are the basis for the bracelet. Next, sit in a circle and pass remaining strand clumps to be chosen by bracelet wearer. Demonstrate a variety of friendship bracelet techniques, such as knot end, twist, braid, interweave, etc. Ask a friend to tie it on their wrist. This bracelet will be a keepsake that is appreciated long after the program has concluded.

Where to Find It/How to Make It: You can find embroidery floss and instructions for making friendship bracelets at craft stores and quilt shops. You can also make friendship bracelets from leather cord and colorful beads.

Full Court Press

Creative Processing Techniques for Athletes

Teachable moments often occur on the playing field. When they do, what better way to address them than with the main focus of the sport itself? The game ball!

Concepts: Some athletes are challenged by the cerebral processing following a teambuilding activity, compared to the more kinesthetic action during the event. By using a familiar object, such as a game ball, and allowing them to kinesthetically manipulate this object during discussion, the length and depth of discussion often improves. In short, this style of processing places the participant in familiar surroundings or a "safe place."

Props/Materials Needed: A ball familiar to the group or sport team.

Directions:

- Traditional sport balls have segments in their outer layer. Basketballs, for example, are divided into eight sections. Tennis balls, baseballs and softballs have only two. Soccer balls have quite a few more.
- The facilitator provides a ball where each segment has been identified with a number, letter, symbol or written question.
- The facilitator begins by tossing this ball to any participant.
- The segment on which that person's right-hand index finger lands defines the question.
- In the case of numbers, letters or symbols, the facilitator reads from an index card they have prepared with questions in advance.
- If the ball contains questions, the person holding the ball can read the question out loud to the group. Questions can have a direct relationship to the game. For example: How does the collaboration of the team during this last activity compare to the teamwork you see on the field? What skills do you use during the game that would have helped you here?

Gem Story

Storytelling is a traditional technique for helping people remember significant events. Why not use a story to get your point across?

Creator: Rich Allen, Impact Learning

Concepts: Here is a story to help participants discover their own "gems" of learning.

Props Materials Needed: A small gem stone for each participant.

Directions:

- Tell the story. Be animated in your delivery. The more memorable you make the story, the greater the impact the stones will have for the participants.
- Adjust the story as you need to make it your own and to have meaning for your participants.
- As you are telling the story, pass out a few stones when you get to the part about when he discovers he has diamonds, rubies, etc.
- Then, after you finish the story, pass out the rest of the stones. You will be amazed at how many people— even adults—were concerned that they were not going to get a stone like the first three did.
- To close the story, talk about how you hope the participants were able to pick up a few "gems" during the program and that they will value them like precious stones.

Here is one possible story for this activity.

The Gem Story

A traveler was on a long journey. Each morning he awoke and traveled along his path. One morning he woke up and set out again on his journey. However, he soon noticed that on this particular morning the path appeared to be getting more and more narrow. He began to grow concerned that he had taken a wrong turn, and decided that he would ask the next person he saw that morning if he was indeed on the correct path. But no one else was on the path that morning. He walked and walked, and it wasn't until noon that he encountered the first person he had seen all day. He entered a clearing in the woods, and there at the far side of the clearing sat a very old man. This old man had long, flowing white hair, a white beard, and had his eyes closed.

The traveler was quite excited to see the old man. He hurried up to him and asked, "Excuse me, but I was traveling along the path this morning, and it began to get very narrow, and I started to wonder if I was on the right path. Can you tell me? Am I going the right way?" The old man just sat there in silence, his eyes still closed.

The traveler tried again, but could get no response. Finally, in frustration, he started to leave. He was at the far side of the clearing when he heard a sound, and he turned around. The old man had opened his eyes, and was staring straight out in front of him. And when he spoke he said, very softly: "You're on the right path. Keep going."

But the traveler was at the far side of the clearing, and wasn't sure if he had heard correctly, so he asked the old man to repeat himself. The old man did say something, but this time it was something quite different. This time he said: "Gather what you find before you cross the river." And then he closed his eyes once again.

Now, the traveler had heard this last part quite clearly, but he was confused—what did it mean? But he could get nothing more from the old man, and finally the traveler did leave, continuing on the path as before.

It was hot on the path that day, and the traveler grew sweaty, tired and thirsty. The path, while growing ever more narrow, was still visible enough to follow. Finally, late in the afternoon, the traveler turned a corner and found himself in front of a river. He was so excited! He ran down to the river, drank some of the water, and used more water to wash himself. When he was fully refreshed he started to wade to the other side, but as he took his first step the words of the old man came back to him, and he paused.

"What did he say?" the traveler asked himself. And then he remembered the words: "Gather what you find before you cross the river."

"Did he mean this river?" wondered the traveler. "Ah, he was crazy!" and he began to move again. But the words of the old man were echoing so strongly in his mind that he found himself backing up to the bank of the river. He looked around.

"If I were to gather something," he asked himself, "what would I take here?"

He looked around and saw trees, shrubs and pebbles by the river's edge—but nothing of any value. But the words of the old man were so strong in his mind that he said, "This may be the strangest thing I have ever done, but . . ." and he bent down and picked up some of the pebbles and put them in his pocket. Then he waded across the river and continued traveling. However, at the far side of the river he soon lost his way and traveled aimlessly until he found another path to follow several hours later. He knew he could never retrace his steps back the way he had come.

Late that night the traveler slept by the side of the road. He woke up in the middle of the night, but did not know what had awakened him. Then he realized that he had rolled over on the pebbles in his pocket, and he shook his head. "That old man was crazy," he said aloud. "I don't know why I picked these up!" He reached into his pocket and took out the pebbles. He was in the act of throwing them away when suddenly the moonlight shone down on what he held in his hand, and he paused.

"No," he said. "It can't be!"

Because what he was holding in his hand were no longer mere pebbles. Now they were diamonds, rubies, sapphires and emeralds—precious gems of all kinds. And he realized what had happened—they had been precious gems all along, but when he had first picked them up they had been covered in dirt, and in his pocket they had rubbed against each other so that the dirt had come off and he could see them for what they were. And then the traveler said the most important thing of all, "Oh. OH! I wish I had gathered more pebbles, before I crossed that river!"

—*Rich Allen, Impact Learning*

Where to Find It/How to Make It: You can obtain small glass stones at many craft stores.

The real man smiles in trouble, gathers strength from distress, and grows brave by reflection.

Thomas Paine (1737–1809)

Goals in Motion

A Magical Technique for Identifying Goals and Barriers

Here is an interesting reviewing technique that leaves a lasting record.

Concepts: While some techniques leave only memories, this technique provides a written record. A teambuilding activity, The Magic Carpet, will be used to demonstrate this technique.

Props/Materials Needed: Several small plastic tarps, shower curtains or plastic tablecloths, masking tape, pens, two flipchart pages (or posterboards).

Directions:

- Place a few plastic tarps in close proximity to each other and invite your participants to stand around the perimeter of each tarp. The ideal tarp size holds approximately eight people.

- Supply each group with a length of masking tape and a few pens and invite participants to individually write down their goals for the program today. For example, those things that would make for a wonderful day or things that they hope will happen. Encourage everyone to share their goals with the other members of their tarp team.

- Next, invite each person to firmly affix their goal tape to the top side of the plastic tarp, and then instruct the group to flip over their tarp.

- Distribute another round of tape.

- On this side, invite the group to write the barriers and obstacles that they might encounter in achieving the goals they placed on the other side of the tarp. Again, encourage each person to share what they have written. When they are finished, ask the group to attach these barriers to the tarp, and then invite the entire group to stand upon the tarp.

- The challenge is for each group to flip their tarp, or magic carpet, from the barrier side to the goal side, with two constraints. First, no one should be lifted up (this limits the amount of spotting needed). Secondly, no part of any participant's shoes or body may contact the floor surrounding each magic carpet. Good Luck!

- During this phase, especially if there is any element of competition in the group, most tarp groups attempt to flip over their own tarp independently. In the few cases where space allows for this solution, some teams cheer "Hey, we finished first!"

- As mentioned in the Half Time Review technique, there is a teachable moment happening, even as individual tarp teams attempt to complete the task. Invite them to pause for a moment and review the original instructions and challenges. "OK, we flip over the tarp, without lifting people up, and without stepping off the carpet." "Not quite," says the facilitator, "the instruction said without lifting people up, and without touching the floor. No one said you could not leave the carpet!" An audible "oh!" exclamation emits from the group, as participants realize that they could have been collaborating with neighboring teams, rather than trying to unsuccessfully compete with them. They have just missed the perfect "win-win" scenario.

- After additional time, and with groups sharing tarps, all groups find themselves on their own tarp, goal side up. Now comes the value in this technique. Participants have just shared their goals and aspirations for the day (or for the next business quarter, or for the next school year . . .), and also what they perceive as the barriers for achieving these goals. This information is not only personal, it is valuable. Invite each person to take their goals and barriers from the tarp, and attach them to two flip chart pages labeled "goals" and "barriers." You now have a written record of the goals and barriers for your group, and a permanent record of their needs analysis and the various obstacles that they wish were not there.

As an example, consider the case of a group of summer camp staff members. In performing this activity during staff training week, the camp director has not only assisted the group in creative problem solving, voicing concerns, setting goals, working together as a team, and learning from their mistakes, but also has a record of each person's goals for making this summer the best summer yet. We know of some camp directors who keep this list on the back of their camp office door, and refer to it daily. "Let's see, how can I help my newest counselors reach their goals this summer . . . ?" Secondly, the director has a list of what their staff perceives as the barriers to accomplishing their goals. "Seems like many folks agree we could use a shelter, in case of rain, at our outpost camp." This is an excellent list to share with the camp board of directors, for future action.

While the magic carpet example is useful here, it is not unique. With masking tape and pens, you can attach goals and barriers to a variety of objects, including soft toys for group juggling, both sides of the low ropes course element The Wall, the starting point and destination for trolleys, and the various islands used for River Crossing or the Muse.

Group Drawing

This activity developed out of a desire to experiment with different ways to facilitate journaling with students during a semester long challenge course class taught by Jennifer Stanchfield. It has become a favorite closing activity for her group work.

Creator: Jennifer Stanchfield

Concepts: This is a group's artistic representation of experience presented in a fun, non-threatening, interactive and creative way.

Props/Materials Needed: A sheet of paper for each group of three to five participants and a colorful marker for each person.

Directions:

- Have the group divide into groups of three to five people. Give each person a marker and each group a large piece of paper.
- Instruct the group to work together to create a symbolic representation of their experience. Remind them that this is not an art contest—just a chance to depict their experience together.
- Allow each group five to ten minutes. Using markers and a short time period helps reduce the intimidation factor for participants who might be concerned about their artistic ability.

- Each group is given the opportunity to share their drawing. The descriptions are often filled with humor and profound insights that help end the experience on a high note.

- Sending these drawings home with the group can help remind them of positive experiences, changes, and group or individual strengths.

- This activity can be used as an evaluative tool for facilitators reflecting the outcomes of an experience and the effectiveness of programming.

There is an art of which every man should be a master—
the art of reflection. If you are not a thinking man,
to what purpose are you a man at all?

William Hart Coleridge

Group Juggle Metaphor Drawing

Group Juggle has been a favorite adventure activity, frequently used as an icebreaker, for goal setting or as a group problem-solving initiative. This engaging reflective activity was adapted from experiences during Jennifer Stanchfield's time as a recreational therapist at The University of Utah Neuropsychiatric Institute. Jeri Claspill and Greg Smith used a similar activity during family challenge course groups. This activity has been used very effectively with adolescents, adults and family groups and with some younger populations as a group process activity.

Photo courtesy of Jeff Baird, High 5

Props/Materials Needed: Group Juggle worksheet and pen or pencil, paper and markers for group members to draw their own. Balls and other soft throwable props for Group Juggle.

Directions:

- Play a round or two of Group Juggle (See Quicksilver by Rohnke and Butler) as appropriate for the group. As facilitators we ofen ask the group to set realistic goals and choose which objects to keep in the game.

- Invite participants to list the skills they used during the activity and keep this list in a visible place—groups will often list skills such as "focus," "slowing down," "letting go of items that get in the way," "making choices," "planning ahead" etc.

- Hand out the Group Juggle worksheet, or have the group members draw a picture of themselves juggling a variety of objects. Include a few on the ground.

Photo courtesy of Jeff Baird, High 5

- Ask participants to fill in the drawn balls with the responsibilities, stressors and activities they are juggling in their own lives, including: work, family, health, homework, money, grief, peer pressures. Allow participants about ten minutes alone with their Group Juggle drawing to think about their answers. People find value in this opportunity to think about their lives.

Photo courtesy of Jeff Baird, High Five

- Invite group members to share one or several of the balls they have filled in. Participants always have the option to pass. Participants gain an appreciation for shared experiences in this activity. Adolescents are often surprised to hear that other kids are feeling the same kind of stress or concerns that they are.

- Next, have group members look back to the list they made earlier of the strengths and skills they used during the group juggle game.

- Have each participant write a sentence for themselves using one or more of the skills used in the game and apply it to their real life juggles.

There are three principal means of acquiring knowledge. . .
observation of nature, reflection, and experimentation.
Observation collects facts; reflection combines them;
experimentation verifies the result of that combination.

Denis Diderot (1713–1784)

A Teachable Moment

Drawing by Paul Stanchfield

Half Time Review

Mid-Activity Reviewing Techniques

Sometimes the teachable moments come before the end of the activity. Here is a technique for reviewing at the midpoint of an activity.

Concepts: For those activities that present difficult challenges to the group, initial planning may not be enough to accomplish the task. While failing at a task can be a valuable learning lesson, it is sometimes necessary for the facilitator to stop the group before the point of no return, and have them consider the outcome of their efforts in advance. The Half Time Review provides the opportunity for the group to reconsider their initial plan, and to make mid-stream corrections.

Props/Materials Needed: None, although an inflatable sportcaster's microphone or toy microphone can be a useful prop. From a professional football game perspective, it can also be helpful to have a flip chart and markers so that participants can sketch player positions and play patterns for their own teammates.

Directions: The facilitator has two options for the half time review.

- They can inform the group that there will be a half time progress review. This style informs the group in advance, and they may choose to use this review as a valuable mid-point resource.

- Alternatively, the facilitator can wait for a teachable moment to occur, and ask the group to perform a "half time review." This second approach is a bit more spontaneous for the group, but requires the facilitator to be ready in advance.

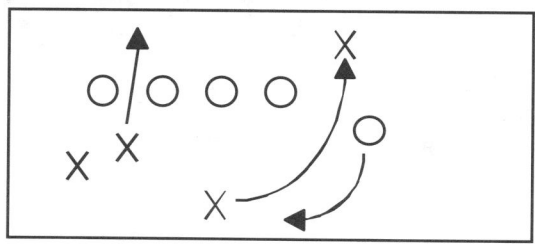

Hand Signals

A Stop and Go Device

Thanks to Mike Anderson for sharing this simple but powerful technique for determining group consensus and readiness.

Contributor: Mike Anderson, Learning Works Training and Development Inc.

Concepts: In some cases, especially early in an adventure-based training, audiences may feel more comfortable voting as a group rather than voicing their opinions individually. Here is a colorful method for determining the consensus and readiness of a group, without having to say a word.

Props/Materials Needed: A wooden hand painted red on one side and green on the other. One for each participant.

Directions:

- The facilitator presents each participant with a red/green voting hand.
- During the course of the meeting, program, or challenge activity dicussion, group members can instantly register their agreement or disagreement with key points by displaying either the green (agreement) side of their hand, or the red (disagreement) side.
- These hands can also be used for voting on specific topics.

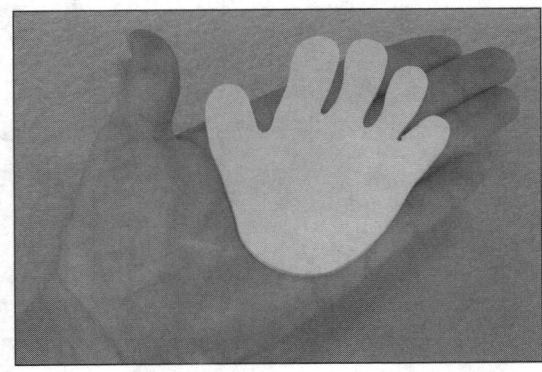

Where to Find It/How to Make It:

Palm-sized wooden hands are available at craft stores. You can also have participants make their own, from red and green paper, by tracing their own hand.

Having My Say

Processing Till the Cows Come Home

While most processing sessions are designed to discuss the teachable moments occurring within a group, it is occasionally possible to simply open the door to conversation, with limited guidance, and 'let folks have their say.' As humans, there are three things that we truly own: our name, our reputation, and our story. This activity is an opportunity for each person to share their story.

Photo courtesy of Jeff Baird, High Five

Concepts: This format of group processing allows everyone to share their voice. Some Native American councils and Quaker religious ceremonies employ this style of opportunity so that all might be heard, especially on challenging decisions. This style of reflection is ideal as a closing ceremony or final group debriefing session.

Props/Materials Needed: None, although comfortable seating is helpful since this process might go on for an hour or more, depending on the size of the group.

Directions:

- The facilitator tells the group that they have an opportunity to have their say. Explain that other participants give each speaking person their attention and they can count on the same attention in return. It is helpful to have a few participants ready to share early in the process, as examples for other members of the group.
- Do not be concerned with silences in the group. Be patient. Good things will happen.

One of the first places we observed this activity being successfully used was at the National Challenge Course Practitioner's Symposium (NCCPS) in Boulder, Colorado. Tom Leahy's outstanding event is listed on his website at: www.leahy-inc.com. With a group of approximately 180 people, this session was completed in about two hours.

Hieroglyphics

Ancient Pictures—Modern Lessons

Thousands of years ago, distant civilizations left information for future generations. What would your team like to tell future generations about what happened here today?

Concepts: Hieroglyphics, pictograms and petroglyphs incorporate a large amount of information into a few simple images, and these messages have lasted for thousands of years.

Props/Materials Needed: Sidewalk chalk, masking tape, a concrete floor, sidewalk, flipchart, whiteboard, wall or other suitable surface for drawing.

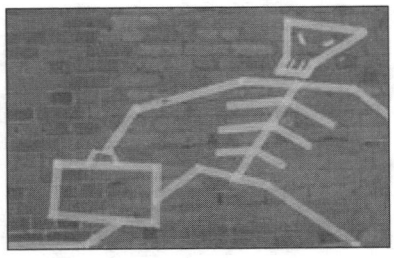

Directions:

- After identifying some of the key learnings from a recent activity, the facilitator asks the group to summarize these concepts

- Invite the group to reduce these concepts to basic symbols, pictures or pictograms. The group then creates a historical record of their efforts using just a few symbols.

- Here is your group's opportunity to share their story with future generations.

Where to Find It/How to Make It: Sidewalk chalk is typically a seasonal merchandise in many areas of the country. Find it at your local toy or craft store. Buy several different bright colors. You can also buy glass marking foam and paint in different colors, suitable for decorating the windows of a conference room, office or classroom. Look for this in the automotive section of your local department store—right next to the fuzzy dice.

High Five

Here is a classic activity that is easy to present.

Contributor: Jennifer Steinmetz, Rock Top Therapy Center.

Concepts: To have each participant process their experience, using their hands as a guide.

Props/Materials Needed: Copies of High Five Hands (see illustration), or allow participants to trace their own hands onto a piece of paper, paper, writing utensils.

Directions:

- Instruct the group to trace their hand onto a piece of paper, or pass out copies of the high five hands to each participant. Instruct them to write on each finger the following attributes:
    - Thumb: your strengths
    - Index finger: talents
    - Middle finger: what you want
    - Ring finger: promises you are willing to make
    - Pinkie finger: what you need from the team
    - Palm: your commitment to the team—an "I will" statement
    - Wrist: support system, what gives you strength

- This is a good activity to set the tone and create focus at the start of a programming day. At the end of the day, pass out the hands again and spend time reflecting on their hands. After everyone has had a chance to share, have participants flip their papers over, pass their "hands" around the group and invite everyone to write something positive for each participant.

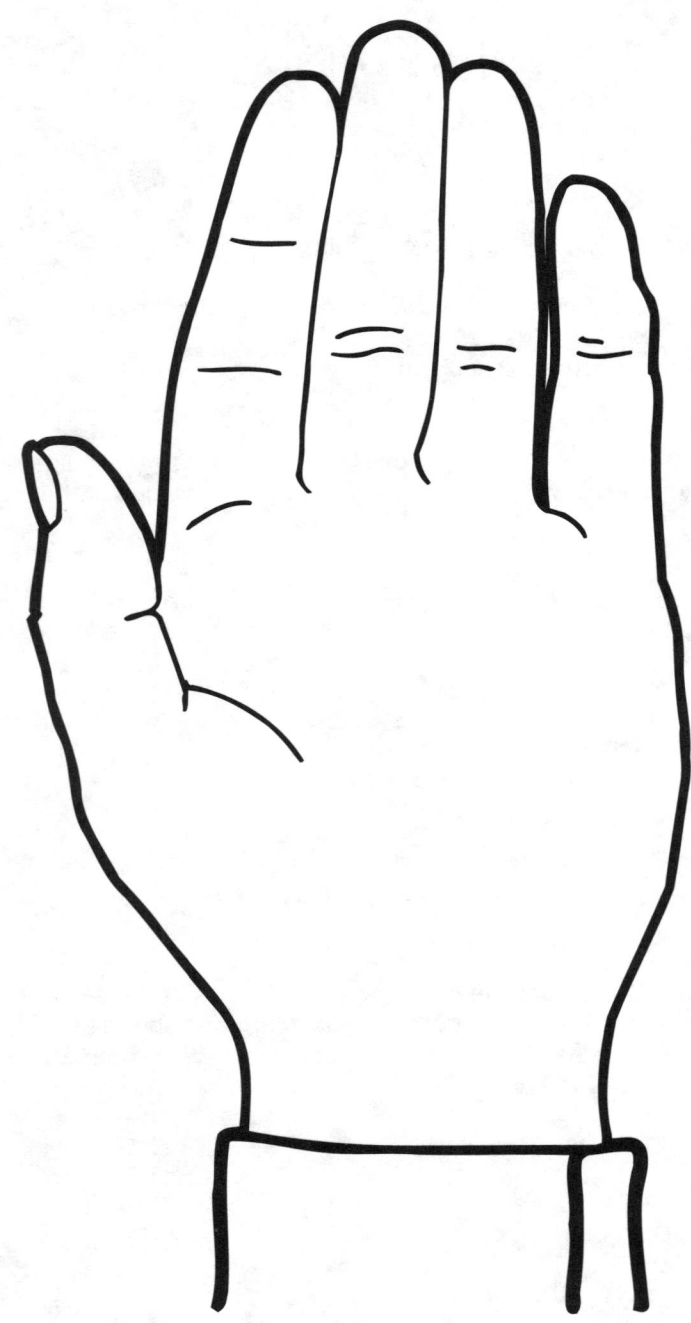

A Teachable Moment

House of Nails

This activity is typically presented as a problem solving activity. Now you can use it as a processing tool after your group has figured out how to balance all of the nails on the head of a single nail.

Inspired by: Karl Rohnke and Faith Evans

Concepts: To demonstrate the unity of shared experience.

Props/Materials Needed: A nail for each participant in groups up to 15. One additional nail in a block of wood or PVC cap as shown.

Directions:

- While the group is gathered in a circle, open a discussion around what the job of a nail is. What does it do?

- Hand out large nails (16p) to each participant.

- Ask the participants to ponder what action, memory, contribution, or learning (pick an appropriate frame) played a part in building their experience today.

- When everyone has thought of a treasured memory, ask them to indicate this with a thumb up. When all thumbs are up, ask a thoughtfully selected person to hold the vertical nail, representing the program.

- Place a nail on the floor in the center of the group and ask each participant to lay a nail in the prescribed place and share their memory. (See illustration)

- When all nails have been placed, add the last one and carefully balance ALL the nails on the head of the vertical nail. Oohhs and ahhhs will follow. It is fun to note the shape created . . . a tent, a mountain, a teepee, a cabin roof.

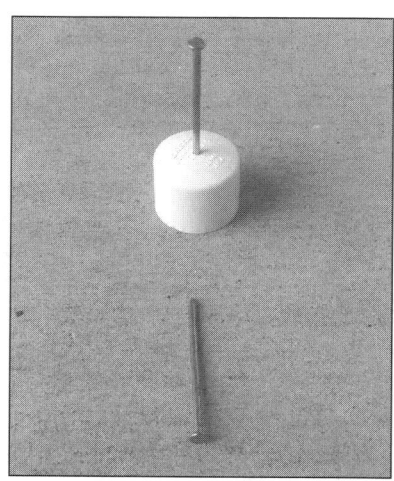

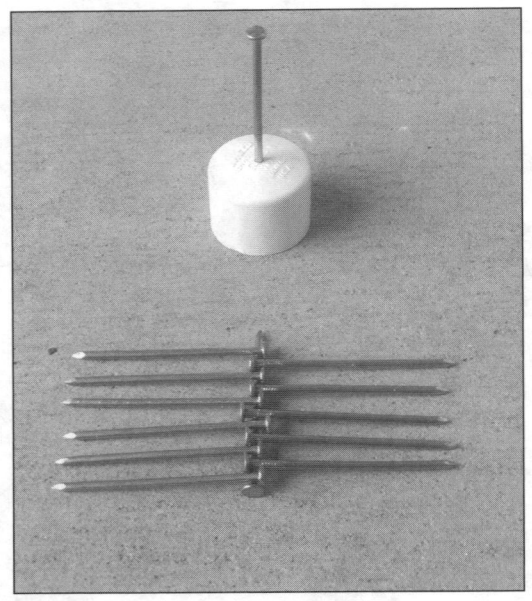

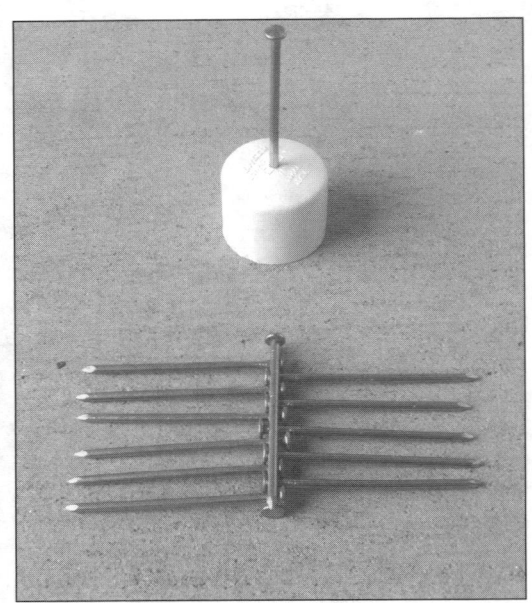

• Nails may be taken home as a momento of the program. Be careful, sharp objects may not be the best momento for all groups.

Where to Find It/How to Make It:

This activity is also called Porcupine Progression, Plenty of Room at the Top, or Nail It. You can buy large nails at most hardware stores. Buy a prepackaged kit from: Training Wheels, Project Adventure, or Grip-It Adventures.

How's the Weather?

The Daily Weather Report

For those of us who work primarily in the great outdoors, weather conditions influence our lives on a daily basis. Here is technique for using various weather conditions to express our feelings and thoughts.

Concepts: While it can sometimes be difficult to express our thoughts and feelings in a group setting, especially with new team members, it is often possible to share them by using common and familiar objects.

Props/Materials Needed: Illustrations of various weather conditions, or pillows made in the shape of weather patterns (such as sunshine, clouds, lightening bolts, snowflakes, tornados, stars, comets, etc.)

Directions: Here are three possibilities for using weather conditions as reviewing tools at the completion of the challenge activity.

- Method I—Pass out cards with various weather conditions to each participant, and ask them to hold these up so that all members of the group can see each one. Next ask the group to identify which weather pattern most accurately describes the performance of the group during the last activity. Point to a few of the more unusual weather patterns and ask if these too could be accurate. Why or why not?

- Method II—Place all the weather illustrations visibly in front of the group, and ask each person to take one that they feel accurately describes their impression of the performance of the group during the last challenge. Ask them to share their reason for choosing this card with another participant, or with the entire group. Invite others who agree with this choice to voice their opinions as well.

- Method III—Place all the weather illustrations visibly in front of the group, preferably on the ground. Give each participant a short piece of rope or webbing (about four to six inches long), which we refer to as a "worm." On the count of three, invite everyone to toss their worm onto the illustration that they feel most accurately describes the performance of the group.

This technique of instant voting encourages each person to form their own impression and vote independently of others in the group. This can be helpful when peer pressure, corporate culture or cultural norms impose on individual choice. In this case, participants do not wait to hear "how their friends are voting" but rather make up their own minds. Facilitators should protect the anonymity of group members and not say, "hey, who put a worm there?" Rather they might say, "I see there is one worm on the blizzard illustration. Can you imagine why a person would choose that one?"

Additionally, the facilitator can also ask members of the group what the "weather" is like in their group right now. Encourage discussion, stories and solutions to "waiting for the weather to change," "correcting the weather," "climate control devices" and other weather related topics.

Where to Find It/How to Make It: Clip art photos of weather conditions can be found in computer software, on-line at several internet websites, and at teacher supply stores. You can also make your own illustrations and weather patterns that are specific to your area of the world.

Image Chips

Image Chips are tactile, perfect for those groups that like or need to hold onto something while they are processing, similar to Treasure Chest.

Creator: Mike Anderson, Learning Works Training and Development Inc.

Concepts: A collection of small, painted wooden images designed to provoke, inspire, encourage, and create interaction between friends and strangers. This activity can be used as an icebreaker or a debriefing tool.

Props/Materials Needed: A number of painted wooden images.

Directions: Here are a few techniques for using image chips.

- Place each of the images face up on a flat surface. Allow everyone the opportunity to survey the images and pick one with which they identify. Allow each participant the opportunity to share their reasons for choosing the image they did. Some may share lighthearted reasons, while others will find profound meaning in their image.

- After the completion of an adventure activity or series of activities, use the image chips to help prompt thoughts or ideas about the activity. Like other debriefing tools in this book, image chips work well when they are placed face up in front of the group and each team member identifies an image that best represents their experience.

- A single image chip can be picked from the collection to help process specific aspects of the activity.

- As a final wrap up for the day, use the image chips to identify feelings they have relating to their day's experience.

- As an alternate closing activity, invite participants to present an image chip to someone else in the group, and tell them why they have chosen this image chip for them.

Where to Find It/How to Make It: Many craft stores have image chips. To buy a set of Image Chips: Mike Anderson, mike@lwtd.com or Grip-It Adventures.

Impression Feet

Impression Feet are small plastic feet about 3/4" long that have a heart cut out of the heel. This makes them great for participants to hang onto shoelaces, keychains, backpacks, and necklaces. These tokens are perfect to reflect on how, when we walk through life, we leave an impression, and that the heart reflects walking with kindness.

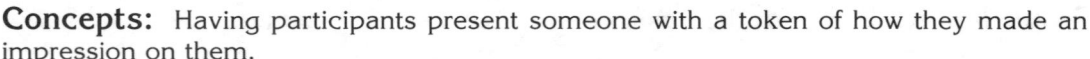

Inspired by: Wendy Caldwell

Contributor: Bridget Widmer

Concepts: Having participants present someone with a token of how they made an impression on them.

Props/Materials Needed: One impression foot for each participant.

Directions:

- At the beginning of the programming day, ask the group to watch the contributions of each of their team members (not just the team members they know).
- At the end of the day, present a collection of colored impression feet in the middle of the circle, one for each person.
- Ask each person to present a foot to another person in their team, and state what that person did that left a good impression on them.

It is pretty amazing how even children as young as first grade can sit still, wait, listen and articulate what their team members did that made them feel good. Kids sometimes want to exchange their foot for a different color, but since it is a gift, they seldom trade. It is wonderful how recipients will value these simple tokens. They love it when they get a new color in a new year or on a different program.

Where to Find It/How to Make It: Sold in sets of 75 by Training Wheels.

Index Card Castles

This activity was presented at the Mid-States, American Camp Association conference in 2001.

Concepts: To have each group write down the foundations of learning they experienced during the program and build a card castle.

Props/Materials Needed: Index cards, pens, pencils, crayons, or markers.

Directions: This is a great activity for large group debriefs.

- Have the group break into smaller groups. Divide any size group into smaller groups of 3-4 participants.
- Give a generous stack of colorful index cards and markers to each group.
- Instruct each group to write down some of the teachable moments that they experienced throughout the day. Use a new card for each new concept. These teachable moments create the foundation of the group's learning.
- After several minutes of writing time, instruct each group to build a card castle with their index cards. It can be as unique as they want it to be. You can also provide tape (which adds a completely different dimension to these castles).
- Instruct participants to build their castle with the foundation cards they created.
- Invite participants to connect their castle to at least two other castles. They can do this however they want, but each group must build their own castle, not a combination group castle. Usually they will use a line of blank index cards to create pathways from one castle to another. If they are asked to connect to only one other castle, the "global village" aspect of this activity will be lost.

- As each group finishes have them step back from their castle and stand along the outside of the "village." It will be obvious that each castle is indirectly connected to every other castle in the room. In very large groups, it will truly look like a global village from the outside, because one castle on one end is connected to the castle on the far end as well.

- A few closing comments about connection is an effective way to complete this activity.

The best rules to form a young man, are, to talk little, to hear much,
to reflect alone upon what has passed in company,
to distrust one's own opinions, and value others that deserve it.

Sir W. Temple

Index Card Debrief

Take a Card, Any Card

This activity combines debriefing with the icebreaking activity Back to Back and is a great way to process in large groups.

Concepts: Creating an active, one-on-one debriefing session.

Props/Materials Needed: Index cards with processing questions written on them, or blank index cards and pens for the participants to create their own debriefing questions.

Directions:

• Write processing questions on index cards and pass one out to each participant or invite participants to write their own processing questions.

Back to Back instructions:

• Have participants find partners and stand back to back.

• When the facilitator calls out "front to front" each person finds a new partner and begins discussing the question that is on their cards.

• When the facilitator calls out "back to back" the duo *exchange* cards, turn around and stand back-to-back with each other. It is amazing how the talking will stop as soon as people are not facing one another!

• When the facilitator calls out "front to front," each person finds a new partner and begins discussing the new question that is on their new card.

• After a few exchanges, bring the group back together and ask for volunteers to share some of their discussions.

I Would Like to Thank . . .

An Award Winning Presentation

Just watch any award show and you will see that an outstanding performance brings with it praise for all those who assisted in the process. Here is your chance to thank those people who made this all possible.

Concepts: A corporate manager in a recent train-the-trainer program remarked that they did not need much feedback in order to do their jobs. Consequently, they did not tend to provide much feedback to their staff, even when requested. The good news is that we can each improve at the things we choose to practice. Sometimes saying thank you, is not just good for the recipient, it can be great for the speaker as well. Here is a chance to help your group learn the value and power of saying thank you and you're welcome, in whatever language is appropriate.

Props/Materials Needed: None, but a good facilitator example to follow is important.

Directions:

- As a final debrief for the program, invite participants to specifically thank those people who have made their experience memorable today. Encourage them to say thank you, and mention why they are offering this thank you. Recipients should respond with "you are welcome." It is suggested that you remind participants, especially with corporate audiences, that we can become better at those things we practice. Here is your chance to practice giving praise to a member of your team.

- Facilitators should be ready to offer an occasional thank you during this activity, to model an appropriate response, and to keep the praise sincere. Do not be alarmed if there are some silences during this activity. It may take some participants a few minutes to compose their thoughts related to thanking other people.

- As a second alternative to this activity, and a somewhat theatrical and often humorous one, participants can be presented with an award trophy (sort of a bronze plated talking stick), and invited to make a one minute acceptance speech for the "you invent the name here" adventure award. An old athletic trophy (you know, the one you have been keeping in the attic since high-school) is perfect for this award. A podium to stand behind it also appropriate, when available. You will improve the quality of acceptance speeches if you allow participants a few minutes to prepare their comments in advance. A few index cards and pens or pencils are helpful. You can even offer specific awards to each member of the group for their contributions that day. And the award for "the best, far-fetched, I can't believe it actually worked—but it did" honor goes to . . . Chris Cavert!

Jars

This is a great activity for long term groups.

Contributor: Chris Cavert, FUNdoing.

Concepts: Many people show up to a program knowing the traditional "concept" buzzwords like teamwork, communication, trust, participation, leadership, support and problem solving. However, these concepts are just the lids of the metaphorical jars.

Props/Materials Needed: Small jars (preferably unbreakable and transparent), masking tape, permanent markers or pens, small strips of paper or index cards.

Directions:

*   Ask, "What is inside of the jar! What are the ingredients?" The ingredients are the "skills" (something observable) that make up a concept. To bring this process from the metaphorical to the visual, when a concept is brought up (one related to the group's program objectives), write the concept on some tape and put the tape on the lid of one of the jars.

*   Next, have the group explore what "skills" go with each concept—this discovery can happen any time throughout the program. When a skill is accepted, have someone write it down on a small slip of paper and stick the paper in the jar.

*   At the end of the program the group will have created a list of skills they can now use to enhance the concepts they continue to explore.

Journaling

Journaling is an effective reflective activity that can be used with nearly every group. For kindergartners or adults, multi-day programs or one-day experiences, journaling can be a powerful individual tool. The use of journaling can become a lifetime reflective skill. Not only does journaling aid in reflection, but it also can assist educators with writing requirements. It gives participants a tangible memoir of their experience and growth. For many ongoing groups, journaling can be a way to ensure that opportunities for reflection are happening regardless of what happens during program time. Trying to fit adventure activities into a traditional class time period is often difficult; processing is often missed because limited time. One way to ensure that reflection is being performed by participants is to use journal assignments.

If journals are shared, it can be a valuable way for participants, educators or facilitators to evaluate and identify outcomes of the program. Ongoing experiential education programs that have used journaling as part of their curriculum report that participants demonstrate a progression in the group development process through their journal entries. It gives group facilitators, students and teachers an understanding of group development, the benefits of the programs initiatives and feedback about the progression of the course. Teachers involved in using journaling as part of semester long adventure education course report that students demonstrated increased insightful thinking and improved writing skills from their practice of journaling.

Journaling can involve a variety of mediums: the written word, worksheets, drawings, scrap booking, and audio or video documentary. Journals can take many forms: traditional journal books or diaries, worksheets, sketch pads, artwork, scrap books, photo journals, or cartoon books.

Journaling Ideas

- Encourage participants to make their own journals.
- Invite participants to create artistic representations of their experiences.
- Give participants specific questions to answer to initially aid in the journaling process.
- Create a portfolio of experiences as a way of journaling.
- Use art activities as part of journaling. Teachers or recreational professionals can coordinate with their program's art department for implementing collaborative projects using alternative forms of media for journaling such as photography, video and audio documentation.
- Creating a worksheet to fill out aids the journaling—make it visually interesting with questions placed in different shaped writing spaces, or by using drawings. We

recommend The Me I See by Wood-n-Barres Publishing. It is a wonderful resource for templates for journaling.

- Use an alternative medium such as scrap booking, photo journaling, or audio and visual documentaries. There are a variety of interesting digital media readily available to groups—from cell phones to small recording devices—digital review can help you create a multi-media record of the group's experiences.

In 2000 and 2001 Jennifer Stanchfield worked alongside physical education teacher Donna Richter and School Psychologist Lynn Reining to develop a semester long ropes challenge class curriculum for senior high school students. During that time Donna and Jen experimented with journaling as a means to ensure that reflection was occurring as well as to meet the school district's writing requirement. They found it become much more than that. The student's statements gave incredible insight into the value of the experiential activities, and how they were meeting physical education standards and developing important assets in students. With the students assent the statements were shared anonymously with school administrators and parents to demonstrate the success of the program. As teachers, Jennifer and Donna gained insights into the sequencing of activities and the success or weakness of specific activities which helped them to continue to adapt and refine the adventure curriculum.

Journaling Assignment Sample from Middleton High School, Middleton, Wisconsin

One of the principles of experiential and adventure education is the principle of action and reflection. It is an idea presented by the educational philosopher John Dewey. He believed that humans do not truly learn from an experience until they spend some time reflecting on it and analyzing how the experience is meaningful to them and relevant to their lives. We are hoping this course will be interesting, fun, and that you will learn new skills. We hope it will be relevant to your life both inside and outside of school.

One of the ways we hope to help facilitate this process is through journaling assignments. We hope it will help make this class something that will be meaningful and relevant now and in the future. We want you to have a record of the work you put into this course and the skills you have learned.

Your writing should reflect your reactions to the activities and their relevance to other aspects of your life.

We want to see more than just a description of what happened in class.
We want you to focus on the "So What?" and the "Now What?"

Examples of questions you could answer in your journal assignments might be:
What were your feelings during the activity?
What did you like and dislike?
What were some of the statements you were telling yourself during the activity?
Were you uncomfortable doing anything? If so, what?
Were any of your reactions typical of you?
Do the experiences in class relate to other aspects of your life? How?

Samples of Student's Journals

One Student's Progress Throughout the Semester

"I am not that big of a fan of other people in my outside life so was not entirely enthusiastic about the activities today. I don't know that I will rush out and make any ground shaking changes in the way I act because of today's lesson. I will however be able to come to class with a positive open mind from now on. My goal for the semester is first and foremost to get it over with (after all I am a senior). I may however, also find time to enjoy it. I have spent three and a half long, lonely, years conducting myself one way in order to get ahead in a class. For Ropes I'll have to try doing things a little differently. My goal is to be more open and accepting of others, and try to be successful in the tasks I am presented with. I can definitely come to class with a more friendly less cynical way of thinking."

"The real test for me was the telegraph game. I don't like people and I don't like physical contact. Holding hands is a big thing for me. Not to sound negative, but some of my classmates are not my favorite people. I sucked it up and went along with it. The competitive nature of the game helped me put any thoughts like that out of my head and focus on the goal. Maybe that's what you were trying to do with today's activities, teaching us to put our differences aside and focus on achieving a goal. It kind of worked. Clever."

"I've noticed lately that I've gotten a lot more talkative. I don't know if that has anything to do with this class, but the effects are definitely showing. I'm more social, and therefore happier and more successful at getting my ideas across. I'm not really a leader in the group, but I'm definitely playing a key role. I am confident I wouldn't be voted off the "island" any time soon."

"Sam and I really stepped up as leaders at the start. It leads me to think of myself as more of a leader. I guess I never really thought of myself as a leader before, but I've started to act like it in the last week or so. Maybe I have always been that way but haven't noticed it till now. That's pretty cool."

One Student's Thoughts on the First Day of Games and Initiatives

"Today was fun! It was more like a regular gym class, but still enjoyable. The really cool part was that it wasn't as ickily competitive as a typical gym class. The competition was friendly, and it was a very fun game. People were encouraging, not cruel, something I—a nonathlete—have experienced very often. I really thought that this gave hope to people, especially me that competitive sports are really not all there is."

Another Student's Final Entry

"But then, up there on the platform, I decided that the fear wasn't getting me anywhere. So I decided to jump. I counted down and then I flew. It was a leap of faith. A leap of trust, confidence, spirit and will. I knew this was what I had wanted to gain from this class. I have learned to trust others, to give it my all. The jump was just a disguise, a cover up. It was really a test of what you have been teaching us all semester. You taught and I learned. I took the test and I passed. I got to the bar and I grabbed it."

Journaling (a few more ideas)

Finding the Right Words

Here are a few suggestions for making journaling fun, interesting and interactive.

Concepts: While composing our thoughts, at least enough to write them down, we often internally process our words. Here are a few suggestions for providing interesting formats for expressing ourselves in words.

Props/Materials Needed: Unique papers and writing tools.

Directions:
No matter what the writing assignment, encourage creativity by providing unique papers and writing surfaces (in nonstandard and free form shapes, such as diamonds, rain drops, trees, and triangles), writing tools (such as etching, colored pencils and markers, glitter paints, and stencils), and presentation techniques (power point presentations, adhesive walls, flip charts, picture frames, journalling books, and sketch pads).

Where to Find It/How to Make It: Check your local library for books related to poetry styles, drawing cartoons and writing lyrics for songs. You can also find resources on other writing styles, including: limericks, haiku, rhymes, rap lyrics, iambic pentameter and prose. There are a variety of creative printing techniques too, such as calligraphy, hidden messages (with lemon juice ink), crayons, scrimshaw, T-shirt art, fabric paint, spray paints, and glitter markers. Visit your local fabric and craft store to find other creative writing tools.

Key Consensus

Here is a metaphoric model activity that is simple to facilitate.

Concepts: Creating the perfect atmosphere to talk about unique issues and having the right key to open or close those discussions.

Props/Materials Needed: Keys of various sizes and shapes, one for each participant.

Directions:

- Place a variety of different keys on a keychain.
- Pass this collection around the group and ask each person to talk about different issues that are occuring on within the group. For example, roles within the group, conflict resolution.
- Discuss some aspects of keys, (i.e., they unlock things; each key is unique; they come in various shapes, sizes, and colors; it can create stressful situations when keys are lost, etc.).
- As the group discusses their issues, assign a metaphor for each issue to a key.
- Assign a "key carrier" and have them carry the group metaphors to each activity.
- Get the keys out before each activity and discuss things that the group needs to lock or unlock to be successful.
- At the end of the program give each participant a key and tell them to go and create their own experiences and metaphors!

Where to Find It/How to Make It: Visit any store that cuts keys. They may have defective keys that they are willing to sell or donate. You can also purchase blank, uncut keys. Antique and old-fashioned keys create special interest.

Knot Race

Here is an activity for those participants who have a difficult time standing still and listening for any length of time. Adding movement after each question keeps the group focused and engaged.

Concepts: Creating an active sharing circle.

Props/Materials Needed: A long rope and three different colored bandanas.

Directions:

- Tie three knots in a long rope and then tie this rope into a circular loop. Color code the knots with three different colored bandanas.

- Each bandana will have a different question or category. For example, the blue bandana can represent a fact-finding question, (i.e., Who was the leader in that activity?). The red bandana can represent an analysis question (i.e., How well did we work together as a team?). And the purple bandana can represent a transference question (i.e., How was this like everyday life?). You can have a list of pre-made questions or let the participants come up with their own questions.

- Invite the participants to pass the rope around in the circle until someone says stop. Wherever the bandanas stop identifies the next participants to answer these questions.

Other suggestions for bandana categories:

Give a compliment to the person who has the red bandana.

Have each bandana represent the same question each time it is passed.

For example:

The red bandana could represent a feeling you experienced in the activity.

The blue bandana could represent something you would do differently next time.

The purple bandana could represent ways in which the group was supportive.

Labyrinth Walk

Reflection in Motion

A few years ago at the AEE Northeast Regional Conference, some wonderful folks created a labyrinth using flagging tape. Even though the entire labyrinth fit within an area roughly the size of a tennis court, it easily required a full ten minutes of quiet reflective time to walk the entire path. What a peaceful experience.

On a recent trip to New York City, Jim even saw a labyrinth painted on the surface of a parking lot, near the farmer's market off Broadway. We are not sure which is more unusual, a farmer's market in downtown Manhattan or a labyrinth imposed in the midst of one of the biggest cities on the planet.

Concepts: The labyrinth is an archetype, a divine imprint, found in historical and religious traditions in various forms around the world. By walking a replica of the Chartres labyrinth, laid in the floor of Chartres Cathedral in France around 1220, we are rediscovering a long-forgotten mystical tradition that is insisting to be reborn.

The labyrinth has only one path so there are no tricks and no dead ends. The path winds throughout and becomes a mirror for where we are in our lives. It touches your sorrows and releases your joys. Walk it with an open mind and an open heart.

Props/Materials Needed: You will need an entire spool of rope, webbing, or surveyor's flagging tape to create a labyrinth for quiet reflection (500–1000 feet should be sufficient). Small paving stones may be another option. There are a variety of labyrinths and mazes, including corn mazes out there.

Directions:

- Upon completing an activity or after journaling, the facilitator encourages participants to reflect on their experience while traversing the labyrinth.
- The typical goal is to reach the center of the labyrinth and return to the outside without crossing any lines, and without talking.
- Movement with meditation and introspection are key elements of the labyrinth walk.

Where to Find It/How to Make It: For more information about this labyrinth, see the book: *Exploring the Labyrinth: A Guide for Healing and Spiritual Growth,* Melissa Gayle West, 2000, Broadway Books, New York, NY ISBN 0-7679-0356-0 or contact the Worldwide Labyrinth Project: 1100 California Street, San Francisco, CA 94108. Website: www.gracecathedral.org.

Later Letters

The Check Is in the Mail

This popular activity was shared by several facilitators. It is a perfect way for participants to engage in renewed self-reflection long after the program is complete.

Concepts: To allow participants to receive a letter from themselves at a later date to remind them of their experience during the program.

Props/Materials Needed: Paper, envelopes, stamps, and pens or pencils.

Directions:

- Give each participant a piece of paper, pen or pencil, and an envelope.

- Ask each person to write a letter to themselves describing their experience from this program.

- After participants have finished writing, have them seal the letter inside the envelope and write their mailing address on the front of the envelope.

- Mail the letters back to their authors at a strategic time. If you have the ability to keep up with a calendar, ask the participants to place a date on the back of the envelope that is when they would like to receive the letter. Then you can mail the letter to them a few days before they wished to receive it. A tracking system and good organization are key to making this work.

- As an alternative, before sealing each envelope, other members of the group can include greetings, mailing addresses, birthday wishes, email addresses, sketches, or photographs. Do not forget a greeting from the group's facilitator.

Learning Rope

A variation by Chris Cavert of the activity, Circle of Rope, inspired by the book, Reflective Learning *(Sugerman, Gass, Garvey, Doherty).*

Contributor: Chris Cavert, FUNdoing.

Props/Materials Needed: A long rope, at least 3/8" diameter. Many hardware stores sell colorful, inexpensive rope. You will need about 50 feet of rope for this activity.

Directions:

- Beginning at the very onset of your program day, place an overhand knot in the rope for every piece of knowledge presented to the group.

- For example, at the beginning of the program you might present the Five Finger Contract (*The Caring Classroom,* Laurie Frank). A knot goes in the rope to remind us of safety, another for commitment, one for respect, another for responding and the final one for encouragement. Discuss each concept before adding another knot.

- As more knots go into the rope we review the previous knots to instill reminders of what has been important to remember.

- This rope travels with the group during the program.

Variation: As a participant keepsake, purchase some ornate rope for this activity. During the close of your program, discuss how the rope and the information in the knots helped out during the program. With a little "experiential magic" transfer the knowledge from each knot into the rest of the rope and all the other knots—so every knot has all the knowledge. Then, with sharp scissors, have each participant cut off one of the knots and tell the group what knowledge in the knot will help them the most. This segment of the rope is theirs to keep.

Leave Your Mark

Handprints

Michelle learned this powerful activity while working at the Saint Francis Academy in Atchison, Kansas. On the final day of a ten-day program, the kids would get to paint their hand and press it onto the wall of the building. It helped them verbalize what they were leaving behind and the changes they were going to make. Some kids who visited the program at a later date knew exactly where their handprints were. How is that for leaving your mark!

Photo courtesy of Jeff Baird, High 5

Concepts: Leaving a permanent mark at a place where the experience happened.

Props/Materials Needed: Paint, a water source to wash hands, a paint brush and a permanent surface for the handprints (such as a wall, tire, sheet, sidewalk, mosaic tiles, or door).

Directions:

- Discuss with the group things they want to leave behind, i.e., bad attitude, poor grades, cursing, personal baggage.
- After some self-reflection, encourage participants to share.
- After each participant shares what they are leaving behind, let them paint their hand and leave their mark.
- Allow participants to wash their hands after they place their handprint.

Lights, Camera, Action!

Scene One, Take One

We all have favorite scenes from Hollywood movies. Here is an opportunity for a group to review their favorite scenes from their adventure experience.

Concepts: Here are four techniques for using a standard movie scene clapboard to review scenes from your most recent adventure-based learning activity.

Props/Materials Needed: A movie scene clapboard, or some participant imagination.

Directions:

- Method I—As a reviewing technique, the facilitator can recreate the scene of the most recent activity and replay it exactly as it happened. Next, the group can "reshoot" the scene, and alter the outcome as desired.

- Method II—At the completion of the activity, the clapboard is passed around the group and each member has the opportunity to share a scene with the group.

- Method III—At the completion of the program, the clapboard is passed around the group and each member has the opportunity to show a future scene where they will use the skills they have learned today in a situation at home, at work, at school, or in their life.

- Method IV—"CUT"! The clapboard could be used as a tool for "stop action" mid activity. If the facilitator or group member wants the group to "freeze frame" a moment in time and evaluate where they are as a group before continuing the task, the clapboard can be used to facilitate a stop action.

  For additional theater related activities see: *Theater's Games for the Classroom: A Teacher's Handbook,* 1986. Viola Spolin. Northwestern University Press, Chicago, IL USA ISBN: 0810140047

Where to Find It/How to Make It: You can find movie scene clapboards at The Trainer's Warehouse, Training Wheels, toy stores, or make your own with two boards that have been hinged together.

Looking Ahead

Making Predictions of the Future

Sometimes it is easier to find what you need when you know exactly what it is that you are looking for.

Concepts: Looking Ahead encourages group members to identify the group behaviors, talents and skills that they feel would be beneficial to the success of the group in advance of the activity. Not surprisingly, groups tend to demonstrate those attributes that they deem important enough to make this prediction list.

Props/Materials Needed: A clipboard, prediction sheet (paper), and pencil, pen or marker.

Photo courtesy of Jeff Baird, High 5.

Directions:

- Prior to presenting the next challenge to the group, the facilitator leads a discussion related to the skills, talents and attributes that have helped the group be successful up to this point.

- After explaining the next challenge, the facilitator asks the group, prior to problem solving, to list the talents and skills that they feel would be helpful in solving this challenge. The facilitator can also provide a list of group skills (such as teamwork, clear communication, creative problem-solving skills, resourcefulness, advanced planning, delegation, resource management, time management, inclusion and cooperation) that the group can circle or check as part of their prediction list.

- After the initiative has been completed, the facilitator encourages different members of the team to look for each of the skills identified and to be ready to discuss when these talents were observed.

Lycra Tube

The Perfect Place for Processing

This ingenious activity makes a comfortable place for the entire group to sit.

Concepts: To provide a comfortable place for the group to process.

Props/Materials Needed: One Lycra Tube per group.

Directions:

- With the entire group inside the lycra tube, each person backs up until the lycra is fully stretched.
- Next, instruct the group to simultaneously sit down in the lycra tube.
- This creates a comfortable setting in which to process, especially for those times when reviewing will require more time. You could do other processing activites, like Chiji Cards, while sitting in the lycra tube.
- If it happens to be a sunny day and there are few trees in sight, the lycra tube can be used to provide shade for the group. Just stretch the lycra tube into a large circle, and lift the top of the lycra tube over the heads of all participants before sitting down. The stretch within the lycra tube will create a canopy that blocks the sun. This also creates a visual barrier between your group and other groups or nearby distractions.

Where to Find It/How to Make It: You can purchase lycra material at most fabric stores. Ask for the highest quality of lycra to ensure the longevity of your lycra tube. You will need 5 yards (4.6 meters) of lycra per tube. See the lycra tube information in the book *Teamwork and Teamplay* by Jim Cain for more information. Or you can buy a lycra tube from several sources including: Adventure Hardware, Training Wheels, Grip-It Adventures, Leahy and Associates, or ask your local challenge course vendor.

The Magical Box

Finding the Magic at the End of the Activity

Thanks to Jim Tonery and Clare Marie Hannon for sharing their version of this wonderful processing activity. We have made a few of our own modifications here. A perfect activity for youth or adult programs.

Concepts: The magical box utilizes a "give and take" mentality which encourages participants to consider the skills that they received as a result of the learning program, and also the talents that they have to offer as a result of this education.

Props/Materials Needed: This activity can be performed with only your imagination, or with an unusual or ornate box or container.

Directions: Here is a processing activity that can be initially demonstrated by the facilitator, and then passed around the group.

- Begin by holding either an imaginary or actual container (the more unusual, decorated or ornate, the better).

- The first part of the activity is to reach into the box and remove some valuable skill or talent that was experienced during the program. For example, a participant might suggest that they are taking out of the box some communication skills that they gained during a recent activity.

- The second part encourages each person to put back into the box a valuable skill or talent that they have to offer to the group. This second part is essential so that the box never becomes empty. A participant, for example, might put back into the box courage that they experienced while on the climbing wall or zipline.

Where to Find It/How to Make It: Try searching at an craft or gift store that features items from foreign countries. Ten Thousand Villages, Ikea, Pier One Imports and other international stores often carry unique foreign made containers in a variety of styles, shapes and materials.

Making Music

Expressing Ourselves Musically

Here is a technique for the group to present their interpretation of the reviewing session in a musical fashion.

Concepts: While some participants are comfortable using words, concepts and even photographs or illustrations to represent their opinions, there are others who find expression using the arts a more suitable and creative technique. The activities presented here explore the musical talent world of multiple intelligence theory, and encourage participants to try a new method of expressing themselves. For those programs using arts integration into traditional classroom environments, music has been used to express subjects ranging from historical events to mathematics and science.

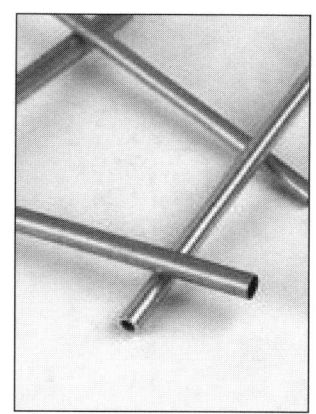

Props/Materials Needed: Musical instruments, chimes, drums, or just the pipe chimes or water concert equipment mentioned here.

Directions:

- At the completion of an activity, the group is asked to review their contributions and performance in the previous activity.
- Next, the facilitator invites the group to create a musical interpretation of these contributions, using the materials provided.
- As with many classical forms of music, some information about the selection is appropriate, and after the performance, a standing ovation.

Where to Find It/How to Make It: Pipe Chimes—You can make an inexpensive set of musical pipe chimes from electrical steel conduit, found at most hardware stores. The dimensions shown here are for standard 1/2" conduit (which actually has an outside diameter of 11/16"). These dimensions create pipes which will be in tune with a piano. Drill a hole completely through each tube, near the end, and hang each pipe from a short length of cord or string. A nail (16p) makes an ideal striker. Invite the group to create a symphony celebrating the contributions of the group.

Note	Length (inches)	Length (mm)
A3	27.72	704
A#	26.93	684
B	26.16	664
C	25.42	646
C#	24.69	627
D	23.99	609
D#	23.31	592
E	22.64	575
F	22.00	559
F#	21.37	543
G	20.76	527
G#	20.17	512
A4	19.60	498
A#	19.04	484
B	18.50	470
C	17.97	456
C#	17.46	443
D	16.96	431
D#	16.48	419
E	16.01	407
F	15.55	395
F#	15.11	384
G	14.68	373
G#	14.26	362
A5	13.86	352

Variation: Water Concert: This additional music making activity can be performed by presenting a group of six to eight participants with a pitcher of water and enough glasses and metal spoons for each participant. Allow each group a few minutes to create 'a symphony performance' by using water to tune the pitch of each glass and the metal spoons for striking.

Masks

Here is a very powerful activity that requires some careful facilitation.

Concepts: To see ourselves as others see us, both inside and out so that we may begin to understand our uniqueness.

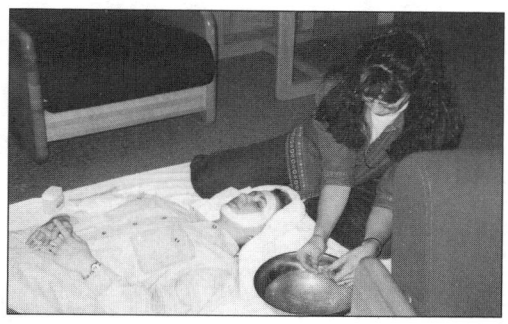

Props/Materials Needed: First aid gauze, often used in wrapping broken arms, cut into 2–3" strips, with approximately 40 pieces per person. Also cut some small 1/2" triangular pieces to fit around the nose and other contours. Carapace "original formula" plaster bandages, extra fast setting, are recommended. Size: 3 inches wide by 3 yards long. They are available at medical supply stores. You will also need some large bowls filled with warm water, towels/sheets, paper towels, plenty of Vaseline, and some reflective, instrumental music to play in the background.

Time Needed: 1–1½ hours

Preparation: Set several mask stations by laying towels or sheets out on the floor. Leave plenty of space between each station. The towels and sheets are essential for keeping the plaster drippings from the floor. Pre-cut the plaster gauze and put these pieces into plastic bags for easy distribution. Set out the bowls of warm water as each pair of participants start the vaseline process.

To mentally prepare the group for the seriousness of this activity, talk to them about trust and how to care for others. This activity will require someone to "give up control" of their sight and in doing so, will force them to trust their partner. Talk to them about caring for others and how they would like to be cared for. Explain that they should use a soft calm voice and tell their partner what they are doing when they are doing it, i.e., "I'm going to apply a piece to your left cheek." Tell them to position themselves so that a part of their knee or arm is in contact with the receiver at all times. This will help alleviate any abandonment feelings during the application and drying process.

Directions:

- Talk to the group about personal reflections. How do people see them on the outside and how is that different from what is on the inside? What is unique about you? etc.

- Tell the group that this is a quiet activity to allow for personal reflection. Play reflective instrumental music in the background.

- Have the group choose partners (or assign them). Ask participants to decide which person will apply the mask first and which will go second.

- The mask receiver will lie down on the towel or sheet and close their eyes. Instruct the person doing the mask to put a VERY generous portion of Vaseline on their partner's face, covering at the hairline and around to the front of the ears and down the neckline. Make sure that the eyelashes and eyebrows are well covered. The Vaseline is what keeps the plaster from permanently adhering to the face and hair, so it is important to apply enough to cover the face completely, but still allow the plaster to define the face. If the receiver has a beard, apply an extra generous portion of Vaseline.

- The person applying the mask (the giver) then proceeds to dip each strip of gauze into the water, smear the plaster together, and place it on the face of the partner. Start with the outline of the face and work inward.

- Apply two to three layers of pieces and cover all of the face, including the eyes. Make sure verbal warnings are given before the pieces go over the eyes (talking is allowed).

- The only place left exposed should be the nostrils for breathing. Even the mouth should be covered. This works best when the giver shapes the gauze on the face of the partner so that the facial features are well defined.

- Few people are allergic to these products, but be cautious.

Very Important: It is recommended that the giver does not remove their hands/knee from their partner at any time—especially when waiting for the gauze to dry and the application process is finished. While this is happening, play soft music and allow no talking, other than placement statements. When all of the gauze has been put on the face, allow five minutes for it to dry. It will get warm as it dries and hardens. You can do a small squeeze test to see if it gives a little or if it has hardened. After the mask has hardened you can help participants remove their mask. Facilitators may need to help with 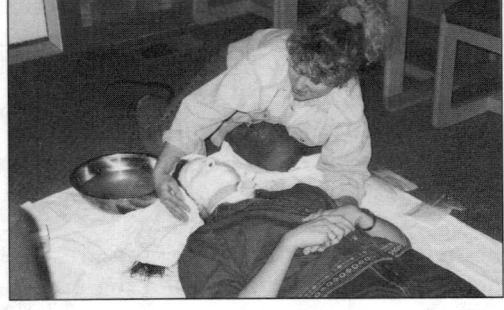 this and assure the participants that there is nothing to fear. Ask the mask receiver to scrunch up their face underneath the mask several times so it starts to release from their face. The mask giver and/or facilitator can start to work the edges of the mask to find a spot where the mask is starting to come off of the face. Gently work the mask off of the face. After the mask is off, the mask giver should walk their partner to a sink so they can use paper towels and water to remove the Vaseline from their eyes and face. This will require a lot of paper towels. To allow the mask to finish drying, wad up several paper towels and put them in the face of the mask. 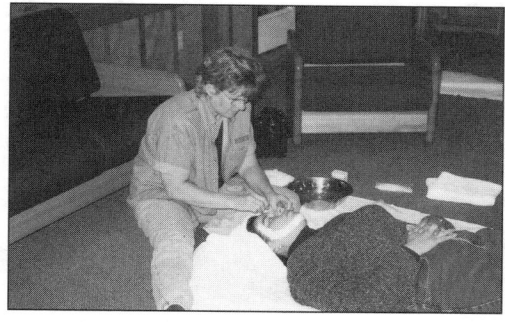 Place the mask with the other completed masks on a tabletop until everyone has finished.

When this is done, have participants switch and the receiver becomes the giver.

A great way to start the debrief for this activity is to have each mask maker present the mask they made to their partner and share something unique they see in them.

An added exercise would be to have them decorate the masks in whatever way they feel is appropriate. This exercise should be thoughtfully sequenced during a longer program. A lot of reflection and insight can be gained from this exercise, too. You could have them share how they feel about themselves while holding their masks, both at the beginning and end of the program.

The following reflective questions are appropriate.

1. What happened?
2. What were some of your feelings?
3. Were you afraid?
4. Did you trust your partner?
5. What did you learn?
6. What does the mask represent?
7. How do others view you?
8. How do you view yourself?
9. Is there anything 'under the mask' you want to share?
10. What do you want to tell your mask maker?

Be sure to have them tag their mask on the back side with their name so they can find it easily at the end of the program.

Where to Find It/How to Make It: Plaster can be purchased from: Carapace, A LOHMANN Company, Tulsa, OK 74147–0040. To purchase online: www.superiormedical.com or 800-268-7944.

A Message for Future Generations

Helping the Next Team

Thanks to Tom Heck for sharing this auditory technique. Tom mentioned that he was working with a wilderness-based program for youth-at-risk populations. During a 30 day program, the teenage participants typically experienced all the stages of group formation (forming, storming, norming, performing and eventually transforming). Near the end of each program (typically the evening of day 29), Tom would present a battery powered tape recorder to the group and encourage them to share their thoughts about the program for the next group. This tape would then be played for the next group, about the time that they were in the "storming"' stage (typically near day 4). The voices of other participants, many of whom were exactly like themselves, were comforting, expressive, and provided some necessary insight to help the group reach the next level.

Contributor: Tom Heck, TeachMeTeamwork.com

Concepts: Facilitators, especially in youth-at-risk settings, can often be perceived as 'one of them' rather than 'one of us' by the at-risk member of the group. The recorded messages mentioned here come from people who are 'like us' rather than 'like them,' and as such are more often welcomed and listened to by members of the group.

Props/Materials Needed: A portable recording device.

Directions:

• Before inviting the group to record their thoughts, it is a good idea for the facilitator to know the group formation level that the group is presently experiencing. This activity is best suited for groups that have reached the performing stage. This activity is also best unscripted, raw, and typically in the often graphic language of the team members themselves. The goal here is an honest, credible description, from people who know, to the next generation of explorers.

- This recording is then presented to a future group, with a simple introduction, at a time when such information can assist the group in moving forward. The storming stage can be an ideal time.

- Although these messages are frequently kept confidential and only shared within the groups, here are a few examples of the content these recorded message might include:

"we were just like you are now,
28 days ago, and we made it through"

"these facilitator dudes said we could trust them, yeah right.
But you know, after 3 weeks with these guys, they were right"

"When I was where you are now, I wanted to quit, to yell, to run off,
anywhere but here. I even tried to. But these guys
helped me get through it, and tomorrow I'm going home again.
Now I know I can make it through anything."

To learn more about youth at-risk populations, read: *Shouting at the Sky-Troubled Teens and the Promise of the Wild,* 1999, Gary Ferguson, St. Martin's Press, New York, NY USA. ISBN 0-312-20008-0.

Message in a Bottle

Helping the Next Team

If you do not happen to have access to a digital recording device or a tool for producing the beeping sound in the reviewing activity Voicemail, here is a non-digital version, of the shipwreck variety, that is sure to work too.

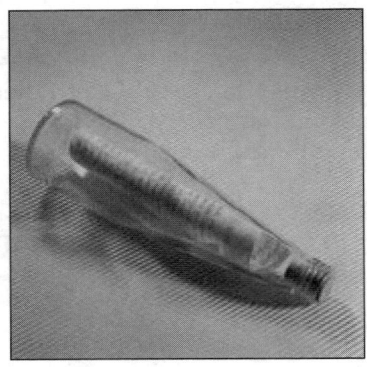

Concepts: The classic message in a bottle is either a call for rescue from some unusual location, a final will and testament, or the location of a secret treasure. This framing allows the group to consider their present situation and write accordingly.

Props/Materials Needed: A clear, plain-looking plastic or glass bottle, paper, pen or pencil, and a cork stopper for the bottle.

Directions:

- At a "teachable moment" of an activity (which is typically either the completion of the activity, or a useful discussion point during the activity), present the group with a clear bottle, paper, pencil, and cork.
- Ask them to write one of the following styles of messages: a rescue note (asking for specific help, such as send us a long rope) or the location (description) of a secret treasure (valuable resource) that will help them complete the task.
- The facilitator can limit the size of the paper and the sharpness of the pencil to further challenge the group.

Metaphoric Cards

Postcards
Chiji Cards©
Expression Cards
Metaphor Cards

This category of engaging participant directed tools uses pictorial images, metaphors or symbols in a variety of ways to represent a participant's or group's reactions to an experience. Providing a tangible image upon which participants can attach their thoughts helps give these ideas substance and shape in quite profound depth. Metaphoric Cards are useful as introductory activities, for processing a specific experience, for closure or even as a tool to help participants resolve conflict. Metaphoric card activities are appealing to participants and are appropriate for all age groups.

Concepts: Group sharing is often more in depth when participants attach their thoughts or feelings to a symbol or picture. Because participants share about a card rather than directly about themselves they are often more willing to share. More reserved members are frequently drawn to expressing themselves through the use of these symbols.

Props/Materials Needed: There are a variety of great metaphor cards created by experiential facilitators. The Chiji Cards created by Steve Simpson, Buzz Bocher and Dan Miller of the Institute for Experiential Education are a popular and appealing deck of metaphor cards. The word chiji means "important moment or opportunity" in Chinese. Mark Rose and Carrie Reilly of Executive Training-Team Quest at The University of Oklahoma have also created what they call Expression Cards. Michelle Cummings created Metaphor Cards, which are laminated, making them especially durable for outdoor programming.

Postcards are readily available cards that contain interesting metaphorical images. This activity can give you an opportunity to use all those postcards you never sent from your last vacation! Some participants might relate to a word written on the back of the postcard rather than the picture itself.

Directions:

- As an introductory activity participants can choose the card that best represents a strength they bring to the group, a goal they have for the day, course, or program, or ask participants to choose a card that best represents how they feel at that moment.

- As a pre-brief in the early parts of a program, spread the cards out before the group and have them pick a card that best represents where they are at that moment. At the very beginning of the day/program, spread the cards out before the group and have them pick a card that best represents where they are at that moment. Ask them how they are feeling and to pick a card that matches where they are mentally coming into the day. Go around the group and ask each participant to share why they picked the card they did and why that card represents them or where they are. If you start the day with this activity, it is good to end the day with this same activity.

- As a debriefing activity, spread the cards out before the group and have them pick a card that best represents an experience or a feeling that they had during the activity or at the end of the day. Ask participants to share their choice of card. Participants can each pick their own card, then draw it or write about in their journal.

- **Group Consensus:** The group is given the task of deciding on one card that best represents what they achieved as a group. This is a great method for groups that are ongoing or have been together for a period of time. The outcome can be very rich.

  - The process of deciding on just one card involves participants sharing about their ideas relating to many different cards and making an argument for their interpretation. The dialogue can be very profound with this method.

  - For very large groups, subgroups can be formed each having their own set of cards or objects. When they come back and share the

Photo courtesy of Jeff Baird, High 5

object they picked it can be interesting to compare and contrast what the other subgroups chose.

- **Three Card Story.** A popular way to use the cards is to tell a story of their experience. The group can come to consensus on three or four cards that represent their journey. A powerful closing Jennifer Stanchfield learned while co-facilitating with Dave Lockett of Steven's Point, Wisconsin involves the group using consensus to pick three objects or cards that tell the story of their progression or "journey" as a group during their training. She asked the group to pick three cards, one that represents "Where we were," one that represents "where we are now," and one to represent "where we are going." This is especially powerful for groups that are going to be working together as a committee, task force, corporation, or other long-standing organizations.

- **Appreciation Activity.** Ask participants to think about the person sitting to their right, and to pick a card that represents something that they have appreciated about that person during the program.

Where to Find It/How to Make It:

Create your own cards by cutting out photos from magazines or greeting cards. Download images to create cards from public domain Internet websites.

Chiji Cards, Expression Cards, and Training Wheel's Metaphor Cards are readily available from a variety of vendors in the experiential education field. Independent bookstores are a great place to find interesting images on postcards.

Mood Dudes™

How Ya Feelin'?

There are several ways you can use Mood Dudes™. They are helpful for counseling sessions or any program in which you would like people to discuss their feelings. There are five faces depicting sad, happy, disgusted, shocked, and anxious emotions.

Creator: Creative Therapy, www.ctherapy.com. The Mood Dudes™ art work is trademarked by Creative Therapy.

Concepts: Having tangible feelings faces for participants to hold onto while talking about their feelings.

Props/Materials Needed: Squeezable Mood Dude™ faces.

Directions:

Here are a few suggestions on ways to use Mood Dudes™.

- Put them in the center of your sharing circle and let your participants pick and choose which feeling they want to talk about or have experienced.

- Use them with individuals and have them talk about an experience with each expression.

- Use them with character development programs.

Having something tangible for your participants to hold onto while talking eases the experience of talking in front of others. They are made of stress reliever material and are 2¾" × 2¾" in size. Those who are really nervous about talking in front of others may be squeezing the heck out of the faces! You can buy the faces individually or in a set of five.

Where to Find It/How to Make It: Creative Therapy, www.ctherapy.com; Training Wheels, set of five only; Adventure Hardware, set of five only.

Other "Mood" products you can use in conjunction with the Mood Dudes™ are: Mood Postcards, Mood Posters, Mood Cube, and Mood Magnets.

On the Level

The Right Tool for the Facilitator

Some simple props can help participants frame a review session. Here, a common hardware tool is used to identify a category related to the group's performance.

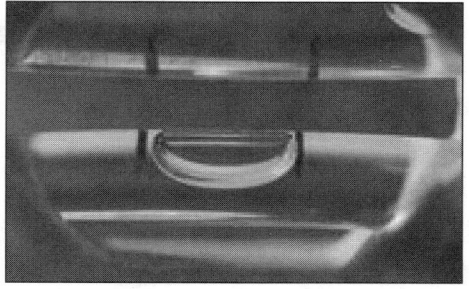

Concepts: A simple diagnostic tool, in this case, a standard builder's level, provides a tactile tool that participants can identify with, and that creates categories for describing the performance of the group.

Props/Materials Needed: A standard builder's level, available in most hardware stores.

Directions:

- At the completion of the activity, the facilitator presents the group with the level, and explains that it is typically used to make sure that structures are level and true.
- In some cases, it is possible for two different builders to read the same level, and yet come up with different ideas about the trueness of a particular structure.
- In the case of the most recent activity, this level can be used to identify the performance of the group. Which of the following categories do you think best describe the performance of the group?
- Dead Center—This bubble reading indicates that the group is perfectly level, right on target, and that there is no room for improvement.
- On the Level—Not quite perfect, but definitely within the lines.
- Half a Bubble Off—This level reading indicates that the group is not quite there, that some adjustment is needed, or that a greater effort is required to reach perfection.
- Off the Mark—This reading indicates that the group feels they were not exactly on target, but that they did "good enough." This category is sometimes described as the "anything not worth doing, is not worth doing well" category. Plenty of room for improvement here, but the group may not want to put any more effort into this particular task.

- At the South End of the Field—This reading indicates that the group feels that their efforts are below the standards set by their company, their customers, and even themselves. Readings at this level should include the opportunity to try the task again.
- Other hardware related questions include: It is possible to be "level" in one plane or direction, and yet be "off" in another? Do you think it is possible to be so focused as a group on one goal that we forget to work with the other important, but lesser goals?

Where to Find It/How to Make It: You can find a variety of levels at most hardware stores.

To listen closely and reply well is the highest perfection
we are able to attain in the art of conversation.

Francois de La Rochefoucauld (1613–1680)

Partner Watch

Feedback from Another Participant

Many organizations encourage mentoring, coaching, 360 degree feedback sessions and other forms of job related and performance feedback. In a similar manner, the Partner Watch technique allows a participant to receive helpful feedback directly from another participant.

Concepts: It is helpful for participants to understand the role of feedback. An example from the facilitator before the activity helps provide guidelines for appropriate feedback. Some organizations may have a focus or theme for the program, and the partner watch can align with this theme (such as watching for leadership skills, application of a recently learned corporate skill, empowerment, creative problem-solving, decision-making, etc.)

Photo courtesy of Jeff Baird, High 5

It is also possible, during the pre-activity partnership formation, for each participant to solicit specific feedback from their partner. For example, "I'd like to work on my problem-solving skills. Please watch me to see if I utilize all the resources available during this challenge."

Props/Materials Needed: None.

Directions:

- Before beginning an activity, the facilitator invites participants to form partnerships of two to three people.
- Next, the facilitator explains the partner watch technique, and encourages careful observation during the activity.
- After the completion of the task or challenge, partners are asked to review the activity together, and share observations and feedback related to their partner's performance.

A Pencil That Never Lies

Every Word Is the Truth

For many professionals, a yearly performance appraisal is a yearly lesson in humility. Sometimes the words just don't seem to match the individual's perception of their contributions and they are left to ponder the relevance of each word. Here is a reviewing technique that encourages us all to look at the words, and to come to terms with their relevance to our present situation.

Concepts: The observations of a member of the group are written down during the activity and shared with the members of the group at the completion of the task. Rather than discuss the validity of each viewpoint, participants are encouraged to consider all comments as unrefutable facts, and to focus their discussion on this assumption and the resulting consequences.

Props/Materials Needed: A clipboard, pencil/pen, and paper.

Directions:

- Prior to the presentation of the next activity, the facilitator requests a volunteer to take the role of observer/recorder. This person is presented with a clipboard, paper and pencil, and asked to make a written record of the performance of the team, including opportunities for improvement.

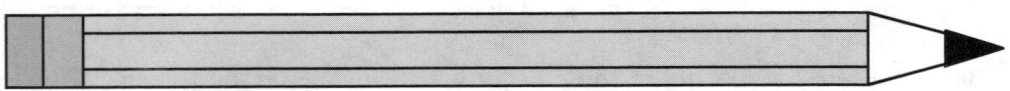

Photo courtesy of Jeff Baird, High 5

- When the recorder is ready to share their observations with the group, the facilitator informs the group that they are to consider every word from the recorder as a truthful fact—and then encourage their discussion about what to do if this was in fact the case.
- As an alternative to a single observer the group can be presented with the clipboard, paper and pencil, and asked that each member write down some observation during the activity that will be discussed during the following reviewing session.

Playing Cards

Chris Cavert shared this simple technique that uses standard playing cards.

Contributor: Chris Cavert, FUNdoing.

Concepts: The benefits of this activity are that it is less threatening for participants to speak to just one person at a time rather than the whole group. Sometimes participants are more open if they are not speaking to their facilitator. Remember good processing can happen even if the facilitator is not present to hear it! This is a useful activity not only to process a specific experience but also to provide closure for a session or program day.

Props/Materials Needed: Playing cards, primarily non-face cards, and those between one (ace) and five, are best. This is a great way of using those incomplete card decks you have with missing cards.

Directions:

- At the completion of the activity, the facilitator passes out a playing card to each participant.
- The suit of each card describes the category of your response, and the number shown on the card identifies the number of ideas you need to share on this subject. For example, a four of spades suggests mentioning four things related to new thoughts that you dug up during the activity.
  - Hearts ♥ generate conversations about something from the heart.
  - Clubs ♣ describe things that grow (new ideas, new thoughts, a new point of view).
  - Spades ♠ are used to dig in the garden, and describe planting some new ideas or things that you dug up during the activity.
  - Diamonds ♦ are gems that last forever. What are some of the gems of wisdom you gathered during this activity?

Where to Find It/How to Make It: You can create some unique cards for your organization. 4-H club advisors can create a pack of "head-heart-hands-health" cards that illustrate various heads (thinking, graduating, wearing various hats, smiling), hearts (friendships, healthy, love, pulse rate), hands (helping, working, holding various tools), and health (foods, fitness, exercise). Try using the colors, themes, values, and mission of your organization to create your own unique card deck.

Plus Delta

What Is Good, What Needs Improvement

Here is a simple and straightforward processing technique that encourages the group to consider what is positive (plus) about their performance and potential improvement opportunities (delta).

Concepts: Rather than identifying team behavior in conventional good-bad categories, the plus delta model provides a positive spin to both sides of the evaluation. Positive attributes are obviously positive in nature, and delta attributes become positive opportunities for change.

Props/Materials Needed: A flipchart and markers can be helpful.

Directions:

- At the completion of the activity, the facilitator presents the plus-delta model to the group.
- Sketching a vertical line down the middle of a flip chart, with a plus sign (+) on the left and a delta sign (Δ) on the right is typically helpful.
- Group members are now invited to identify positive attributes about their performance, and likewise to identify attributes that they would like to alter or change in the future.

Photo courtesy of
Jeff Baird, High 5

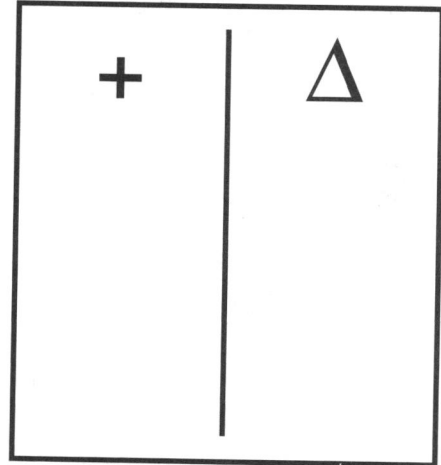

Pocket Medic Debrief

Is There a Doctor in the House?

This activity was created while on a day hike at a wilderness camp for emotionally disturbed teenagers. Since you never go anywhere without your first aid kit while working with youth audiences, it was the perfect choice (and quite frankly the only prop available) to use for a debriefing tool when the group spontaneously needed to huddle up. After an amazing debrief with these "wounded" kids, the pocket medic debrief was formed! Highly recommended for therapeutic groups.

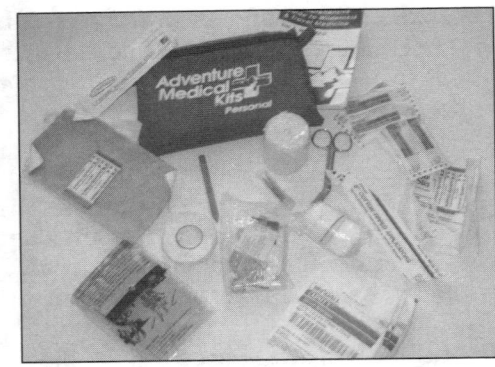

Concepts: Using first aid kit supplies as metaphors for debriefing.

Props/Materials Needed: A first aid kit with a wide variety of supplies.

Directions: You probably already have this equipment and never realized it could be an excellent processing tool.

- Pull out your first aid kit and lay out all of the supplies inside.
- Explain what each piece is and what it is used for.
- Ask each participant to be thinking of which items represent experiences or similarities to themselves as you explain each item.
- Invite participants to share how they identify with the different items in the kit.

Here are a few examples:

- Splinter grabber: Able to pull things out of difficult situations.
- Safety pin: Multi-purpose tool, able to perform many functions in different situations.
- Sting relief pad: Is able to take the "sting" out of situations.
- Antiseptic towlette: Able to clean small wounds and wash things clean.
- Double antibiotic ointment: Used to cover small wounds. Prevents infection in minor situations.
- Sterile gauze pad: Used to cover wounds for them to heal.
- Fabric bandage: Used to cover small wounds after cleaning.
- Knuckle bandage: Used to cover small wounds in specific areas.
- Telfa dressing: Does not stick to wounds.
- Sterile wound closure strip: Used to hold things together.
- Moleskin: Used to cover "hot spots" before a blistering situation occurs.
- Molefoam: Has thicker skin.
- Acetaminophen: Used to reduce pain.
- Ibuprofen: Used to reduce inflammation.

Pocket Processor

You can expect more "a-ha" moments from this activity than most others! This is particularly true in the Human Continuum activity described below. It is suitable for adult and youth groups.

Creator: The Institute for Experiential Education, Buzz Bocher, Steve Simpson, and Dan Miller.

Concepts: The Pocket Processor is a processing tool based on the theory of the yin and the yang. This theory describes two ends of a continuum with each end having the seed of the other. A healthy being does not stay at one point on the continuum, but flows continuously between the two extremes. The Pocket Processor helps participants examine the flow along the continuum.

Props/Materials Needed: One deck of Pocket Processor cards.

Directions: There are several ways to use the Pocket Processor.

- **Basic Use.** The most basic use of the Pocket Processor is to debrief an activity by spreading all the cards out and asking each participant to choose the card that best represents some kind of progress made (either individual or group progress). Then allow each person to explain his or her choice (e.g., "I chose the competing/cooperating card because I am naturally very competitive, but I successfully fought off my desire to complete the initiative faster than the other group.")

- **Variation 1.** Rather than allowing each person to pick a card, the facilitator may ask the group to come to consensus on the one card (or two or three cards) that best exemplifies progress made by the group. The narrowing down of the cards then may become the topic of discussion and the participants will start processing all of the issues to narrow it down to the top one.

- **Variation 2.** Fifty-four cards can be overwhelming. Facilitators may choose to narrow the options to a smaller number of cards (seven to twenty) before spreading them out.

- **Frontloading.** The Pocket Processor is an excellent frontloading tool. If a group has multiple goals or a poor idea of what their goals are, spread out the cards prior to the day's activities. Then have the group pick out one or two themes that they want to work on that day. After the day's activities are complete, pull out the cards chosen and ask them to assess their progress on the goals that they set for themselves at the beginning of the day. Goals can be individual or for the group. Rather than setting group goals, a facilitator may frontload by allowing each member of the group to choose his or her own card.

- **Human Continuum.** It is important to remind participants that the two phrases on each card are extremes of a continuum, not dichotomies. One way to convey this information is through a human continuum. Directions:
  - Have two sides of a room (or an open space) be two extremes of a continuum. You can place a piece of webbing or rope to mark the center.
  - Then read the two sides of the card and allow every participant to physically place himself or herself anywhere on that continuum. For example, a facilitator can say, "this side of the room is always taking charge. The other side of the room is always allowing others to lead. I want each of you to find the place on the continuum where you most fit today."
  - The human continuum then lends itself to discussion (e.g., "If most of you usually take charge, what impact does that have on completing the task? Are the same people in your group always taking charge, the same people always allowing others to lead? If so, what are the pros and cons of this arrangement?")

Where to Find It/How to Make It: To make this activity you could use index cards and write down categories on each card and use it the same way as described above. To buy a deck: Institute for Experiential Education, www.chiji.com, Training Wheels, High 5 Adventures, Adventure Hardware, Grip-It Adventures, Project Adventure, or your local challenge course provider.

Poetry Dog Tags

This clever set of dog tags was actually designed for dogs! They were designed for your favorite pooch to wear a phrase or word around their neck. Leave it to creative facilitator, Jennifer Steinmetz, to find other uses for them!

Contributor: Jennifer Steinmetz, Rocky Top Therapy Center.

Concepts: Have the participants choose words or goals from the dog tags laid out before them.

Props/Materials Needed: A tin of Poetry Dog Tags.

Directions:

- The basic concept is that the group would look over the different words printed on the dog tags and put together a goal, match a feeling, use as a metaphoric model or discussion piece, or whatever else you come up with! There are 250 tags in the box along with two chains to hang your thoughts on. The set was actually designed for dogs to wear a phrase or word around their neck, so some of the words/tags are pet oriented.

- Some of the words in the set are: attitude, away, beautiful, beyond, breath, consume, delicious, diva, existence, fast, fall, forever, friend, ghetto, heaven, hip, imagine, intoxicate, karma, love, meditate, never, omen, outside, photograph, perfect, rain, sacred, serious, together, and so on.

- The tags are one inch by half an inch, so they are much smaller than army dog tags.

- Invite the group to come up with a goal for the day and put it on a chain to wear from initiative to initiative.

- Re-evaluate after each activity how they did on their goal or what they could do to improve their performance as a team.

Where to Find It/How to Make It: Chronicle Books, www.chroniclebooks.com; Training Wheels.

Processing Cube

An interesting way to create new and innovative processing tools is to visit any toy store or page through a toy catalog. That's how this activity was created! See what other creative toys are out there and then tweak them to make them work for your processing sessions!

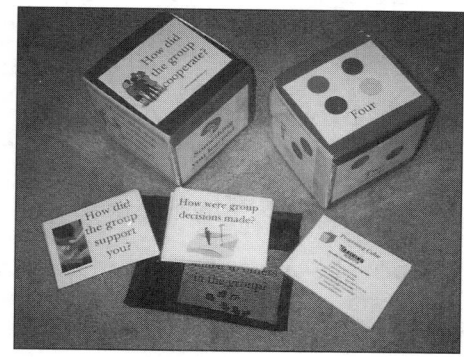

Creator: Michelle Cummings

Props/Materials Needed: A Processing Cube. This colorful cube is 6 inches on each side and has clear plastic windows. Choose a selection of processing questions that will best suit your group. This is a great debriefing activity for all types of learners: kinesthetic, visual, and auditory.

Directions: There are a couple of different ways to present this activity.

- Ask the group to form a circle and toss or roll the dice to one another. Whichever question lands face up is the question that the person answers.

- Toss the cube around the circle, like in the activity "Group Juggle". At random the facilitator calls out, "Stop," and whoever has the cube at that time answers the question that is face up.

- Another way to add some fun to this activity is to include drumming or have some music playing while the cube is being passed around the circle. When the drumming or music stops, the participant holding the cube answers the question that is on top. You include auditory learners at a higher level when you add music.

Customizing Your Cube: You can custom design cards to fit the needs of each group. The cube can be changed every time you use it. To customize cards for each group hand out blank index cards and colored pens or markers. Let the group members create their own questions. This involves the participant in the planning process and they will have more investment in answering the questions they come up with on their own.

Youth Groups: Pass out blank index cards and crayons/magic markers and let the kids draw pictures and their own questions. Kids often prefer their own questions to yours!

Corporate Groups: For corporate programs, create questions that include the group's corporate logo, mission statement, or core values. Most corporate groups really enjoy the customizing of their programs.

Staff Trainings: A fun way to spice up your staff trainings is to create Processing Cube questions that ask about specific topics from this training. For example, after a ropes course training, include questions like "Demonstrate how to tie a bowline on a bight knot." or "Where are the three fire extinguishers located?" or "What would you do if a participant got stung by a bee?". Then toss the cube around the circle. Whatever question lands face up when you catch it would be the question that you would answer.

Where to Find It/How to Make It: A beach ball works well for a do-it-yourself processing cube. Write different questions on each panel of the beach ball. You can find the processing cube at: Training Wheels, Adventure Hardware, Sportime, Grip-It Adventures, or check with your local ropes course provider.

Puzzles

A puzzle is defined by it's parts. Even the smallest piece has significant importance. Puzzles allow participants to identify their role in the group.

Concept: Puzzles can be incorporated into reflective learning in a variety of ways. Puzzles create a unique atmosphere in which each participant can contribute an equal piece. Puzzle pieces can work as a metaphor for the role participants take in activities. They can act as a space to create artistic representations of a participant's strengths or contributions to the group. They can create a "picture" of the group and its experiences and goals piece by piece.

Props/Materials Needed: A blank jigsaw puzzle.

Directions: There are many ways to use puzzles. The only limit is your imagination. Here are a few of our suggestions:

- Each person decorates a puzzle piece. You can have them color on their puzzle piece to represent the learning that they wish to take away from the program.

- **For counseling sessions:** have the client or family color a different piece to record their progress and milestones. You then have a colorful memory puzzle of everything they have accomplished and learned.

- **For schools:** These are great for field trips! It can utilize bus time on their way back to school. After your trip to the museum give each student a puzzle piece and some crayons as they get back on the bus. Have them color what they learned on their puzzle piece. When you get back to school the students can put the puzzle together.

- **To close an adult program** you can have a group identify goals by having participants decorate puzzle pieces to represent the learning that they are going to take away from the program.

- **What is your piece of the puzzle?** In newly formed committees and other action groups members need to assign roles early on—through creating artwork, or strength and goal words—group members can explore, express, and define their roles in a

group and the strengths they bring to the group. Allow participants to take their puzzle piece home with them.

- **In a conflict situation,** the puzzle pieces can be used effectively as a communication tool. Expression can be enhanced when a person uses a puzzle piece to represent their feelings and actions. It is also helpful for participants to name their part in a conflict and the piece they might take on to change it.

- **As a memento of group experience:** Iron on puzzles can create a unique puzzle for your group as well. Using your computer you can create whatever you want to iron onto the puzzle. Some examples would be group goals, a mission statement or a group photo. Then using a color printer, print your finished piece onto the iron on transfer paper. You then iron that piece of paper directly onto the puzzle and as a closing activity, have the group put the puzzle together to reveal the finished piece.

- **As name tags for a small conference or business meeting:** Write each person's name on a puzzle piece and glue a pin to the back. They then have to find the person(s) they connect with.

Where to Find It/How to Make It: There are several types of blank puzzles available. One type is called the Community Puzzle. You can purchase these puzzles from: www.communitypuzzle.com, Training Wheels, Project Adventure, Adventure Hardware, and Grip-It Adventures. The Community Puzzle consists of large universal blank puzzle pieces that fit together in any order. Since the Community Puzzles are universal, they will connect with any other Community Puzzle; if you had a group of 300 you could get enough puzzles so that each participant could decorate their own piece and then add it to the large puzzle.

The Community Puzzle comes in two sizes. The large puzzle consists of 48 pieces, 24 large center pieces and 24 border and corner pieces. The center pieces are roughly 4" x 4". The Community Puzzle Jr. is a 16 piece puzzle. It has four center pieces and twelve border and corner pieces. It is based on the same concepts as the large Community Puzzle, and can be used for individuals and smaller groups.

You can sometimes find small blank puzzles at teacher supply stores as well. These puzzles are generally not universal puzzles. They are usually smaller puzzles that have about 12 pieces. You can find these at office supply stores or on the internet.

There are some companies that carry large dry erase board puzzles. This would be a tool you could use over and over. You can make your own dry erase board puzzle using a jig saw. Take a large dry erase board and draw onto it the puzzle pattern you want it to have. Then use your jig saw, follow your pattern, and cut the board into puzzle pieces.

Prior to the creation of pre-made blank puzzles for group work, a common resource for large blank puzzles was the toy store. The large child character puzzles designed for ages three to five found at toy stores and spray painted white can be a great option. This puzzle will be more challenging to put together since there will be no guide to help them (the pieces are not universal and the picture is covered.)

The real art of conversation is not only to say the right thing at the right place but to leave unsaid the wrong thing at the tempting moment.

Dorothy Nevill

Raccoon Circles

The "World Wide Webbing"

"Invented is a strange word. I tied a knot in a piece of webbing"

Tom Smith, on the creation of the first Raccoon Circle.

Raccoon Circles are 15 foot (4.6 meter) long segments of tubular climbing webbing that can be used to create community and bring participants closer together for a variety of active learning activities. These circles can also be used to create smaller processing groups when working with large audiences.

Concepts: The close proximity of other participants creates an atmosphere of connection and respect when using Raccoon Circles. With a 15 foot long segment of webbing, eight adults or ten children can easily find a space. For larger groups, you can tie several Raccoon Circles together. You will need about 15 inches (38 cm) of webbing length for each person, and the water knot will take up about one foot of webbing, too.

Props/Materials Needed: A few Raccoon Circles in different colors.

Directions: Here are several processing and discussion activities that can be performed with a raccoon circle.

Elevation

- At some point during an adventure-based learning program, the facilitator may wish to ask the group a question so that they can decide where to take the group next. Using a single Raccoon Circle and with everyone "connected," ask the group their views on the topic you wish to know more about. For example, "please lift your portion of the Raccoon Circle to the level of understanding you have related to the current challenge. Shoulder high: I have enough information to begin. Stomach high: I'd like to discuss this more. Knee high: could you explain again from the beginning?"

- This approach will give the facilitator a visual response to key questions they have, and allow participants to respond without needing to speak.

It's Knot Our Problem, Is It?

- The knots found in a piece of webbing can be helpful (the water knot helps to hold the Raccoon Circle together), or harmful (this Raccoon Circle is all twisted up and knotted!) Pre-knot a variety of short segments of webbing, and let the participants choose one that reflects the kinds of knots (problems or difficulties) they are presently dealing with in their lives, or some of the challenges, worries or fears that they are experiencing today.

- Discuss what needs to happen to remove the harmful knots (addiction, social problems, lack of resources, dysfunction), and keep the helpful ones (connection to family, friends, resources).

- Discuss what techniques are available to assist in removing the harmful knots (identify resources) and what needs to keep happening to reinforce and fully appreciate the helpful knots.

- For the pre-knotted webbing collection, use a variety of webbing, narrow, wide, long, short, different colors, different styles of knots, some easy, some hard. (Jim used a 10,000 pound hydraulic press to knot a few of them. We do not think those knots will be coming out any time in this century!)

Just to show you how such activities can work, consider this real-life story:

" . . . We had been working with a group of 13 and 14-year-old girls. They were all struggling with issues (you know, the kind of stuff that breaks your heart). We had just completed a check-in with them. Clearly it had been a rough day for most of them and they had so much on their minds. We decided to use the activity A Knot Between Us. We used the analogy of the Raccoon Circle as the road of life, where the knots signified the bumps in the road or the problems they were facing. We invited each girl to name their knot (problem) and then to work collectively to untie them. This was such an incredible experience!

When we processed after the initiative the girls candidly discussed their behaviors. They learned so much about themselves and working together. One girl really needed help, but found it hard to ask; one was thrilled that the girls helped her even when she didn't ask. Another girl noticed that she kind of sat back and let the other girls untie her knot (solve her problems), one girl noticed that sometimes well meaning friends try to help you out and actually make things worse. This was truly the right initiative at the right time with the right group!"

Jennifer Steinmetz
Rocky Top Therapy Center

Reflection with Music

- During processing and debriefing activities, try playing some of the following music to reinforce the circles theme of the Raccoon Circle. There is a wide range of music styles here. So, please listen before you decide to play any of these for your audience. Make sure that the song you choose carries the lyrics, issues and values that you want to share.

- The facilitator can play music in the background as the group discusses the last activity, or the music can be the focus, and a discussion can begin after the song, based on the lyrics, theme or style of music.

Song Title	Artist	Album Title
"Circle of Life"	Lebo M.	*Lion King Soundtrack*
"(All my Life's a . . .) Circle"	Harry Chapin	*Greatest Stories Live*
"Circle of Friends"	Paul Winter Consort	*Double Album*
"Circle Dream"	10000 Maniacs	*Our Time In Eden*
"Circle"	Barbara Streisand	*Higher Ground*
"Full Circle"	Collective Soul	*Disciplined Breakdown*
"Perfect Circle"	R.E.M.	*Murmur*
"Circle"	Sarah McLachlan	*Fumbling Toward Ecstasy*

Lots of Knots

Here is a simple technique for encouraging group members to say more during a processing session.

- For each comment made by a member of the group, one knot can be untied from the rope.

- At some point before the first processing session of the program, the facilitator offers the group a segment of rope or a Raccoon Circle.

- The group is then asked to tie as many knots into this segment of rope as possible. If there is room for one more knot, then please add one more knot. Encourage each member of the group to include at least one knot of their own.

- At the beginning of a processing session, the facilitator produces the knotted rope and explains to the group that for each comment made by a member of the group, one knot can be removed. Each group member is encouraged to remove the knot they created by offering their own comments during the session.

- One unique feature of this style of reviewing is that while the participant is manipulating the knots, they are able to express themselves, effectively working both sides of the brain at the same time.

Believe It or Knot

Thanks to Mike Anderson for this excellent get-acquainted activity that encourages everyone to talk within the group.

- With the entire group holding a Raccoon Circle, the knot is used as a pointer to identify the person talking.

- Begin by passing the knot to the right around the group. Someone says "right there!" the knot stops, and the person nearest it has the opportunity to disclose some interesting fact about themselves, such as, "I have been to Spain twice in the past four years!" It is now the responsibility of the rest of the participants to decide whether they believe that this information is true or false.

- After several questions from the group and some discussion, the group gives their opinion of the validity or falseness of the disclosure, and the person providing the comment can tell the real story. This single comment version of Two Truths and a Lie proceeds a bit more quickly for each person than the full blown version. Use either, as time permits.

- After a person has revealed the true nature of their comments (true or false), they say "left" or "right" and then "right there!", and a new person has the opportunity to disclose something to the group.

- The level of disclosure to the group is often a measure of the closeness, unity, and respect within the group. For example, a disclosure such as, "I have two dogs as pets," is a lower level of disclosure than "I repeated the seventh grade in school." Depending on the group setting and the purpose of this activity for your group, different levels of information or disclosure are appropriate. As the group becomes more unified, this activity can bring out greater disclosure between members of the group, family members and members of a team.

The Talking Knot

- This closing activity is a variation of the opening activity Believe It Or Knot, where the knot tied in the Raccoon Circle acts as a pointer and the facilitator or other participant instructs the group to move the knot to the right (clockwise) or to the left (counterclockwise), then stop, and the person nearest the knot or pointer has the opportunity to speak.

- Suggest the type of comments a person could make by giving the group a verbal example or two. For example, you might suggest that participants think of a quotation that applies to their experience, or a movie title that describes this experience, or a theme song. You might also encourage the speaker to say their good-byes to the group during this time.

- This technique chooses the person, rather than allowing a participant to make their own choice of when to speak.

- As a variation, use the Raccoon Circle as a talking stick by allowing participants to move the knot around the circle, and when a person is ready to speak, stopping the knot when it is in front of them.

- Another variation, called One (Thought) for the Road, uses the format of the activity Believe It or Knot. In this version, someone suggests moving the knot to the right (or left), then saying "stop," and the person nearest the knot has the opportunity to express a brief closing thought, or simply say "thank you" or "pass."

The Meter

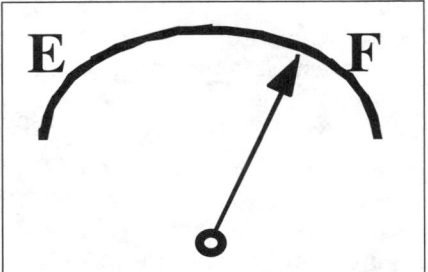

- With one Raccoon Circle, make an arch shape like the one shown here. This is your fuel gauge, or any type of meter that you wish.

- Ask participants to stand outside the meter, at the position that best relates to them. For example, the amount of energy that you have right now could be just like a gas tank gauge (empty, half a tank, full).

- This activity acquaints participants with each other, indicates preferences, and lets us find out about each other.

- This activity also can be used by a facilitator to gain some useful knowledge about the participants in the group. For example, the number of hours spent working out each week, or the number of books read in the past six months, or the number of frequent flyer miles accumulated in the past year, or the number of brothers and sisters in your family.

- Thanks to Tom Heck and Roger Greenaway for sharing examples of this simple but powerful activity.

A Circle of Four (In the Loop)

Thanks to Rick French for sharing this interesting get acquainted, debriefing, and/or closure activity.

- Spread a few Raccoon Circles around on the ground. Use enough for the entire group, with about four people in each circle.

- As a goal setting activity, ask the participants to share with the others in their circle the goals they have for themselves and for the group that day.

- After a few minutes, ask each circle to tell the whole group some of these goals.

- A facilitator should be available to write these goals down on a large piece of paper.

- Ask the participants to all go to a new circle with four new people in it.

- Continue goal setting, or ask another goal oriented question, and record the responses.

- For debriefing, this Circle of Four activity, which can easily be done with a different number of participants, allows simultaneous discussions so that the whole group can have a chance to express their feelings. This may allow a debriefing process that takes a bit less time when a large group is involved, while not diminishing the need to share and discuss.

- After each topic of discussion, participants can be encouraged to join another new circle, with four new people.

- As a closing activity, let the group reflect back on the original goals mentioned above, and evaluate whether those goals were met during the event. This format is also a nice way to say good-bye to a variety of folks, in small groups, using some discussion and a close proximity of participants to each other.

Sign In Please

- Dr. Tom Smith once mentioned that he often encouraged members of the group to write words of encouragement or significant phrases directly on the Raccoon Circle using a permanent marker or waterproof pen. He also encouraged them to sign their name. At the completion of their time together, he would cut the group's Raccoon Circle into small pieces, so that everyone in the group could take away some portion of the whole "spirit" of the group. Names and words will be most visible when you choose a dark color marker, and a lighter color Raccoon Circle webbing (yellow, light gray, orange, etc.)

W.A.M.F.

- W.A.M.F. stands for Wrapped Around My Finger, and pretty much explains this entire activity.

- Begin with an unknotted segment of webbing. One person in the group begins wrapping the webbing around their index finger, and while doing so, provides the group with some information about themselves (where they were born, family members, school experiences, childhood pets, dreams, goals, favorite foods, etc.). The goal is for this person to continue talking until the webbing is completely wrapped around their finger. When they reach the end, they can allow the webbing to unwind, and pass it along to the next person in the group.

- This particular technique allows a bit more time for folks to talk about themselves, and also provides a kinesthetic activity coupled with a verbal activity for exploring some of the multiple intelligence opportunities, and whole brain learning possibilities.

- There is also a popular theory that for folks that may be a bit shy about speaking to even a small group in public, the activity of wrapping the webbing around their finger occupies that portion of the brain which creates inhibition. By wrapping and rapping at the same time, the speech center becomes less inhibited, and more information is typically shared!

- This is also a useful method for encouraging participants to talk at length about their experiences, rather than one or two word answers.

Connectedness

When Tom Smith first used the word "connectedness" some folks wondered if this was a real word. Lately, this word has been showing up in some pretty interesting places. Most recently, in the published results of the National Longitudinal Study on Adolescent Health. In the Journal of the American Medical Association (*JAMA*), Resnick, et. al. reports that parent-family connectedness and perceived school connectedness were factors that protected youths against nearly every health risk behavior measured in the study (see the first article mentioned below for details). Clearly, connection between people, between people and the organizations they belong to, to the environment and to the global community is a valuable thing. The Alameda Study conducted in California in the late 1990's also illustrates that in addition to many significant social factors (such as poverty, access to healthcare, community, substance abuse and other social pressures) the presence of connectedness within a community has an overwhelming effect on the overall health of the community. Edward Hallowell mentions some of these findings in his book simply titled *Connect*. You are encouraged to read some of these findings the next time you are trying to justify the need for community building activities in your classroom, adventure program, learning community, or corporation. The facts are in, "connectedness" is one of the most outstanding methods for improving the health of your community—and with Raccoon Circles, you have hundreds of methods for creating connectedness. Good Luck!

Protecting Adolescents from Harm: Findings from the National Longitudinal Study on Adolescent Health, Resnick, Bearman, Blum, Bauman, et.al., *JAMA*, September 10, 1997, Volume 278, Issue 10, pages 823–832.

The National Longitudinal Study on Adolescent Health: Preliminary Results: Great Expectations, Klein, *JAMA*, September 10, 1997, Volume 278, Issue 10, pages 864–865.

Connect: 12 Vital Ties That Open Your Heart, Lengthen Your Life, and Deepen Your Soul, 1999, Edward M. Hallowell, Pantheon Book, New York, NY ISBN 0–375–40357–4

Try using the word "connectedness" for a Google search on the internet. You will find dozens of articles, websites, and links that are worth researching.

The Value of Connection

Since co-authoring *The Book on Raccoon Circles* with Tom Smith, Jim Cain has seen the value of connection through new eyes. With co-author Kirk Weisler, Jim Cain is writing a new book focused on creating an environment of connection in the workplace. This book includes stories of organizations that are working hard to create such environments and activities for the "do it yourself" crowd. This book is filled with dozens of activities, stories, resources, and ideas for creating a connected work environment for little cost, but with significant impact.

The Value of Connection—In the Workplace, 2006, Jim Cain and Kirk Weisler, Visit the Teamwork and Teamplay website for more information on this book.

Where to Find It/How to Make It: You can find tubular climbing webbing at your regional outdoor store, especially one that sells climbing equipment. You can also purchase Raccoon Circles from Adventure Hardware, Training Wheels, Grip-It Adventures, Sportime, and other challenge course providers.

Additional Resources: *The Book on Raccoon Circles,* by Tom Smith and Jim Cain, contains more than 100 adventure-based learning activities that can be presented with only a simple piece of tubular climbing webbing. This 272-page book is available from Learning Unlimited at 1-888-622-4203 or www.learningunlimited.com. You can also download a PDF collection of raccoon circle activities from the Teamwork & Teamplay website at: www.teamworkandteamplay.com/raccooncircles.html.

The Group Loop Activity Guide—22 Fun Group Activities That Enhance Community, Teamwork, Leadership and Creative Problem-Solving, by Tom Heck. Phone (828) 665–0303 www.tomheck.com

Lines and Loops—Community Building Activities with Webbing, by Chris Cavert. Twenty-two pages of activities, illustrations and references. Phone (928) 526-6386 chris@fundoing.com   www.fundoing.com.

Random Ricochet

Chris Cavert developed a game called Ricochet using an oddly shaped, knobby ball that bounces unpredictability. Here is an interesting way to use these balls as defriefing tools.

Concepts: A creative way to randomly select the next person to answer a debriefing question.

Props/Materials Needed: One ricochet ball and a hard surface.

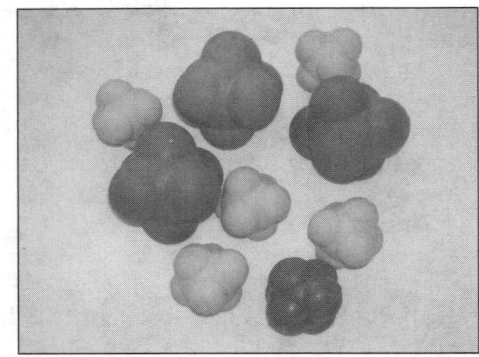

Directions:

- Have the group stand in a circle and toss the ball up in the air, into the center of the circle.
- Whoever the ball bounces to is the next person to talk or answer the debriefing question.
- This is a great tool for taking the heat off of the facilitator as the one who is always choosing different people to answer each question.
- Invite group members to have their hands ready to catch the ball.

Where to Find It/How to Make It: Some pet stores will have these in their toy or ball section. They are also called Reaction Balls. To buy: Sportime, Training Wheels, www.justballs.com, Fundoing, Adventure Hardware, Grip It Adventures, Challenge Options. For additional activities using this ball, read: *Ricochet and Other Fun Games with a Ball,* 2001, Chris Cavert, Learning Unlimited, Tulsa, OK USA, ISBN: 1-885473-88-5

Rap Songs

This past summer a group of middle school students from an inner city area in Massachusetts came to High 5 Adventure Learning Center for a two day challenge course experience. On the second day one of the students arrived saying they had a song to share with the group and facilitators. He and three other students performed a foot stomping rhythm with their melodious interpretation of their experience at High 5 and their goals for the upcoming day. Here is a copy of their rap.

Yo Check It

We're going again on the Ropes Course in Vermont.
Everybody waitin' till We drive by.
Everybody know that we near.
Throw your hands up and throw a High 5.
We worked the ropes course like
Bill Nye the Science Guy
If you ain't feeling the ropes course thing
You should manage it.
To all of us this place is a challenging
So buckle up it is a long drop no sound.
All I could say is good luck and don't look down.

This is High 5 keepin' me with a frown
I thought I was lost but now I've been found
This song was written with so much essential
I also wrote this to ya because I'm feelin' sentimental
When I first walked on that log
I didn't know what was going to happen
I thought I was going to fall
But I had my spotters there to look out for me.
With no doubt and panickin'.

Listen Dave now that we're in this place
I'm the spotter here to make it safe

Don't let that log shake,
A shake ya
If you hit the floor that'd be a ground shaker
I'll be here to be your fall staker

They led us to this "Whale Scale"
That's for sure
I thought we had it down packed until we keep on tapping the floor
We were at the point where we wanted to give up
Every time we touched the floor
We had to stand back up

When I first heard of High 5- to go I was wishin'
But when I got there they changed my jokin' vision
Now in life I've got a new way of thinking
And a new way of living
And here's something new that I'm spittin'
I can't wait till we hit the High elements and then we'll be chillin'
Today the high stuff is what we'll be hittin'

I'm on this V line with my partner
Holding my hands up like I'm building a shelter
Trying not to fall
Trying not to drop
But if I go, I got the spotters in their spots

Directions:

- Allowing your groups to express themselves musically taps into another learning style.

- Have participants divide up into groups of two to three.

- Instruct each group that they are to come up with a rap song that reflects their experiences during the program.

- Allow each group as much time as they need to create their rap. For residential groups, allowing evening "down time" to create longer songs usually lets participants put more energy into the task. For those groups that are together for only a single event, allow 15–20 minutes to come up with a shorter song. For groups such as schools, set aside some time in class for them to work on their songs.

- Each group performs their rap song for the rest of the group.

Reflective Readings

Using Stories to Make the Point

Some of the best children's stories make valuable reading, even for adults. Here is an example of how a story can be used to reinforce the lessons learned in an experiential learning activity.

Concepts: Stories are just one more way to reinforce learning. From the standpoint of Edgar Dale's Cone of Learning, the greater the involvement of the participant, the greater the retention of information. Stories, especially those told in the oral tradition (without pictures, sound or other special effects), allow the listeners to form their own images to match the words. These images can be unique for every person in the group—just as the learning from each experience is unique.

When a story is carefully chosen to reflect the needs of the group or to reinforce the learning of an experiential activity, both the activity and the story are enhanced.

Photo courtesy of Jeff Baird, High 5

Props/Materials Needed: Visit your local library for inspirational readings for children and adults. The Outward Bound International publishes an extensive book of readings. Corporate programs might enjoy books such as *Who Moved My Cheese, FISH,* and other current best selling story books. But the all-time favorite on our list is the classic, *All I Really Need to Know I Learned In Kindergarten* by Robert Fulghum. The activity mentioned here uses Fulghum's "Mermaid" story from this book.

Directions:

- Select an adventure-based learning activity and identify the significant lessons presented. For example, topics such as perseverance (Shackleton's epic Antarctic journey), inclusion (the mermaid story from Robert Fulghum), change *(Who Moved My Cheese),* tolerance *(Little World,* by Joanna Carolan), fun in the workplace *(FISH),* and additional topics such as leadership, creative problem solving, overcoming adversity, celebrating diversity, unity, community and connection—all provide links between adventure-based learning activities and a significant number of books, readings and stories on the same subject. These are your opportunities.

- As an example, the following activity on inclusion is valuable when working with populations that have a diversity of talents and personnel. But this simple activity is made even more powerful and memorable when a reflective reading is used to reinforce the simple concept of inclusion.

Shaping the Future

Exploring Inclusion and Connection

- This activity begins with a facilitator holding a bag filled with a collection of wooden shapes.
- Within the bag, each shape comes in a variety of colors.
- Participants are invited to each take a piece, but not to look at it, nor can they show this piece to anyone else. They are allowed to hold this piece, feel the shape, talk about it, describe it and otherwise try to share information about their piece, but they *cannot look at it.*
- The facilitator provides the following minimal instruction to the group, "find your people." Simply stated, everyone is looking to find the other group members that are holding a piece of wood similar to theirs.
- After a few minutes, the facilitator calls out "one more minute" and encourages everyone to find their people. At the end of this minute, everyone freezes in place, and the facilitator allows them to look at their piece.
- Some groups form easily, as their shapes are easy to describe. Others are a bit more difficult to sort out. Some groups have other shapes mixed in (that is OK). And then there is the case of our one and only "star" in the group. Here is a person with star qualities, but unfortunately, there is only one star in the bag.
- The facilitator now begins the reviewing component of this activity, and asks, "Where are my square shapes? Where are my Triangles?"

- Next the facilitator can ask the "star" participant to talk about their experience of trying to fit into other groups, and to find their place in the group.

- Finally, the facilitator can ask all the red team members to hold up their piece of wood. "Aren't these some of 'your people'?" Group members reply "yes, but we couldn't see their color." Which creates another teachable moment—aren't there people right now in your organization, that are part of "your people," but you just don't know that yet. What can you do to find them? A discussion related to inclusion, invitation, and connection is suitable here, followed by the facilitator's command, "Now you have one more minute . . . find your people . . . and make sure no one is left behind!"

- At this point the activity has reached a natural conclusion, so now it is time for the icing on the cake—the story that makes this activity even more valuable. At this point, the facilitator reads the three minute long story, "The Mermaid" from Robert Fulghum's book, *All I Really Need to Know I Learned in Kindergarten.* "Giants, Wizards and Elves was the game to play. . . ."

We encourage you to try this style of reflective reading. Your groups are sure to remember these lessons long after the sunburn has faded.

Where to Find It/How to Make It: The colorful wooden shapes described above are available from Adventure Hardware at 1-800-706-0064 or www.adventurehardware.com.

The 15th Anniversary Edition of *All I Really Need to Know I Learned in Kindergarten* by Robert Fulghum has some additional new stories. Visit your local bookseller, Amazon.com, or www.robertfulghum.com.

Little World: A Book About Tolerance, 2002, Joanna F. Carolan, Banana Patch Press. 1-800-914-5944 Hanapepe, HI, www.bananapatchpress.com.

The Outward Bound Book of Readings with stories from around the world is published by Outward Bound International, 1192 East Draper Parkway, Suite 322, Salt Lake City, Utah 84020 USA Email: obinternational@outward-bound.org.

Rhythm Processing Experiences

Kenya Masala and The Rhythm Of Life! team has talented, energetic drummers and dancers who bring passion and energy to every presentation. Kenya is committed to creating highly effective learning and community building experiences through drumming. He builds an atmosphere of enthusiasm, inviting full participation, authentically motivating individuals and groups of all ages and backgrounds, nationally and abroad. If you have not experienced Kenya, you need to!

Photo courtesy of Kenya Masala

Creator: Kenya Masala, www.rhythmoflifedrumming.com.

Concepts: For groups that are already pretty expressive and communicative, provide them with another creative way to express their learning, understanding, or emotional state. Though it has been tried with more mellow groups with some success, it is best with really energized "risk taking" groups, or in groups where there is already a good deal of safety and rapport.

Photo courtesy of Kenya Masala

Props/Materials Needed: A number of hand percussion "toys" (bells, rattles, shakers, tambourines, small drums, etc.).

Directions:

- Place a number of hand percussion "toys" in the middle of the circle.
- Move around the circle one person at a time, asking each person to choose an instrument when it is their turn.
- Instead of the person sharing verbally, ask them to create a short piece of music or rhythm that expresses their experience about the day, or the last activity, etc.
- Once they have completed, they can have the option of sharing more in a verbal manner, or simply letting the music speak for itself.

This leads to some great laughter, and sometimes a deeper understanding of communication than can be had using words. You can often hear folks chatting about what they shared long after the circle is complete.

Right Tool for the Job

Hand Me a Wrench. No, the Other One . . .

Young children are amazing when it comes to tools. They have no filters or pre-conceived ideas about what things are for, so a wrench can be used as a hammer, and a screwdriver makes a perfect chisel in their world. Sometimes they are able to solve their own problems using tools that we think are inappropriate, but in fact, work just fine!

Concepts: This activity fits into the category of "forced choices" in reviewing. Although the tool selected may not be the ideal tool for the job, figuring out how to use it to solve the challenge requires creativity, problem solving skills and tenacity.

Props/Materials Needed: A small toolbox filled with unusual tools (such as hose clamps, unusual wrenches, garage sale nicknacks, antique kitchen utensils, etc.) and other interesting objects.

Directions:

- When participants reach a difficult portion of a challenge activity, a facilitator can ask, "would you like a tool to assist you with this stage of the process?" and then produce an object from the toolbox. This tool becomes the ideal problem solver. The only task is to understand how such a tool can assist the group in completing the task.

- To encourage the group, the facilitator can remark, "my Dad said this was the right tool for this job—we just need to figure out how to use the darn thing." This "forced choice" takes some creativity to apply, but often results in an usual and successful new approach and solution.

Where to Find It/How to Make It: Visit the yard sales and garage sales in your neighborhood, Ebay on the Internet, and your grandparents' junk drawer. Training Wheels sells a unique set of laminated Tool Cards. See Tool Cards activity later in this book.

Self Facilitation

Empowering the Group

A good facilitator leaves no fingerprints.

Jim Cain

The role of the facilitator is certainly critical in the presentation of adventure-based learning activities. According to author and educator Richard Wagner, the facilitator can be the "make or break" portion of an adventure-based learning program. Occasionally however, you may encounter a group that has been actively engaged in the team process for a significant amount of time, and that is very capable of running their own debriefing session. They may also be able to run their own activity (provided that the activity does not require facilitator

Photo courtesy of Jeff Baird, High 5

intervention for content or safety considerations). For such instances, here is a simple technique with enough structure to assure a successful outcome.

Concepts: Empowering a team to conduct their own reviewing session is just one more step a facilitator can take to strengthen their relationship to the group. A unique activity is presented here that can be presented, conducted and reviewed by members of the group, with minimal interaction from a facilitator.

Props/Materials Needed: The necessary equipment for the initiative or challenge, plus two additional information sheets. First, a detailed challenge information sheet, complete with hints in case the group falters in the completion of the task. Second, a group reviewing sheet, with sufficient explanation for the group to follow. Examples of these documents are illustrated on the following pages.

Directions:

- The facilitator begins the activity by asking each group of six participants to elect one person to act as "communicator." This person then visits the facilitator, collecting equipment, direction sheets and information related to the successful completion of the task. Having these participants present the task to the group, rather than the facilitators themselves, begins the transfer of power. These communicators are aware that some hints or clues exist, but will not read them until the group elects to use them. This means that the communicators can also act as group members, without influencing the outcome with privileged information.

- When the group has finished the task at hand (in this case, to assemble the entire contents of the equipment bag (PVC tubes and connectors) in such a way that no holes are left open), the communicators then share the reviewing questions with the group. In order to encourage the greatest participation, each group member is asked to read one of these questions to the rest of the group and to write down the answer. All groups can share their findings when everyone has finished.

Most of the facilitator preparation for this activity occurs well in advance of the actual delivery of the activity. The activity title, The Network, can easily be altered to meet the needs of the group. For example, this collection of tubes might be similar to the International Space Station, and debriefing topics might include international collaborations, diversity and unity. For marriage encounter or partner enrichment programs, couples can work on the network together, and then discuss how well they worked together, or identify possibilities for improvements in their working relationships. The example on the next page, The Leadership Network, has been used to focus on leadership issues during the activity and after, during the debriefing session.

After assigning an appropriate name to the activity, the next task for the facilitator is to create a written description of the activity. Appropriate text, photographs, sketches or illustrations are helpful. It is also useful to prepare a short collection of hints or insights which might assist a struggling group in finding the solution for themselves. These hints are also presented in written form, on the original information sheet, but folded under (or placed within an envelope) until needed by the group.

Finally, the facilitator prepares a series of appropriate questions to explore the various events that are likely to occur during the activity. The network, for example, often requires some early analysis, grouping of similar parts, construction, and ultimately, the ability to keep what is working, and rebuild what is not. The self-debriefing questions should reflect such events.

At this point, the facilitator is prepared to present the activity to the group. Since the activity and debriefing sessions will be self-administered, the facilitator is free to assist groups needing more help, or to observe the groups without distractions. This style of empowering groups also enables one facilitator to work with many groups simultaneously.

Where to Find It/How to Make It: The activity illustrated in this example is called The Network, and utilizes a collection of PVC tubes and connectors known as Teamplay Tubes. These tubes are available from Adventure Hardware at 1-800-706-0064 or www.adventurehardware.com.

The Leadership Network

The Project. Your group has been asked to construct a leadership network using *all* of the PVC tubes and connectors contained in the equipment bag. Just like any water system network, this leadership network must have no leaks. That means that each tube will be inserted into two connectors, and that each connector will have a tube in each opening and that the whole system will be interconnected. Your network design is a "stand alone" architecture, so for this activity, you are asked not to collaborate with other groups (they are attempting to solve the same problem with exactly the same pieces). When you are finished, there will be no holes left open in your design.

Some Valuable Information. First attempt to build your network without looking at the following three hints. If you are having some problems after 10 minutes, feel free to check the information below. When you are finished, fill out the leadership evaluation form on the back side of this sheet.

Hints

- **Connectors Have Priorities.** Consider: which of the connectors should you attempt to use first, second, and last? Clue: count the number of openings and start with the highest first.

- **Diversity Works Throughout the Process.** By using some long and some short tubes in the beginning, you will have a supply of long and short tubes at the end. This can be helpful.

- **Stress Levels.** Tubes that fall apart more than two times are trying to tell you something! And networks that contain too much "internal stress" from unusual angles, connections that are forced, and designs that are based more on brute strength than on finesse, are likely candidates for reorganizing (i.e., attempt to lessen the stress level of the network!).

Leadership Evaluation

Please answer as many questions as your group can in the time allowed.

1. What types of team behavior were demonstrated by each member of the group? (i.e., what was the role of each team member: decision maker, creative genius, worker bee, problem solver, etc).

2. Was there an obvious leader in the group, or did the group share leadership?

3. How was leadership decided, shared, or avoided?

4. Which of the following styles of problem solving was used by your group (circle one):

   1. trial and error   2. analyze, plan, perform   3. a really good guess and a whole lot of luck

5. After your group decided on a plan, did the group change the plan during the activity? If so, why?

6. How many ideas were considered during the early stages of the activity? Was each idea, and each person, given an opportunity to be heard?

7. Describe how each member of the group was given an opportunity to contribute to the group's success.

8. How would you rate your group's overall completion of this task?

9. In general, were the participants in your group more concerned about completing the task, or in caring for the members of the group? On the "American football field of leadership" below, mark where your team stands.

Completing the Task End Zone	10	20	30	40	50	40	30	20	10	Care for the Members of the Group End Zone

10. If you had the opportunity to perform this task again, what would you suggest to do differently?

11. If you were asked to give advice to a new team trying to accomplish this assignment, what information would you provide them to help them be successful?

12. If you were going to hire an employee to complete this task, what skills would you be looking for?

Shuffle Left, Shuffle Right

Reviewing in Motion

Some folks have remarked that it takes more energy for an 11 year old boy to stand still, than it does for them to move! For participants that need to move during a debriefing session, here is a perfect solution. This is a facilitator favorite, submitted by several people.

Concepts: Providing some kinesthetic movement during a reviewing session can maintain the energy of the group, and keep those high energy folks engaged by being active.

Props/Materials Needed: None.

Directions:

- Begin by asking the group to form one large circle. Groups may decide to place their arms around their neighbors, hold hands, or simply stand unconnected next to each other.

- The facilitator offers the group the chance to "have their say." This may be related to a particular question, or the previous activity, or be open to any viewpoint that a person in the group wishes to share. It is often helpful for the facilitator to go first, and demonstrate the style (and length) of a response.

- The activity begins with the group shuffling to the left.

- At some point, the facilitator says "stop!" and then gives their comment to the group.

- Next, they say "shuffle right," and the entire group shuffles right, until someone else says "stop" and has their say.

- When it seems that no one has anything left to say, count down from 10, 9, 8, 7, 6 . . ., if someone still has something to say, they should call out, "Stop!" Have them say, "shuffle left."

- This activity continues until the countdown reaches zero.

Solo Experience

The solo experience has been a traditional part of multi-day Outward Bound™ programming since the early sixties. Great thinkers throughout history, such as Thoreau and Descartes, have written about the benefits of alone time free from distraction. In many cultures structured alone time in the wilderness is part of a coming of age ritual. Kurt Hahn, the founder of Outward Bound™, stated that true learning requires periods of silence and solitude as well as direct activity. Many practitioners find structured alone time balances and supports the group process.

Concepts: To give each participant time alone to reflect.

Props/Materials Needed: Basic weather gear and appropriate food and shelter depending on the type and length of solo experience. Participants could be given a journal or drawing assignment during this time.

Directions:

- The solo experience in Outward Bound™ programs involves the participants being led off to a spot by themselves for an extensive time overnight, with limited food and supplies and no reading material other than their journal, to reflect upon themselves and their experience. This idea could be used in shorter-term programs in many different ways. In many programs allowing for participants to take a 15 or 20-minute time separate from the group could be very effective.

- A facilitator plans a structured period for the group to venture out from the program base for a short period of time away from others to reflect. The group would then be called in by some type of call or whistle to rejoin together. (Having them leave their watches could make this alone time more meaningful.)

- Participants could use journals during this time of meditation and reflection— either provided by the program or made as part of the program. Participants could be given specific journaling or drawing assignments to take on their solo.

- A creative example of using a shorter solo experience was shared by a camp counselor at a workshop recently who shared that she has the kids in her group spread out along the shoreline of the lake at camp and sit by themselves and reflect during the time between dusk and dark.

- Participants could be asked to bring something back with them from their journey that represents their strengths or their group experience (much like the treasure chest activity but only using a found object).

Time away from the group can support the group process by giving participants a chance to slow down free from distractions, and possibly to cool down after conflict or intense group experiences.

To find out more about Outward Bound™, read: *Outward Bound USA—Learning Through Experience in Adventue-Based Education,* 1981. Joshua Miner and Joe Boldt, William Morrow and Co., New York, NY USA. ISBN 0-688-00414-8, or visit www.outwardbound.org.

S.O.S.

Help Is on the Way

Concepts: While many elements of review focus on the positive elements of team performance, this activity requires the group to consider those skills and talents which still need additional work to be fully successful.

Props/Materials Needed: None.

Directions:

- The facilitator explains the classic form of the Morse code S.O.S. message [which consists of three short pulses (dots), three long pulses (dashes) and three more short pulses (dots)].

- This code is used by those in need of assistance and is generally an urgent call for help.

- In the case of the most recent teambuilding activity, the S.O.S. message is a call for specific assistance to help the group complete the task with a skill or resource that they do not presently possess.

- The facilitator can limit the length of the S.O.S. message, requiring the group to prioritize the skills or materials they are seeking. Individuals can also submit their own requests for information, skills or resources.

Soul of Sole II

This creative processing activity uses the dominant wear patterns on a participant's shoes.

Creator: Jen Gross Lara, a variation on Adam Clark's Soul of Sole I.

Concepts: Participants answer different processing questions based on the dominant wear spots on their shoes.

Props/Materials Needed: Soul of Sole II reflexology chart.

Directions:

- Pass out a Soul of Sole II sheet to each participant.
- Tell them to look at the bottom of their shoes and identify the dominant wear spots.
- Match your dominant wear areas to the sole map.
- Using the reflexology-inspired questions as a guide, reflect on the day's program.
- Go around the circle and ask each person to share one of the questions that matches their dominant wear spots.

Where to Find It/How to Make It: You can find reflexology charts in most spa and body shops. Copy this sheet and pass it out to your participants. You can purchase hand and foot reflexology charts from: www.reflexology-research.com.

SOUL OF SOLE II

USING THE SOLE OF YOUR SHOE, FIND YOUR 2-3 AREAS OF DOMINANT WEAR.
MATCH YOUR DOMINANT WEAR AREAS TO THE SOLE MAP BELOW.
USING THE REFLEXOLOGY-INSPIRED QUESTIONS AS A GUIDE,
REFLECT ON TODAY'S WORKSHOP.

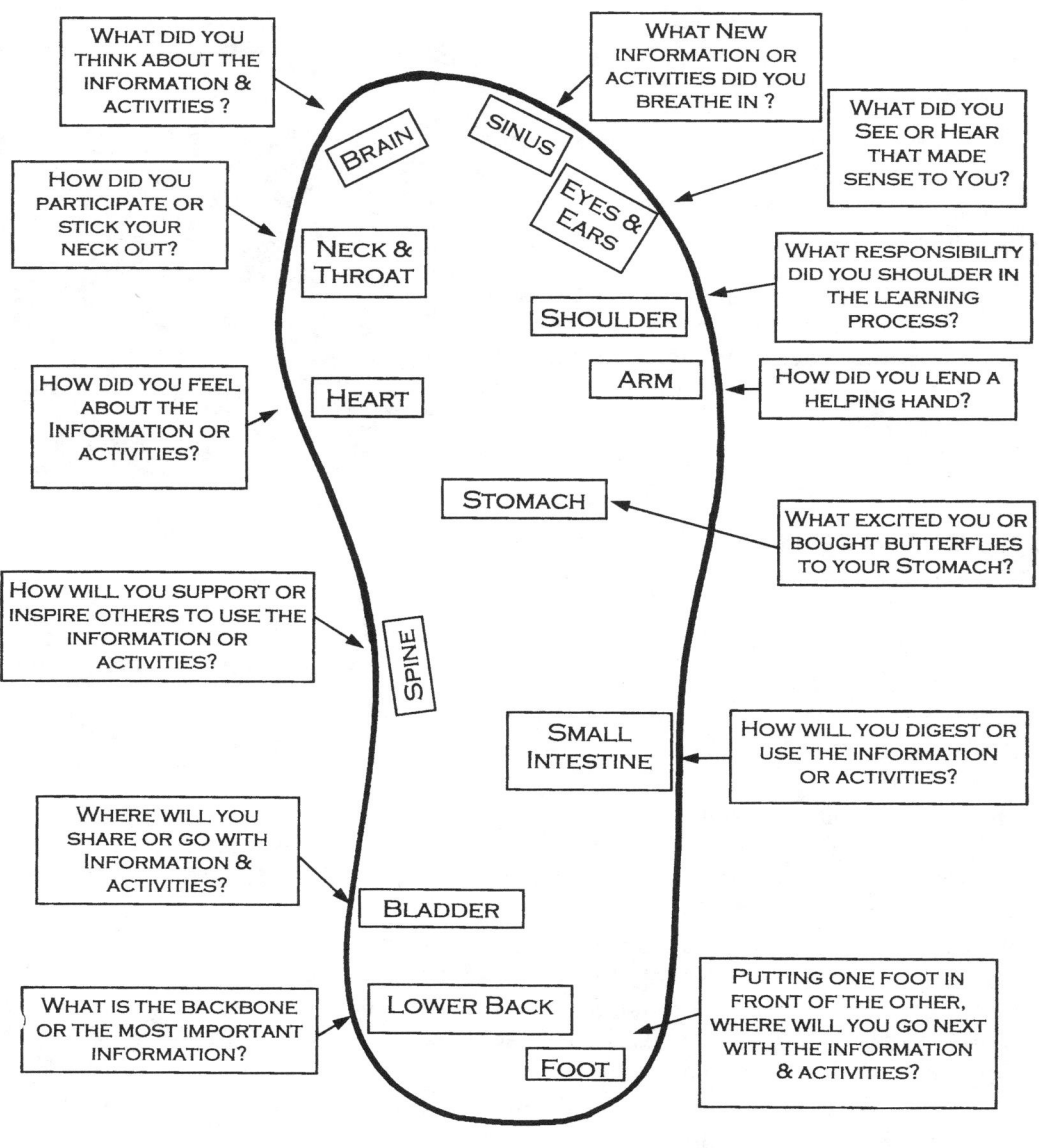

WHAT DID YOU THINK ABOUT THE INFORMATION & ACTIVITIES?

WHAT NEW INFORMATION OR ACTIVITIES DID YOU BREATHE IN?

WHAT DID YOU SEE OR HEAR THAT MADE SENSE TO YOU?

BRAIN

SINUS

EYES & EARS

HOW DID YOU PARTICIPATE OR STICK YOUR NECK OUT?

NECK & THROAT

SHOULDER

WHAT RESPONSIBILITY DID YOU SHOULDER IN THE LEARNING PROCESS?

ARM

HOW DID YOU LEND A HELPING HAND?

HOW DID YOU FEEL ABOUT THE INFORMATION OR ACTIVITIES?

HEART

STOMACH

WHAT EXCITED YOU OR BOUGHT BUTTERFLIES TO YOUR STOMACH?

HOW WILL YOU SUPPORT OR INSPIRE OTHERS TO USE THE INFORMATION OR ACTIVITIES?

SPINE

SMALL INTESTINE

HOW WILL YOU DIGEST OR USE THE INFORMATION OR ACTIVITIES?

WHERE WILL YOU SHARE OR GO WITH INFORMATION & ACTIVITIES?

BLADDER

PUTTING ONE FOOT IN FRONT OF THE OTHER, WHERE WILL YOU GO NEXT WITH THE INFORMATION & ACTIVITIES?

WHAT IS THE BACKBONE OR THE MOST IMPORTANT INFORMATION?

LOWER BACK

FOOT

A Teachable Moment

Step into the Circle

Step Up, Speak Up, Step Back

If you remember raising your hand to speak in class back in elementary school, here is a grown-up version designed to make sure every voice is heard.

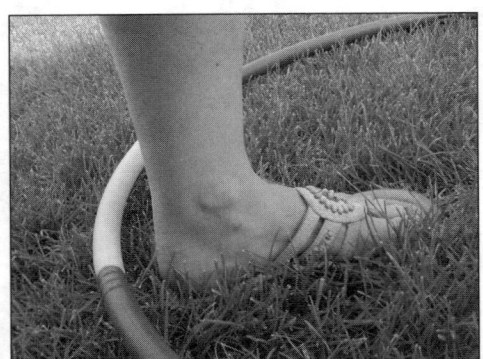

Concepts: If a person cares enough to speak up, there should be a place for their voice to be heard. This simple reviewing technique helps to make sure that every person who has a comment gets to have their say. The circle also creates an environment where every person can see every other person in the group.

Props/Materials Needed: A large circle, drawn with sidewalk chalk, or with a long rope.

Directions:

- At the completion of an activity, the facilitator leads the group around the perimeter of a circle that has been created on the ground.

- Next, the facilitator steps into the circle (modeling what they are about to present), and informs the group that all those entering the circle can have their say.

- Explain that after you ask a question, anyone wishing to answer, or even to voice their comments, is asked to step into the circle, so that each person might be heard. When you are finished, step out again. If someone is speaking and you wish to comment, step into the circle quietly, and begin to speak only when the other person has completed their commentary.

- This process continues until everyone has had their say and everyone is standing on the outside of the circle again.

210

Sticks in a Bundle

Here is an activity that is popular with wilderness programs and is especially useful for those individuals who are visual learners.

Contributor: Mary Ann Loeffler, CTRS Metropolitan State College of Denver

Concepts: When individual strengths are combined, they are unbreakable.

Props/Materials Needed:

1. Four sticks 5 inches (13 cm) long per person
2. A length of twine to tie around all sticks
3. A printed card saying "Sticks in a Bundle are Unbreakable" a Kenyan proverb attached with the twine to the bundle.

Directions:

- In a circle at the end of the day, have individuals think of four strengths that they brought to the program.

- Pick a stick that represents each strength and tie them all together in a bundle. Discuss how one strength combined with others is unbreakable.

- Demonstrate the concept by trying to break the bundle.

- Tie the proverb on the bundle to remind them of the strengths they brought to the team and how the strength of each member contributes to a strong team.

Where to Find It/How to Make It: Collect sticks outside. Use packing twine, string, or yarn. Cut strips of paper big enough to write the proverb and punch a hole in it. Use natural twigs or branches for the sticks and string or twine to wrap around the bundle.

Stones

While living in Madison, Wisconsin, Jennifer came upon beautiful pewter 'stones' in a gift store that were engraved with words such as play, joy, courage, strength, peace, laughter, rejuvenation, trust, in English on one side, and a variety of languages on the other. She started using them successfully as a closing activity for a week-long training. One group participant still wears her stone as a necklace to this day.

Concepts: To let participants choose a word to sum up their experience.

Props/Materials Needed: Pewter engraved stones, natural engraved stones, stones with permanent ink words written on them.

Directions:

- This activity is most effectively used as a closing or after an involved activity or series of activities.

- As a closing activity, lay all of the stones out and have participants choose one that represented their experience during the program.

- Having participants take the stones with them as a memento of their experience and a representation of their growth can be very powerful.

- Giving the pewter stones away can be somewhat expensive, but making your own would be easy to do with rocks and a nice marker or engraving tool.

Where to Find It/How to Make It: You can find engraved stones at many truck stops, novelty shops, craft and gift shops. You can make your own by collecting some smooth rocks and writing words on them with a marker or paint pen, or painting them. Training Wheels sells a set of engraved stones.

Stop 'N Go PRE-brief

Brian Brolin is one of the most creative facilitators we know. He created this ingenious activity in his garage!

Creator: Brian Brolin

Concepts: The Stop 'N Go PRE-brief is a front-loading activity using the colors of a traffic light; red, yellow, and green.

Props/Materials Needed: The Stop 'N Go key chain, or you can use red, yellow, and green marbles, colored tennis balls, rubber balls—or any visual or tactile prop.

Directions:

- Stop 'N Go works best after you are already into a sequence of activities. Before the third or fourth initiative activity, pull out the colored marbles. At this point they have already started to show group behavior patterns. Pull out the colored marbles and say:

  "A traffic light is used to help direct motorists to keep them from crashing. The lights signify things a driver should do to keep things flowing smoothly. Let's take a moment to look at things our group needs to do in order to keep moving forward with no crashing . . ."

- Then introduce the colors and ask the group to give suggestions.
  - RED: What things are happening in the group that need to STOP in order for us to be more successful? Usual answers are to stop teasing, horseplay, put-downs, blaming, etc.
  - YELLOW: What things do we need to be CAREFUL of as we continue? Suggestions can include to keep everyone safe, listen to all ideas, be aware of personal choices and boundaries, etc.
  - GREEN: What things do we want to GO for? These could be group goals, as well as behavior suggestions. Ideas may include being respectful, encouraging more, setting time limits, etc.

- If it would not be a distraction, the marbles are presented to specific individuals who will monitor those ideas for the group. For example, one person could be given the yellow marble and asked to let the group know any time he sees someone's ideas being overlooked by saying "Careful! Are we listening to everyone?." Those participants holding marbles can be asked to report at the end of the activity on what they observed.

- The marbles can also be used in a feedback session, giving specific individual suggestions on things to stop, be careful of, or go for. Hand the marbles around and allow anyone interested in such direct feedback to hold them and get suggestions. Some facilitators have done this with therapeutic programs in the form of "warm fuzzies and swift kicks," where everyone gave one positive and one "constructive" comment to the person beside them. Be sure your group is bonded enough to handle such a potential confrontation, and that they have learned how to be respectful in giving feedback. This would work best with groups that have spent at least several days together.

A residential program for younger boys uses the Stop 'N Go as a pre-teaching tool. Counselors carry a set of marbles with them on a keychain, and use them when transitioning to a new environment. For example, the group has been playing basketball, and now they are headed for the van to go to a movie. The marbles are brought out, and they are asked the questions that help them focus on appropriate behavior: STOP talking loudly before getting into the van, STOP outdoor roughhousing. BE CAREFUL to listen to staff instructions, BE CAREFUL to stay together. GO/DO have fun together, DO portray a good program image in the community, DO be polite and respectful of others. The same application could be used by school teachers as students transition from one area or class to another.

Where to Find It/How to Make It: Brian Brolin, brian@fundoing.com; Training Wheels; Grip-It Adventures; FUNdoing.

Story Bag

The Story Bag is based on the idea of the traditional medicine bag. Items placed in the bag tell stories of courage, pain, adventure, learning and more. These stories can later be shared with others, or simply reflected on in solitude.

Contributor: Brian Brolin

Concept: The story bag can be a great tool to use if you work with the same group for a long period of time. You can create a special time to get out your story bag and share some life lessons with them. This would be a great opportunity to talk about how each person does not have enough time to make all of the mistakes in the world, and that they can learn from others—even their teachers, parents, and counselors. (Who knew!)

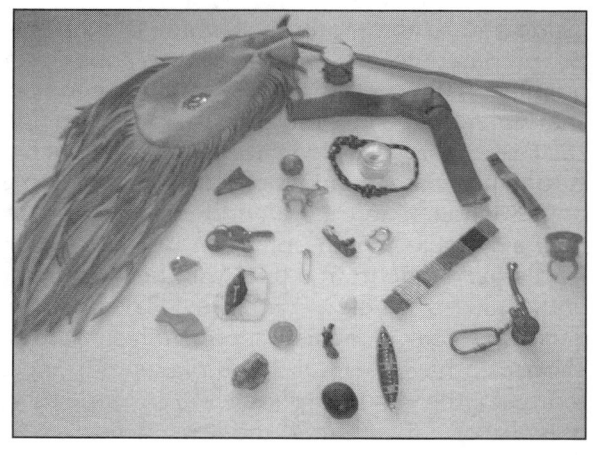

Directions: Medicine bags are found in many cultures around the world. They are often small leather pouches with a long lace that is worn around the neck. African medicine bags have historically contained small ceremonial items like bone totems and special plant roots. Pouches found in Viking sites have contained special carved stones. Anasazi Indian dwellings have yielded small bags containing sage and stone blades. Fur trappers and explorers in the early American West adopted the medicine bag idea from the indigenous peoples they came across, and carried them as good luck charms.

There is no doubt that these bags were, and still are, very sacred to the owner. Items placed in the bag have significance to the owner, and tell important stories. Imagine a young warrior of an ancient civilization out on his first hunt. He has practiced with his bow and arrows since he was a small child, and now he is allowed for the first time to go with the men after meat for the village. He uses all his learning to stalk and track, and eventually shoots his first antelope! He is now considered a provider for his family and relatives. He recovers the arrowhead from that first kill, and carefully places it in the bag around his neck as a reminder of the feeling of finally using his skills for the good of others. He has a story to encourage himself when things are not so good later in life.

Brian has had a story bag for several years. He chooses to share his stories with others, and the items he places in his bag remind him of lessons he has learned in his own travels. He has a piece of obsidian stone he picked up from the inside of a volcano, reminding him of the tenacity and determination it took to get there. He has a crocodile tooth from northern Kenya, where he saved a friend from being eaten by crocodiles by using swimming safety skills he learned as a child. He has a silver tomahawk head pendant reminding him of a story Benjamin Franklin wrote about not giving up on your goals. All of the items are object-lessons that are meaningful to him, and are stories and experiences he enjoys sharing spontaneously with others.

A friend of Brian's in Namibia took the story bag idea, and created a large story basket. He did not want to be limited to the small size of a pouch. Another person uses a dream catcher and he hangs significant items and momentos from the web. The basic idea is the same, of having a visual, tangible, object that acts as an anchor for an important event.

A nice way to introduce the story bag is to dump out all of your pieces that you have inside and let the group pick which trinket/object they would like to hear a story about. Be prepared to tell whatever story goes along with each piece. Depending on the population you work with, you may need to set some boundaries around personal sharing and how the information you share does not get used against you later on.

But a story bag does not have to be such a personal, individual thing. A group that is together for an amount of time can develop a group story bag. For example, students on a backpacking trip can end the day with debriefing significant events of the day. An item signifying a high point can be chosen to place in the group story bag. This might be a small stone from a peak climbed, or a piece of charred wood from a campfire, or a bottle cap from a clean-up project. The important thing would be that the item represents a *group* event or achievement, rather than an individual experience. The group may choose to have several items presented, and then vote on keeping the ones that best represent the group experience. A group story bag is a great way to retell highlights to parents or others after the trip. This would work well with school classrooms or therapeutic groups also.

SWOT Training

A Four Element Analysis

While some processing techniques focus on positive and negative group traits, such as the Plus-Delta Model, SWOT analysis provides a more extensive view of the group's performance. SWOT stands for Strengths, Weaknesses, Opportunities and Threats.

Concepts: Strength issues focus on the positive attributes of the group. This can be especially important when the group may not have been successful in the most recent challenge. This category encourages group members to identify talents and skills that they consider helpful and that they wish to continue using in the future.

Weaknesses identified during the activity, such as limited initial planning or limited utilization of available resources, encourages the group to take a close look at those elements which are less than optimal. By identifying these attributes, team members are able to focus on those attributes which, when strengthened, can lead to the greatest improvements.

Identifying opportunities is a method for tying the skills of the group to useful applications of these skills in the future. This information can lead the facilitator to a specific next activity for the group. For example, a group that identifies great physical strength in accomplishing a task, might be ready for a higher level of physical challenge. A group which identifies creative problem solving skills as one of their talents can be presented with an activity requiring an even higher level of ability.

Analyzing the threat potential to group unity and performance can lead to a list of attributes that the group needs to preserve in order to maintain their high level of team performance. For example, if consensus is deemed necessary within a group contract, then the absence of consensus represents a risk to the team unity and performance. If the team demonstrates the ability to solve challenges, even when critical or essential resources are eliminated, then available resources do not present a threat to the group. In each of these cases, it is good to identify any elements which hold the potential for reducing the performance of the group.

Directions:

- At the completion of the activity, the facilitator presents the SWOT model, and asks the group to identify the various strengths, weaknesses, opportunities and threats evident from the most recent performance of the group.

Props/Materials Needed: A flipchart and markers are helpful, both during the activity, and as a written record for the group to consider upon completion of the program.

He had occasional flashes of silence, that made
his conversation perfectly delightful.

Sydney Smith (1771–1845), referring to Macaulay

Talking Stick

This is a common method for use both as a speaking prompt and a group management tool during reflective discussions.

Concepts: Providing an opportunity for each person to talk without being interrupted.

Props/Materials Needed: The actual prop needed for a Talking Stick can be literally anything you want it to be. It could be a stick you pull out of the woods or it could be something more elaborate that you put some time and effort into creating.

Some possible talking sticks: piece of PVC pipe, a stick from a tree, plastic microphone, recorder, pencil, rain stick, drumstick, ruler, dowel rod, old cow bone, baton, broom handle, a microphone, soda bottle, mailing tube, piece of leather wrapped around a stick, (be creative!), glitter wand, wooden spoon or candle stick.

Directions:

*   The talking stick is useful with those groups that talk over each other and may not listen to what their teammates have to say. The talking stick is just what it sounds like— whoever has the stick gets to talk and everyone else listens.

*   As the facilitator, be creative with who gets the stick next. Consider a finger system of holding out the number in which the next person is to talk (i.e., the next person to talk holds out the number one with their finger, the next person holds out the number two, and so on).

*   Pass the stick sequentially around the circle.

If you use the talking stick a lot with your groups, they can really get into this activity. They will give the stick a name and eventually start asking for the stick on their own. That way they are more in control of their process. Sometimes that works and sometimes you have to intervene. Play with it and make it your own!

Team Resume

Thanks to Tanya Aghazarian for the great idea for this activity. It emerged from a group of high school students that were having trouble getting jobs. They were kind of rough looking kids, purple hair, tattoos, piercings . . . They were creating wonderful resumes and then going to the job interviews but not getting hired. This activity was created to help them learn how to sell themselves without selling themselves out.

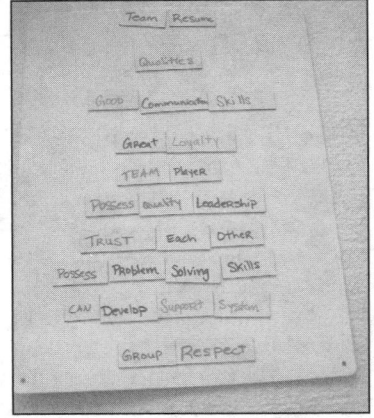

Creator: Tanya Aghazarian and Michelle Cummings

Concepts: Team Resume is a great activity to use when trying to encourage individuals and teams to discuss how to sell themselves and their qualities.

Props/Materials Needed: Magnet boards, word magnets and picture magnets.

Directions:

- Give each individual or team a magnet board, word magnets, and picture magnets.
- Invite participants to look through the picture magnets and come to consensus on one picture magnet that will be used as their individual logo/team logo.
- Then using the word magnets, participants are asked to develop their team resume. Their Team Resume can have any look they want, but they must present it in an appropriate format.
- If you have several teams working at the same time you could set up a scenario in which they are competing for the same job or bid.

Here is some great verbage to read to your participants for this activity.

Resumes or Marketing Documents

Effective resume building can help individuals and teams achieve their goals by taking an aggressive approach in selling your skills to employers, not just listing your past history. Effective resumes are no longer just an inventory of your credentials or a biography of your work history; instead, they are meant to market your strengths to potential employers and sell you above your peers—individuals just like yourself who possess the same qualifications, training and experience as you do, and who are applying for the same position as you.

Selling Your Skills or Achieving Your Goals

In essence, you are competing with your peers for the same position—and just listing your employment history and education does not tell the employer anything different about you than the other 93+ resumes that are already on the hiring authority's desk. So why should they call YOU for an interview instead of anyone else?

Resumes Must Answer: "Why You?"

To compete in today's marketplace, the resume must be much more aggressive in bringing out your skills, achievements, talents, abilities, and accomplishments to demonstrate to a potential employer how YOU can contribute to their performance, profitability, and success. In essence, the resume must answer the question: Why does the company want to hire YOU, as opposed to every other qualified individual who has also submitted their resume? or Why does your team deserve the bid and not the other five teams that are applying for the same job?

Have each team present their resume to you, the hiring authority, and have them give you a presentation as to why they should get the winning bid.

Where to Find It/How to Make It:

Training Wheels and Grip It Adventures sell a custom made team resume kit that has pre-printed magnets with metaphoric pictures and 660 words on them, as well as the magnet boards.

You can find magnet boards and pre-cut magnets at teacher supply stores. Then, using different colored markers, you can write on different words that you would find on a resume. Some suggestions would be:

Team	Group	Constructive
Teamwork	Personal	Great
Teambuilding	Respect	Well
Skills	Resume	Good
Communication	Member	Talk
Qualities	Timely	Rules
Player	Understand	Devoted
Leadership	Understands	Lead
Quality	Levels	Hear
Possess	Level	Manager
Trust	High	Managerial
Each	Clear	Administration
Other	Criticism	Concise
Problem	Amazing	System
Solving	Excited	Feedback
Develop	Solves	Problems
Support	Follow	Excellent

Any words that you would typically find on a resume will work well for the Team Resume.

Thought Balloons

I Wonder What They Are Thinking?

Comic strips and cartoons have used thought balloons for years to help us see what a character is thinking or feeling. We will use the same technique here to review what the other members of our group are pondering.

Concepts: It can be helpful to see inside what another member of the group is thinking and feeling. Often these thoughts are comical, humorous and thought provoking. This technique allows instant feedback and keeps an element of humor, even when the group is facing a serious challenge.

Props/Materials Needed: Large comic strip panels with blank thought balloons, or real balloons, cardboard cutouts of thought balloons with pens and colorful markers, or dry erase board thought balloons with dry erase markers.

Directions: Here are two possibilities for using the thought balloon technique.

- First, participants are given cardboard, dry erase board, or real balloons and markers during the activity, to share their thoughts as they work their way through the challenge. This version allows participants to record their thoughts for the debrief session, so that they can say, "well, just before we dropped the ball, I was thinking . . ."

- Secondly, the group is given a thought balloon or comic strip panel at the completion of the task, so that they can write their own thoughts, feelings, or humorous commentary about the performance of the group.

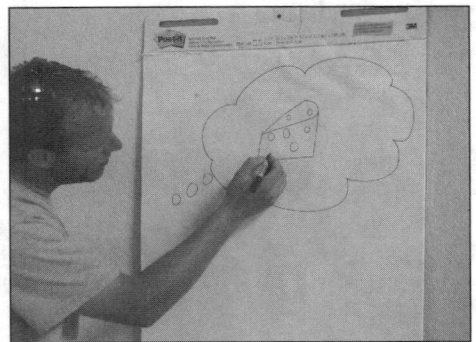

Where to Find It/How to Make It: You can find comic strip panels in nearly every newspaper. Comic book stores, libraries, and on-line websites also carry a variety of comic strips, some of which are ideal for your audience.

Thumbs Up

A very simple, but powerful activity to end a long program.

Contributor: Tom Leahy, Leahy and Associates

Concepts: Giving each participant the time they need to process and giving the group a thumbs up signal when they are finished.

Props/Materials Needed: Your thumb!

Directions:

- These sessions can take as long as they need to. Explain to the group that each person has as much time as they need to share their learnings and what they will take away from the program. Their speaking time will be uninterrupted by others and when they are finished, they will give the group a thumbs up sign.

- When the participant has finished speaking and has given the thumbs up sign, the group echos back a thumbs up signal acknowledging their contribution.

Time Capsule

Helping Future Generations

Here is a simple technique that invites the entire group to reflect on the recently completed task, and then to leave behind some advice for future generations.

Concepts: The idea of identifying skills, talents and team resources that will be valuable 100 years into the future requires participants to not only consider the most recent activity but also the value of such things in the future.

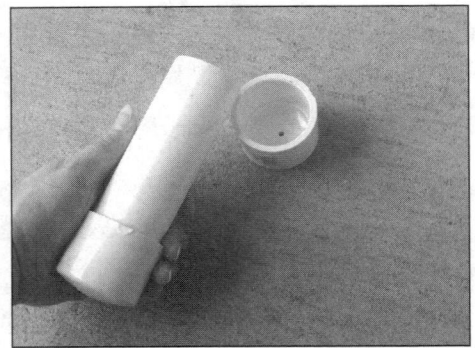

Props/Materials Needed: A unique box or storage container, paper, markers, and index cards. You can make a simple PVC tube time capsule with a one foot long segment of 3 inch diameter PVC tubing and two end caps.

Directions:

- At the completion of the task, present the time capsule container and a collection of paper and writing materials for the group to construct the various elements they wish to place in the time capsule.

- Instruct the group that they are to review the most recent activity completed, and then to leave information in the time capsule that will assist groups in the future to accomplish the task.

- You can suggest such items as: recommendations on team skills that would be useful, drawn pictures of objects that might be helpful in completing the task, hints, clues, riddles, stories and observations.

- When complete, place the objects into the time capsule and seal the container.

Timing Is Everything

Quantifying the Adventure Experience

While there are many techniques for qualitatively analyzing a group's performance in adventure-based learning activities, here is a technique for quantifying that performance.

Contributor: Tom Leahy, Leahy and Associates

Concepts: A technique for using time analysis to quantify the performance of a group during an adventure-based learning activity.

Props/Materials Needed: A chess clock or two stopwatches.

Directions:

- After presenting a new challenge to the group, the facilitator selects one side of a chess clock to represent the time spent by the group discussing and planning the completion of their task, and the other side to represent the time spent actually working to accomplish this goal.

- The chess clock is especially useful as it quickly changes from one side to another, in a similar fashion to the speed at which the group changes from talking to doing.

- As a special note, chess clocks are unique timepieces. The button above the left dial actually starts the clock on the right side, and the button above the right dial starts the clock on the left side. It is helpful for a facilitator to label each of these buttons and dials "planning" or "performing."

- At the completion of the challenge, during the debriefing session, the facilitator can present the clock and ask the group if they are surprised by the quality of their result versus the time spent accomplishing the task. In many cases, groups remark that a bit more time spent planning might have reduced the total amount of time necessary to complete the task. This outcome from the group can be especially helpful when you are trying to encourage a group to spend a bit more time planning before they begin working.

- Because the facilitator has their hands occupied during this activity, it is suggested that this tool is only used for an activity where spotting or other interventions are not required.

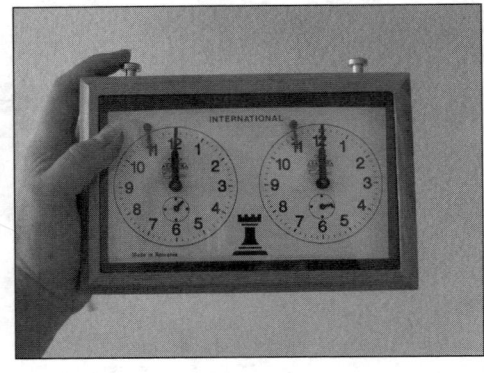

Where to Find It/How to Make It: You can find chess clocks in game stores and via the Internet. Some can be quite expensive. A less costly alternative is to use two inexpensive stopwatches, but remember that you must "stop" or pause the time on one watch while the other watch is running!

There isn't much better in this life than finding a way to spend a few hours in conversation with people you respect and love. You have to carve this time out of your life because you aren't really living without it.

Real Live Preacher, RealLivePreacher.com Weblog, August 27, 2003

Tool Cards

Tom Leahy is famous for asking his participants, "Do you need a tool?" After participating in one of his workshops, Michelle took that concept and ran with it, (thanks, Tom!). Tool cards emerged to give participants a metaphoric visual to attach to their needs.

Creator: Michelle Cummings

Concepts: Most people are familiar with building tools and their uses. Tool cards have pictures of a variety of familiar construction tools. Use the metaphors for each tool to initiate a discussion about valuable team tools.

Props/Materials Needed: Tool Cards (pictures of tools), actual tools or toy replicas of various tools.

Directions: Here are several different ways to use tool cards.

- Debriefing Tool: Spread the cards out before the group and have them choose a tool that best represents an experience or a feeling that they have had. Ask each participant to share why they picked the card they did and why that particular card represents them or an experience they have had.

- Pre-briefing Tool: When used at the beginning of the day, these cards can be a great pre-briefing for the day. Spread out the cards and ask them to pick out the cards representing the "tools" they think are going to need to be successful as a team. Ask each participant to share why they picked the card they did and what team tool it represents.

- Intervention Tool: When a group is having a hard time during an activity and needs an intervention, stop the activity and spread out the cards before the group. Ask them to think about the role they are playing within the activity and then pick a tool card that would best represent the role they are playing. This allows each participant to reflect on their own behaviors and place an external role with that behavior. Invite each participant to share why they picked the card they did and what tool they are portraying.

Where to Find It/How to Make It: You can make these cards yourself with most computer clip art programs and some business card stock. You can also find pictures of tools in tool catalogs and hardware store advertisements often found in the Sunday newspaper. You can buy laminated tool cards from: Adventure Hardware, Training Wheels Inc., or Grip-It Adventures.

Traffic Signs

What Sign Are You?

Innovative reviewing activities often use familiar objects in an unfamiliar manner. Here is an interesting method of using the traffic and road signs we see every day to express our inner feelings and thoughts.

Creator: Jim Cain, Teamwork & Teamplay

Concepts: While it can sometimes be difficult to express our innermost thoughts and feelings, it is often possible to describe them in terms of familiar and common things. Here is an opportunity to do that with some of the most familiar signs we see every day—traffic signs.

Props/Materials Needed: Illustrations of familiar and unique road and traffic signs.

Directions: Here are three possibilities for using illustrations of traffic signs. We recommend these at the completion of the activity.

- Method I—Pass out cards with traffic sign images to each participant, and ask them to hold these up so that all members of the group can see each one. Next, ask the group to identify which sign most accurately describes the performance of the group during the last activity. Point to a few of the more interesting, unusual, or obscure signs and ask if these too could be accurate. Why or why not?
- Method II—Place all the traffic signs visibly in front of the group and ask each person to take one that they feel accurately describes their impression of the performance of the group during the last challenge. Ask them to share their reason for choosing this

card with another participant, or with the entire group. Invite others who agree with this choice to voice their opinions as well.

- Method III—Place all the traffic signs visibly in front of the group, preferably on the ground. Give each participant a short piece of rope or webbing (about four to six inches long), which we refer to as a "worm." On the count of three, invite everyone to toss their worm onto the illustration that they feel most accurately describes the performance of the group.

  This technique of instant voting encourages each person to form their own impression and vote independently of others in the group. This can be helpful when peer pressure, corporate culture or cultural norms impose on individual choice. In this case, participants do not wait to hear "how their friends are voting" but rather make up their own minds. Facilitators should protect the anonymity of group members and not say, "hey, who put a worm there?" Rather they might say, "I see there is one worm on the 'bridge out' sign. Can you imagine why a person would choose that one?"

Where to Find It/How to Make It: Clip art photos of common traffic signs can be found in computer software, on-line at several Internet websites and at teacher supply stores. You can also make your own signs or cards. Consider using foreign language signs for international audiences or diverse work teams.

He had occasional flashes of silence,
that made his conversation perfectly delightful.

Sydney Smith (1771–1845), referring to Macaulay

Treasure Chest

Life Is Full of Great and Wonderful Treasures

Thanks, Veronica Falcinella, for inspiring this great activity. Here is a wonderful technique for turning common items into unique treasures.

Concepts: Using tangible metaphoric props to aid in discussion.

Props/Materials Needed: You'll need a unique treasure chest of some kind, anything from a cool leather bag to a plain cardboard box. Personalizing your treasure chest will make it even more valuable to you as a facilitation and debriefing tool. Your treasure chest can be filled with a wide variety of common household items. Many people have a junk drawer somewhere in their lives—whether it is at the office, the workshop or the home. It is a great place to find items for your treasure chest. Here is a sample list of some of the items you can include in your treasure chest:

Clothes pins	Duct tape	Hackey sack
Safety pin	Whistle	Erasers
Book of matches	First aid kit	Plastic snake
Stapler	Water bottle	Phone numbers
Crayons	Thumb tack	Dice
Flashlight	Small basket	Dominoes
Coffee cup	Deck of cards	Golf ball
Slinky	Can of Spam	Golf tee
Sheriff's badge	Paper punch	Rubber chicken
Toy airplane	Cassette tape	Coaster
Handcuffs	8 track tape	Stick
Keys	Remote control	Ruler
Locks	Batteries	Tape measure
Film container	White out	Beads
Binoculars	Rock	Pictures of grandparents
Magnifying glass	Piece of rope	Pocket calendar
Combination lock	Flower	Fake credit cards

Rubber band	Scissors	Coins
Old business cards	Sticky notes	Watch
Old cell phone	Key chains	Headphones
Pencil	Feather	Timer
Pens	Yo-yo	Bottle cap
Lighter	Small stuffed animals	Tassel
Pocket knife	Compass	Floppy disk
Carabiner	CD	Webbing
Masking tape	Toothbrush	Jacks
Pictures of children	Pop top	Magic markers
Hammer	Dental floss	Lip balm
Glue	PEZ dispenser	The kitchen sink!!!

Directions: Set out the contents of your Treasure Chest before the group. Allow the group adequate time to examine the items before them. Next, invite the group to pick up individual items that metaphorically represent an experience they had during the activity, day or program and then share these with the group. You will be amazed at some of the responses that your participants will give you. Sometimes it is less intrusive if you let participants partner up or present in small groups.

Length: This activity can be used quickly or explored at a much deeper level. As a brief reflection activity, invite each person to pick one item and then provide a one sentence description of why they chose this particular item and how it relates to the activity. You can also make this activity last much longer by asking the participants to deeply reflect why they picked the item they did, why it metaphorically relates to their experience and how they can use such a metaphor in the future.

Safety guidelines: The main safety concern with this activity is to make sure the items in your treasure chest are safe and appropriate for the population of people you facilitate. For instance, you may not want to have pocket knives and matches in your treasure chest if you are working with offenders in a lock-down facility. You can easily replace these items with pictures of knives and matches, as they do make appropriate metaphors that many participants may relate to.

Make sure the items in your treasure chest are not of significant value to you or irreplaceable. Sometimes items from your treasure chest will mysteriously walk off and like real treasure, may be lost forever.

See the treasure chest—mini version for more ideas on how to use this activity.

Treasure Chest-Mini Version

Small Treasures

Photo courtesy of Jeff Baird, High 5

We have often been asked, "What about activities for those of us who lead expeditionary programs and don't have much room in our pack for props?" Jennifer Stanchfield came across a great selection of charms and a beautiful small bag at a local bead shop, inspiring the creation of the mini version of this great reflective activity.

Props/Materials Needed: Small beads, charms, buttons, tiny objects placed in a unique small pouch or interesting container.

Concepts: Using tangible objects as symbolic representations of an experience or personal attribute can lead to very effective processing. Providing a tangible object upon which participants can attach their thoughts facilitates transfer of learning. One strength or this style of processing is that it is non-threatening to participants and facilitators and leaves open the opportunities for creative and meaningful interpretation.

Directions:

- The treasure chest can be used for introductory activities, for processing a specific experience, for closure and as a tool to help participants resolve conflict.
- As an introductory activity, participants can choose the object that best represents a strength they bring to the group or a goal they have for the day or course.

- Invite the group to come to a consensus on one object that best represents their experience as a group, the strengths of the group or something they have achieved during the activity.

- Group members can use the charms to relate the "story" of their experience by lining up four or five objects that demonstrate how they progressed through the activity, the day or the course as a whole.

- Invite your participants to pick their own object and then draw it or write about its meaning or representation in their journal.

- The treasure chest can be used effectively in closing activities by helping the group tie their experience together by picking three objects—one that describes where they were when they arrived, the second where they are now—or what they achieved, and the third where they are going next. Each person picks one object that represents something they are taking away from the program. Allowing participants to take away their charm as a memento of their experience, can be especially powerful.

To listen closely and reply well is the highest perfection
we are able to attain in the art of conversation.

Francois de La Rochefoucauld (1613–1680)

Trigger Bill

Words of Wisdom from the Old West

When you visit Cheley Colorado Camp you will notice, located throughout the buildings, quotes from the Cheley's famous personality Trigger Bill. These quotes can make metaphorical connections during a processing session.

Inspired by: Michael Davis for Cheley Colorado Camp

Contributor: Chris Cavert, FUNdoing

Props/Materials Needed: Index cards with some of Trigger Bill's more famous quotes.

Directions:

- Write some of the quotes listed below, in large print, on a 5 × 7 inch (12.5 × 17.5 cm) index card.
- After an activity pass the cards around the group and ask each participant to choose one quote that closely relates to the experience they just had.
- Each participant is then given the opportunity to share their quote and thoughts with the group. For example, someone might choose, "The things we do mean more than the things we say." This might encourage a participant to discuss someone who gave a helping hand (literally) during one of the activities.

Trigger Bill Quotes:

The things we do mean much more than the things we say.

Most arguments have two sides but no end.

Character is not made in a crisis; it is only exhibited then.

You are doing your best only when you are trying to improve what you are doing.

Friendship is the only cement that will ever hold the world together.

People rarely succeed at anything unless they have fun doing it.

The road to success is always under construction.

Nothing of importance was ever done without a plan.

If only we could forget our troubles as easily as we forget our blessings.

It is better to make mistakes in trying . . . than to make the mistake of not trying at all.

Dream big dreams . . . then put on your overalls.

Nothing great was ever accomplished without ENTHUSIASM.

Do one good deed each day for ten years and you will have helped 3650 people.

Ability is rated by what you finish . . . not what you start.

If you don't like the way the ball bounces . . . then don't drop it.

What we see depends upon what we are looking for.

Good or bad . . . your habits represent you.

Whatever one processes becomes of double value when we have the opportunity of sharing it with others.

Too many people overvalue what they are not and undervalue what they are.

The finest of all gifts are not things but opportunities.

Be content with what you have . . . never with what you are.

Ideas are funny things . . . they won't work unless you do.

Where you are coming from is not nearly as important as where you are going.

Giving love . . . involves giving something of yourself.

Updating Your Resume

Powerful Skills and Talents

While you are probably not likely to list your talents of crossing an imaginary river filled with alligators on your resume, you can mention your ability to assist your group in achieving consensus, working together successfully as a group and resolving conflicts.

Concepts: The skills and talents displayed during an active learning scenario often have direct connection to the skills required in the workplace. For this reason, reviewing the team's performance after the most recent teambuilding activity and identifying the skills and talents required to complete the task is only the first part of the review. The next part, and one that contributes to the "transfer of knowledge" following such a teambuilding activity, is for each member of the group to identify, in corporate resume language, what valuable skills they demonstrated during the last activity.

Props/Materials Needed: This activity can be done verbally, with no props at all, or the facilitator can provide blank resume forms (or company-like job application forms) for the group to fill out.

Directions:

- At the completion of the challenge activity and after identifying the various skills and talents that contributed to the success of the team, ask each group member to identify their contributions to the team and then to express these contributions in high-powered corporate resume language.

- As a follow-up, ask participants to share how they could use this talent in their workplace, with their department or project team.

Virtual Slideshow

In This Next Slide You'll See . . .

Here is a very simple activity that combines auditory, kinesthetic and visual learning styles in a single technique.

Creator: Jim Cain, Teamwork & Teamplay.

Concepts: The slide projector "clicker" theme is used here to show some imaginary images taken by each participant. Often, words can be hard to find, especially to describe all the new experiences encountered in an adventure-based learning program. By starting with images or pictures, participants often feel that they are simply describing the images, rather than being asked to create their own discussion. The clicking sound is auditory, the clicking motion and role-playing of a slide projected image is kinesthetic, and the imagined image is visual. Three learning styles, all rolled into one activity.

Props/Materials Needed: A "clicker" or, since the group is sharing imaginary images, why not have an imaginary clicking device too? "On the count of three, let's all make the sound that a slide projector clicker makes. One, Two, Three . . . CLICK!"

Directions:

- As a facilitator, demonstrate the operation of the clicker by pointing it towards one wall, or distant edge of the group, pressing it (CLICK), and then narrating what your image shows. "In this next slide, you'll see . . ."

- Ask your participants to think of two to three pictures or slides that they would want to present about the day.

- Pass the clicker around the group (or use your tongue to make a clicker sound) and tell them to "click" as they tell the group about each slide.

- Have them point the clicker at their "virtual" slide screen as they are talking about their slide.

This activity has an uncanny way of taking the spotlight away from the speaker and directs it to the slide show. It helps those who are uncomfortable with the group staring at them while they are sharing. The person speaking often gets caught up in the colors, the people and the story they are telling about in their slide rather than focusing on speaking in front of the group.

Where to Find It/How to Make It: You can find metal clickers at many pet stores (used for training dogs), and at Training Wheels.

Voicemail

Please Leave a Message

Here is a simple technique that requires the group to leave a time-limited message about their present assignment.

Concepts: Many corporations require interim status reports on key projects. This technique of keeping management "up to date" on critical issues, resources and task completion is vital to many organizations. In an adventure-based learning situation, our electronic answering machine encourages the group to consider their most important accomplishments and deepest concerns, and truthfully communicate these to their upper level management.

Props/Materials Needed: A digital watch with an alarm, or other device for creating a digital "beeping" sound. A portable voice recorder that can play back the message is even more realistic. Office supply stores often carry inexpensive versions of these devices. In a pinch, a cell phone with voice mail will work.

Directions:

- The facilitator informs the group that their upper level managers have contacted them, and would like an interim status report on their progress in completing the task on time. The managers have left a telephone number, and would like the group to leave a brief message in the next ten minutes. The facilitator can limit the length of the message (from thirty seconds to two minutes) that can be left on the voice recorder.

Walk a Mile in Your Shoes

Kim Kickert shared this activity during an outstanding processing workshop. This is a great one for long expeditionary programs and for facilitators that need to travel with minimal props!

Inspired by: Kim Kickert

Concepts: Getting participants to think about others.

Props/Materials Needed: The shoes on your feet!

Directions:

- Have each participant take off one of their shoes and throw it into the center of the circle.
- Next, invite them to choose a shoe at random, find the shoe's owner, and stand next to them, forming a circle with the entire group.
- Have each person share why they would want to walk a mile in the shoe of the person whose shoe they have.
- This is a great activity to talk about the positives in each person's life.

Web of Commitment

Dr. Jon Johnson or Dr. J, as he's commonly referred to, adds some great insight to this oldie but goodie activity. Thanks, Dr. J!

Contributed by: Dr. Jon Johnson, Ph.D., Director, Team-Leadership.com, San Antonio, Texas.

Props/Materials Needed: A ball or reel of accessory cord rated with a minimum of 90 pound breaking strength.

Concepts: For some years now groups (any size from eight to twenty-five) have frequently ended their day on the challenge course with a Web of Commitment. In this closure a ball or reel of ninety-pound test string typically found in hardware stores—the rainbow colored string adds lots of color—is fed into a circle of participants by one of the facilitators. The ball of string starts with one person and they make a statement about the day that is true for them. It could be something new they learned today, or something powerful that they are going to take away from the program. After each person shares they toss the ball of string to someone in the circle who has not received the string yet. As they toss it they hold onto their end of the string so that in the end the group has formed a giant web.

To make this closure more powerful three other things may be added:

- **Levitation of a member.** Once the web is completed ask people to stand up if they are not already, and to take the slack out by leaning back. Ask them to get a tactile image and "feel" of this web and invite people to notice what it suggests to them. If the group is large enough—usually around twenty is sufficient—you may invite them to select someone to honor here at the end of the day by using the web to lift them off the ground.

  Remind the group about the challenge of choice. Have everyone lower the web to the ground and the person selected lies across the most supportive part of the network in a spread-eagle posture. On the count of three, raise, pause to shout his/her name in unison, then on three lower the person back to the ground.

- **Personal reflection** is a variation that invites people to engage their imagination. Each person is given a pen and a card that has a statement like the following at the top and room to write below:

Reflect upon the power of collective thought and collective action that you have witnessed here today, and imagine what might happen if this power were to continue to grow within this group in the days to come. Write down what you think of as you imagine possible outcomes. Please write only what you would feel comfortable sharing with the rest of the group here, and sign it with your name.

To start this activity tell the group, "When you get the string you are to read what you wrote on the personal reflection card you were given a few minutes ago. After you have read what you wrote on your card and the group has recognized your contribution, you are to look across the circle and make eye contact with someone across from you who will let you know they are ready to be next. At no time should your hand-off be to someone directly to your right or left.

Once you have found the person who will go next, you are to walk across the circle and hand them end of the string, but do not let go of the string entirely. Instead, find your way back to where you were in the circle and keep holding onto the string. Now as each additional person reads their reflection and crosses the circle, everyone who has gone before will continuously feed the string through their point of contact and forward on into the growing web of connectedness."

• **Poetic Summary.** If the personal reflection has been used, the following poem or ideas from the poem can speak to the group about their shared experience of the web before they leave the program. The intention here is to reinforce the dramatic power and vivid image of team leadership that the web can represent.

Becoming Smarter

If becoming smarter's worth thinking about,
Then trust must always be balanced with doubt . . .
But think about too what the wise man said,
When he shared with us what he saw in his head.

Like when Einstein reflected on the work he had done.
And he told us that intellect was not NUMBER ONE.
More important to him in the act of creation
Was the faculty of his imagination.

Now you all were asked to engage this today,
And each one responded with something to say.
Each contribution was attached to a string,
At the end what we had was a curious thing.

A network of powerful thoughts and projections,
Tied to an artwork of personal connections.
As we all held it up for the next to cross under
This web of our visions made some of us wonder.

If at a thousand words one picture is valued
The weight of this web can surely be tallied.
This analogy somehow seems quite appealing,
But what's the currency in which we are dealing?

If from the learning zone you take this one thing,
Take your own mental image of all of this string.
It has no center—it's not fixed or tied,
Yet all the points 'round it are all unified.

The connections made here share no central stem,
The leadership's happening . . . out on the rim!
With less centralized power, command and control,
A bright synapse snaps 'tween the parts and the whole.

Poem courtesy of Dr. Jon Johnson

Where to Find It/How to Make It: Hardware stores, challenge course vendors, and climbing stores will have test rated rope and cord.

Well-Oiled Machine

This large group closer is perfect for groups that need an active, fun or even silly ending.

Concepts: A "well-oiled machine" has many pieces and parts that all work together to make the machine work properly. This concept also works for teams.

Props/Materials Needed: None.

Directions:

- After your group has worked well together all day long, "like a well-oiled machine," have them take that concept home with them.

- Discuss the idea that machines have several pieces and parts that all work together to make the machine work properly. This concept also works for teams.

- Instruct them to think of a noise and an action in their head. (whirring, clanging, beeping, swishing, sloshing, chugging, etc. . . . and an appropriate movement to go with it.) Ask for one volunteer to step into the center of the group and start doing their action and noise.

- After this volunteer has performed their noise and action for about five seconds another volunteer steps forward and physically attaches somewhere to the first volunteer and adds a new noise and a new action. Ask them to physically attach so that the machine will be one large working unit by the time everyone adds in their action and noise.

- Then one at a time the rest of the group will enter the "machine," physically attach to another working part already in process and add their noise and action.

- By the time everyone has joined the machine, it will be whistling and bustling about with activity.

What I Know, What I Want to Know, What I've Learned

Here is a propless debriefing technique that provides a framework for the group.

Creator: Faith Evans, PlayFully, Inc.

Concepts: This model is especially useful following a skill-based activity and quickly provides an evaluation umbrella for an entire program.

Props/Materials Needed: None.

Directions:

- Begin by asking participants to share, "What I know" about canoeing, backpacking, leadership, glazing pots, playing the guitar, etc.
- Next, it is valuable to ascertain "What I want to know" in order to direct the program to the needs of the participants and keep them fully engaged.
- "What I've learned" is excellent feedback for the recently completed program or activity."
- As an optional fourth step, you can ask the group to consider, "What else I want to know."

Whose Stone Is It?

This is our variation of "Whose Bandana Is It?" from the book, Reflective Learning by Sugerman, Gass, Doherty, and Garvey.

Contributor: Chris Cavert

Props/Materials Needed: A variety of small, colorful polished stones. Try to provide at least twice as many stones as group members.

Directions: While looking for a cost effective giveaway Chris re-discovered the wonders of polished stones. He likes to present this activity at the end of a program.

- Spread out the stones on a special ceremonial ground cloth (or bandana). Then ask the group to observe the stones for a minute without talking and have them contemplate the positive characteristics of the stones. For example, shiny, curved, intricate, layered, colorful, complex and so on.

- Then, as a group, determine what stone, and its characteristics, relate to a member of the group.

- Next present that stone to the person to take with them as a reminder of the program and what the group saw in that person. Again, emphasize that you are asking the group to come up with positive characteristics about the stone and the person it represents. For example, someone might say, "This stone has layers in it like Patty. Patty showed some of her layers today like, her fun spirit, her competitive nature, and her kindness towards others."

- **Variation:** A fun, interesting twist to this activity is chocolate rocks. You can find them in the same places as the polished stones. They are not as intricate as the stones but they have enough color variation in them to work. Once everyone has a rock, take yours and put it in your mouth and chew it up. The looks are great. Casually mention, "We're all that, and more," referring to what was told about us by our group mates and that we have much more to share. Invite others to eat up or save their rock for later.

Where to Find It/How to Make It:
Polished stones are available at souvenir, craft, and gift stores.

Word Search

The Language of Leadership

A novel way to "seek and find" the elements of your reviewing discussion.

Concepts: Here is a reviewing technique which incorporates the linguistic style of multiple intelligence. By visually searching for key words and phrases that identify important teambuilding and leadership topics, participants individually and as a group consider the possibilities of each of these being a part of their recent challenge.

Props/Materials Needed: A large-scale version of a word search puzzle.

Directions:

- At the completion of an activity, the facilitator rolls out the word search puzzle before the group.
- Participants are asked to find as many words as possible, especially those related to the topic at hand (such as leadership, teamwork, cooperation, creative problem solving, etc.).
- You can even consider a word search in a foreign language, or with multiple languages for multicultural groups.

Where to Find It/How to Make It:

Create your own grid pattern. One suggestion is provided below. Be sure to print large enough for members of the group to be able to easily read the letters.

```
L E A D E R S H I P P R I T E A M W O R K
E N V I S I O N C O M M U N I C A T I O N
A E V I F H G I H K P E S K I L L S D W T
R R S L E E H W G N I N I A R T R A Z L D
N G C O N S E N S U S W Z L I S T E N K O
I Y A L P M A E T Q S M E Y B L U C K T R
N E C O O P E R A T I O N H A R D W O R K
G N I V L O S M E L B O R P M K S E P M S
```

Worms

It's the Little Things That Count

Here is a technique for having your say, without having to say a single word. Thanks to Dave Knobbe for this brilliant debriefing technique.

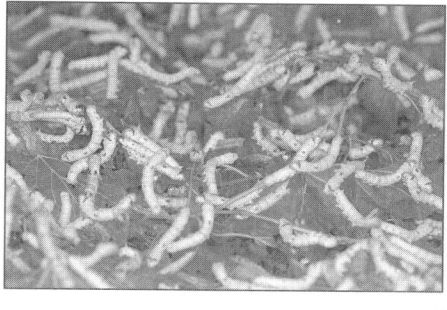

Contributor: Dave Knobbe, Wyman Center, St. Louis, Missouri.

Concepts: The reviewing that typically occurs at the completion of an adventure-based learning activity adds value to the activity and the program in total. In some cases, it is not easy to hear everyone's comments, but the facilitator may still wish to poll the feelings of the entire group. In other cases, some participants may mimic the answers of others, when the facilitator would like to hear each person's individual voice. Here is a simple technique that allows everyone's opinion to be registered, even if their voices are not necessarily heard.

This technique of instant voting encourages each person to form their own impression, and vote independently of others in the group. This can be helpful when peer pressure, corporate culture, or cultural norms impose on individual choice. In this case, participants do not wait to hear "how their friends are voting" but rather make up their own minds.

Props/Materials Needed: Colorful illustrations (traffic signs, weather conditions, thought and feeling cards, emotional faces, affirmation statements), and one short segment of rope or webbing about four to six inches long (which we call 'worms') for each person in the group.

Worms can also be used during the planning stages of a challenge activity, as a method of voting on various plans, techniques, or options. Have a few cards that have words like YES, NO, Agree, Disagree, Plan A, Plan B, Plan C, or even Continue Planning, Start Working.

Directions:

- Place the available illustrations visibly in front of the group, preferably on the ground.

- Give each participant a short piece of rope or webbing (a worm).

- On the count of three, invite everyone to toss their worm onto the illustration that they feel most accurately describes the performance of the group.

- Facilitators should protect the anonymity of group members and not say, "hey, who put a worm there?" Rather, they might say, "I see there is one worm on the 'continue planning' sign. Can you imagine why a person would choose that one?"

There isn't much better in this life than finding a way
to spend a few hours in conversation
with people you respect and love.
You have to carve this time out of your life
because you aren't really living without it.

Real Live Preacher, RealLivePreacher.com Weblog, August 27, 2003

X-Ray Vision

The Power to See Inside Others

While observers are commonly used in challenges and initiatives, why not utilize an observer with super-powers?

Concepts: One of the most interesting multiple intelligences to work with during an adventure-based learning program is the one dealing with gaining a knowledge, understanding or sense of empathy with another member of the group. This ability to work together is enhanced by practicing the skills that encourage this connection. In this case, X-Ray Vision encourages participants to not only observe the visible behaviors of other participants, but also to understand the motivation for their behavior. By sharing their impression of another's motivation and behavior, a door is opened to a greater understanding of each group member, and for everyone in the group.

Props/Materials Needed: A cool pair of glasses (with or without lenses), sunglasses, novelty glasses, safety glasses, goggles, or binoculars.

Directions:

- The facilitator asks for a volunteer to act in the role of observer for the next activity. The facilitator can provide the following information, or simply hand the glasses with the following instruction sheet to the observer.

X-Ray Vision—You have been provided with a unique pair of glasses, which it turns out, give you X-ray vision that allows you to see leadership, power, and what motivates behavior in the participants of your group. After assisting your group in completing this activity, you will be asked to share what you have witnessed during the completion of the task and your best guess as to the motivation of the group members during the activity.

Where to Find It/How to Make It:
Toy stores sell a variety of novelty glasses and oversized sunglasses. Vision centers may have older frames for sale. Hardware stores sell safety glasses that you can paint and decorate.

Education begins a gentleman, conversation completes him.

Dr. Thomas Fuller (1654 - 1734), Gnomologia, 1732

*It gets you nowhere if the other person's tail is
only just in sight for the second half of the conversation.*

Pooh's Little Instruction Book, inspired by A. A. Milne

Bibliography

Reference Books

A Manual for Group Facilitators, 1977, B. Auvine, B. Densmore, M. Extrom, S. Poole and M. Shanklin, The Center for Conflict Resolution, Madison, WI USA.

A Teachable Moment: A Facilitator's Guide to Activities for Processing, Debriefing and Reviewing, 2005, Jim Cain, Michelle Cummings and Jennifer Stanchfield, Kendall/Hunt Publishing Company, Dubuque, IA USA Adventure-based and active learning activities open the door for meaningful conversations about subjects and content that matters. Learn how to go beyond just the activities with more than 100 different tools. ISBN 0-7575-1782-X.

Activities That Teach, Tom Jackson, 1993, Red Rock Publishing, Cedar City, UT USA ISBN 0-916095-49-5.

Adventure Therapy: Therapeutic Applications of Adventure Programming. Gass, M. A. "The Evolution of Processing Adventure Therapy Experiences." Ed. M. A. Gass. Dubuque, IA: Kendall/Hunt Publishing Co., 1993.

All I Really Need to Knot I Learned In Kindergarten—15th Anniversary Edition 2003, Robert Fulghum, Ballantine Books, New York, NY USA ISBN 0-345-46617-9

Book of Metaphors—Volume II, 1995, Michael A. Gass, Kendall/Hunt Publishing Company, Dubuque, IA USA ISBN 0-7872-0306-8.

Connect: 12 Vital Ties That Open Your Heart, Lengthen Your Life, and Deepen Your Soul, 1999, Edward M. Hallowell, Pantheon Book, New York, NY ISBN 0–375–40357–4

Drawing on the Right Side of the Brain: A Course in Enhancing Creativity and Artistic Confidence. Edwards, Betty. Los Angeles, CA: Jeremy P. Tarcher, Inc., 1989. ISBN 0-87477-513-2

Effective Leadership in Adventure Programming. Priest, S., and M. A. Gass. Champaign, IL: Human Kinetics, 1997.

Executive Marbles and Other Teambuilding Activities, 1998, Sam Sikes, Learning Unlimited Publishers, Tulsa, OK USA ISBN 0-9646541-2-1.

Exploring the Five Stages of Group Formation Using Adventure-Based Activities, by Jim Cain, 2003, from the Teamwork & Teamplay website at: www.teamworkandteamplay.com

Facilitation at a Glance! A Pocket guide of Tools and Techniques for Effective Meeting Facilitation, 1999, Ingrid Bens, Association of Quality and Participation (AQP)/Participative Dynamics/GOAL/QPC, Cincinnati, OH USA ISBN 1-890416-05-3.

FISH!—A Remarkable Way to Boost Morale and Improve Results, 2000, Stephen Lundin, Harry Paul and John Christensen, Hyperion, New York, NY USA ISBN 0-7868-6602-0

FISH! Tales—Real-Life Stories to Help You Transform Your Workplace and Your Life, 2002, Stephen Lundin, John Christensen and Harry Paul, Hyperion, New York, NY USA ISBN 7868-6868-6*Flow: The Psychology of Optimal Experience,* 1990, Mihaly Csikszentmihalyi, Harper & Row, NY, NY USA ISBN 0-06-016253-8.

The Group Loop Activity Guide—22 Fun Group Activities That Enhance Community, Teamwork, Leadership and Creative Problem-Solving, by Tom Heck. Phone (828) 665–0303 www.tomheck.com

Hot Tips for Facilitators: Strategies to Make Life Easier for Anyone Who Leads, Guides, Teaches, or Trains Groups, 2003, Rob Abernathy and Mark Reardon, Zephyr Press, Tucson, AZ USA ISBN 1-56976-150-7.

Islands of Healing: A Guide to Adventure Based Counseling, 1988, Jim Schoel, Dick Prouty and Paul Radcliffe, Project Adventure, Inc. Hamilton, MA USA ISBN 0-934-38700-1.

Joining Together: Group Theory and Group Skills, 1994, David W. Johnson and Frank P. Johnson, Allyn and Bacon, Boston, MA USA ISBN 0-205-15846-3.

Lasting Lessons: A Teacher's Guide to Reflecting on Experience, 1992, Clifford E. Knapp, ERIC/CRESS Clearinghouse, Charleston, WV USA ERIC Document 348204.

Lines and Loops—Community Building Activities with Webbing, by Chris Cavert. Twenty-two pages of activities, illustrations and references. Phone (928) 526-6386 chris@fundoing.com   www.fundoing.com.

Little World: A Book About Tolerance, 2002, Joanna F. Carolan, Banana Patch Press. 1-800-914-5944 Hanapepe, HI, www.bananapatchpress.com.

Masterful Facilitation: Becoming a Catalyst for Meaningful Change, 1998, A. Glenn Kiser, Amacom, New York, NY USA ISBN 0-8144-0398-0.

More Activities That Teach, Tom Jackson, 1995, Red Rock Publishing, Cedar City, UT USA ISBN 0-916095-75-4.

More Than Activities, 1990, Roger Greenaway, Save the Children Fund, Glasgow, Scotland, UK ISBN 1-870322-21-5.

Multiple Intelligences in the Classroom, Thomas Armstrong, 2000, ASCD Alexandria, Virginia USA ISBN 0-87120-376-6 Probably the "best" book on using multiple intelligences. Easy to read and apply.

The Outward Bound Book of Readings, Outward Bound International, 1192 East Draper Parkway, Suite 322, Salt Lake City, Utah 84020 USA Email: obinternational@outward-bound.org.

Outward Bound USA—Learning Through Experience in Adventure-Based Education, 1981, Joshua Miner and Joe Boldt, William Morrow and Co., New York, NY USA ISBN 0-688-00414-8

Playback: A Guide to Reviewing Activities, Roger Greenaway and David Hilditch, 1993, The Duke of Edinburgh's Award with Endeavour Scotland, Edinburgh, UK ISBN 0-905425-09-X

Processing the Adventure Experience: Theory and Practice, 1992, Reldan S. Nadler and John L. Luckner, Kendall/Hunt Publishing Company, Dubuque, IA USA ISBN 0-8403-7028-8.

Processing the Experience: Strategies to Enhance and Generalize Learning, 1997, John L. Luckner and Reldan S. Nadler, Kendall/Hunt Publishing Company, Dubuque, IA USA ISBN 0-7872-1000-5.

Quicksilver: Adventure Games, Initiative Problems, Trust Activities and a Guide to Effective Leadership, 1995, Karl Rohnke and Steve Butler, Kendall/Hunt Publishing Company, Dubuque, IA USA ISBN 0-7872-2103-1.

Reconsidered, Revised and Expanded with Twenty-Five New Essays. Who Moved My Cheese, 1998, Spencer Johnson, G. P. Putnam's Sons, New York, NY USA ISBN 0-399-14446-3

Reflective Learning: Theory and Practice, 2000, Deborah Sugerman, Kathryn Doherty, Daniel Garvey and Michael Gass, Kendall/Hunt Publishing Company, Dubuque, IA USA ISBN 0-7872-6561-6.

Reviewing Adventures: Why and How? 1996, Roger Greenaway, Published by the National Association for Outdoor Education (NAOE) Sheffield, UK ISBN 1-898555-01-X.

Shouting at the Sky—Troubled Teens and the Promise of the Wild, 1999, Gary Ferguson, St. Martin's Press, New York, NY USA ISBN 0-312-20008-0

Still More Activities That Teach, Tom Jackson, 2000, Red Rock Publishing, Cedar City, UT USA ISBN 0-9664633-5-8.

Teaching with the Brain in Mind, 1998, Eric Jensen, ASCD, Alexandria, VA USA ISBN 0-87120-299-9.

Teambuilding Puzzles—100 Puzzles for Creating Teachable Moments in Creative Problem Solving, Consensus Building, Group Decision Making, Goal Setting, Communication and Teamwork, 2005, Mike Anderson, Jim Cain, Chris Cavert and Tom Heck, FunDoing Publishing, AZ USA.

Teamwork & Teamplay, 1998, Jim Cain and Barry Jolliff, Kendall/Hunt Publishing Company, Dubuque, IA USA ISBN 0-7872-4532-1.

The Appreciative Facilitator: A Handbook for Facilitators and Teachers, 2001, Cheri B. Torres, MTC, Maryville, TN USA ISBN 0-9714416-0-X.

The Art of Facilitation: How to Create Group Synergy, 1995, Dale Hunter, Anne Bailey and Bill Taylor, Fisher Books, Tucson, AZ USA ISBN 1-55561-101-X.

The Bottomless Bag—Again! 1993, Karl Rohnke, Kendall/Hunt Publishing Company, Dubuque, IA USA ISBN 0-8403-8757-1.

The Book of Answers, 1999, Carol Bolt, Hyperion, NY, NY USA ISBN 0-7868-6566-0.

The Book on Raccoon Circles, 2002, Jim Cain and Tom Smith, Learning Unlimited Publishers, Tulsa, OK USA ISBN 0-9646541-6-4.

The Conscious Use of Metaphor in Outward Bound, 1983, Stephen B. Bacon, Colorado Outward Bound School, Denver, CO .

The Essential Elements of Facilitation, 2000, Simon Priest, Mike Gass, and Lee Gillis, TARRACK Technologies, ISBN 1-932298-02-9.

The Facilitator's Fieldbook, 1999, Thomas Justice and David Jamieson, Amacom, New York, NY USA ISBN 0-8144-7038-6.

The Skilled Facilitator: Practical Wisdom for Developing Effective Groups, 1994, Roger M. Schwarz, Jossey-Bass, San Francisco, CA USA ISBN 1-55542-638-7.

The Value of Connection in the Workplace: You Can be the Catalyst for Building Community and Creating a Positive Environment in your Corporation, 2006, Jim Cain and Kirk Weisler.

Who Moved My Cheese? An A-Mazing Way to Deal with Change in Your Work and in Your Life, 1998, Spencer Johnson, G. P. Putnam's Sons. New York, NY USA ISBN 0-399-1446-3.

Proceedings, Periodical and Journal Articles

Action Learning and Groupware Technologies: A Case Study in GSS Facilitation Research, Pak Yoong and Brent Gallupe, *Information Technology & People,* Volume 14, Issue 1, 2001, page 78+.

Alternative Methodologies for Processing the Adventure Experience, Thomas E. Smith, 1986, Raccoon Institute, Cazenovia, WI 53924.

A Model for Debriefing Experience, Simon Priest and Mindee Naismith, *Journal of Adventure Education and Outdoor Leadership,* Volume 10, Number 3, Fall 1993, pages 16–18.

A Model of Group Initiative Facilitation Training (G.I.F.T.), Simon Priest, *Outdoor Communicator,* Volume 20, Number 1, Fall/Winter 1988/89, pages 8–13.

Changing Perspectives on Facilitation Skills Development, M. Berry, *Journal of European Industrial Training,* Volume 17, Number 3, 1993, pages 23–32.

Comments on Facilitator Competencies, R.M.Schwarz, *Group Facilitation,* Volume 2, Number 2, 2000, pages 33–34.

Competencies of Small Group Facilitators: What Practitioners View as Important, Judith A. Kolb and William J. Rothwell, *Journal of European Industrial Training,* Volume 26, Number 2–4, 2002, pages 200–203.

Designing Processing Questions to Meet Specific Objectives, Clifford E. Knapp, *Journal of Experiential Education,* Volume 7, Number 2, 1984, pages 47–49.

Developmental Sequence of Small Groups, by B. Tuckman, 1965, *Psychological Bulletin,* Number 63, pages 384–399. The "original" article on the stages of group formation.

Developing and Supporting Creative Problem-Solving Teams: Part I—A Conceptual Model, Elspeth McFadzean, *Management Decision,* Volume 40, Number 5, 2002, pages 463–475.

Developing and Supporting Creative Problem-Solving Teams: Part II—Facilitator Competencies, Elspeth McFadzean, *Management Decision,* Volume 40, Number 6, 2002, pages 537–551.

Developmental Sequence in Small Groups, Bruce W. Tuckman, *Group Facilitation,* Number 3, Spring 2001, pages 66–81. An interesting follow-up article to his classic stages of group formation article nearly 40 years ago.

Examining the Learning Process Used in Adventure Education, Scott Wurdinger, *Journal of Adventure Education and Outdoor Leadership,* Volume 11, Number 3, Fall 1994, pages 25–27.

Facilitating Problem Solving Groups: A Conceptual Model, E.S. McFadzean and T. Nelson, *Leadership and Organization Development Journal,* Volume 19, Number 1, 1998, pages 6–13.

Facilitating Team Development: A View from the Field, John E. Jones and William L. Bearley, *Group Facilitation,* Number 3, Spring 2001, pages 56–65.

Facilitating the Challenge in Adventure Recreation for Persons with Disabilities, J. Dattilo and W. D. Murphy, *Therapeutic Recreation Journal,* Volume 21, Number 3, 1987, pages 14–21.

Facilitation Excellence: Styles and Processes of Facilitation, J. Van Maurick, *Leadership and Organizational Development Journal,* Volume 15, Number 8, 1994, pages 30–34.

Facilitators: One Key Factor in Implementing Successful Experience-Based Training and Development Programs, Richard J. Wagner and Christopher C. Roland, *Coalition for Education in the Outdoors Research Symposium Proceedings,* Bradford Woods, January 17–19, 1992.

Five Steps to Better Processing, Steve Simpson, Buzz Bocher and Dan Miller, Association for Challenge Course Technology (ACCT) Pre-Conference Workshop Proceedings, January 24, 2002.

Group Development: A Review of the Literature and a Commentary on Future Research Directions, George Smith, *Group Facilitation,* Number 3, Spring 2001, pages 14–45.

Group Facilitating, Doug Miller, *Camping Magazine,* Volume 67, Number 5, May/June 1995, pages 28–32.

How to Design a Debriefing Session, H. Hammel, *Journal of Experiential Education,* Volume 9, Number 3, 1986, pages 20–25.

How to Process Experience, L. K. Quinsland and A. Van Ginkel, National Technical Institute for the Deaf, Rochester Institute of Technology, Rochester, NY, USA *Journal of Experiential Education,* Volume 7, Number 2, 1984, pages 8–13.

Issues and Concerns About Computer-Supported Meetings: The Facilitator's Perspective, F. Niederman, C. M. Beise, and P. M. Beranek, *MIS Quarterly,* Number 20, 1996, pages 1–22.

Journal Writing in Experiential Education: Possibilities, Problems, and Recommendations, Janet E. Dyment and Timothy S. O'Connell, *ERIC Digest,* September 2003, EDO-RC-03-5.

Leader Behaviors Affecting Team Performance: Similarities and differences between leader/member assessments, Judith A. Kolb, *Journal of Business Communication,* Volume 32, 1995, pages 233–248.

Lead Line: Facilitation Through Online Scripting, Jennifer H. Landau. Harry Chesley, Suzana Seban, Lili Cheng and Shelly Farnham, *Group Facilitation,* Number 5, Spring 2003, page 37–49.

Lessons From Skateboarders, Richard Sagor, Educational Leadership, September 2002, pages 34–38. What motivates young people to master the challenges of sports? How can we inspire the same level of motivation in our classrooms?

Participants' Perceptions on the Role of Facilitators Using Group Decision Support Systems, F. Ackermann, *Journal of Group Decision and Negotiation,* Volume 5, 1996, pages 93–112.

Protecting Adolescents from Harm: Findings from the National Longitudinal Study on Adolescent Health, Resnick, Bearman, Blum, Bauman, et.al., *JAMA,* September 10, 1997, Volume 278, Issue 10, pages 823–832.

Reflection Re-Examined: A Hard Look at a Sacred Cow, Clifford E. Knapp, *Proceedings of the 22nd Annual AEE Conference,* Austin, Texas, November 1994, pages 289–293.

Stages of Small Group Development Revisited, B. Tuckman and M. Jensen, 1977, *Group and Organizational Studies,* Number 2, pages 419–427. The revised and updated article.

Teaching Facilitation: A Play in Three Acts, Suzanne C. de Janasz, *Journal of Management Education,* Volume 25, Number 6, December 2001, pages 685–712.

Team and Organisational Learning in a Cross-Functional Community of Practice: The Importance of Privileging Voices, Ed. B. Peile and Wendy Briner, *Career Development International,*
Volume 6, number 7, 2001, pages 396–402.

The Art of Reviewing, Roger Greenaway, *Journal of the Institute of Training and Occupational Learning,* Volume 3, Number 1, pages 47–53. ISSN 1469-977X
http://www.traininginstitute. co.uk/itoljournalf.htm.

The Effects of Facilitation, Recording, and Pauses on Group Brainstorming, A.K. Offner, T.J. Kramer and J.P. Winter, *Small Group Research,* Volume 27, 1996, pages 383–398.

Theories, Practices and Benefits of Debriefing in Outdoor Education, Mark Brackenreg, *Journal of Outdoor Education,* Volume 26, 1993, pages 3–11.

The National Longitudinal Study on Adolescent Health: Preliminary Results: Great Expectations, Klein, *JAMA,* September 10, 1997, Volume 278, Issue 10, pages 864–865.

The Role of the Facilitator in Computer-Supported Meetings, V.K.Clawson, R.P.Bostrom and R. Anson, *Small Group Research*, Number 24, 1993, pages 547–565.

The Supervisor as a Facilitator of Informal Learning in Work Teams, Christina Macneil, *Journal of Workplace Learning*, Volume 13, Number 6, 2001, pages 246–253.

Thinking in Outdoor Inquiry, Clifford E. Knapp, August 1992, *ERIC Digest* EDO-RC-92–3, ERIC Document ED 348198.

What Do We Mean By Facilitation?, Brian Auvine, Betsy Densmore, Mary Extrom, Scott Poole, and Michael Shanklin, *Group Facilitation*, Number 4, Spring 2002, Pages 53–55.

Why Did We Do That? How to Process Teambuilding Games, Tom Heck, *Leadership for Student Activities*, May 2004, pages 12–14.

Writing Activities: A Primer for Outdoor Educators, Alan Brew, *ERIC Digest*, June 2003, EDO-RC-03-1.

With the gift of listening comes the gift of healing.

Catherine de Hueck

Collections of Reviewing Activities by Category

Some of Our Favorite Activities by Category

Occasionally you may want to group debriefing activities by specific categories, creating your own list of favorites. Here is a brief collection of powerful reviewing activities that explore each of the following themes.

For additional information on Reviewing Activities sorted by Category see the section titled Organization of Activities in this book. (See page 35.)

Multiple Intelligence Theory

Mathematical (Quantification): Voice Mail, Timing is Everything
Kinesthetic (Movement): Buzz Ring, Raccoon Circles, WAMF, Knot Race, Raccoon Circles Lots of Knots, Random Ricochet, Concentric Circles
Visual (Artistic): Chiji Cards, Weather Signs, Image Chips
Linguistic (Speech): Alphabet Blocks, Having My Say, Word Search, Journaling
Musical (Rhythm): Rap Song, Making Music
Interpersonal (Knowing Others): Partner Watch, X-Ray Vision, Concentric Circles, Circle of Kindness
Intrapersonal (Knowing Self): Balloon Faces, Journaling, Group Juggling Drawing, Solo Experience.
Natural World (Environmental): Sticks in a Bundle

Processing and the Five Stages of Group Formation

Forming: Comfortable Conversation Starters, Rounds, Domino Debrief, Concentric Circles
Storming: Having My Say, Fear in a Hat, Metaphoric Cards, Tool Cards
Norming: Feeling Cards, Web of Commitment
Performing: Chiji Cards, Efficiency and Effectiveness
Transforming: A Circle of Kindness, Bead Ceremony

Verbal Communication and Discussion

Circle of Kindness, Concentric Circles, Conversation Cards, Creating Available Space, Having My Say, Dominoes, Voice Mail

Giving and Receiving Feedback

Dinner Notes, Half Time Review, High 5, I would like to thank, Later Letters, Shuffle Left, Shuffle Right

Shorter Debriefing Sessions

Concentric Circles, Creating Available Space, One Word Whip, Virtual Slideshow

Non-Verbal Techniques

Bucketful of Ideas, Group Drawing, Racoon Cirlce Elevation

Athletics

Full Court Press, Half Time Review

Personal Contact

Masks, Shuffle Right, Shuffle Left

Goal Setting

Goals in Motion,, Metaphoric Methods, What I Know, Jars

Humorous and Fun

I Would Like to Thank, Group Drawing, Rap Song, Thought Balloons

Younger Audiences

Chiji Cards, Treasure Chest, Metaphoric Methods of all kinds, Artistic Expression Activities including Group Drawing, Drawing as Journal Assignments, Debriefing Tic Tac Toe, Butterfly Life Cycle, Balloon Faces

Small Groups

Metaphor Cards, Treasure Chest, Body Part Bag, Masks, Stones, Racoon Circles, Group Drawing, Journaling and Solo Experiences, Puzzles, Crystal Clear

Closing Activities

Shuffle Left, Shuffle Right, Concentric Circles, Circle of Kindess, Chiji Card—Three Card Story, and Stones

Opening Activities

Comfortable Conversation Starters—Concentric Circles, Dominoes

Search Institute Developmental Assets

Search Institute's 40 Developmental Assets are concrete, common sense, positive experiences and qualities essential to raising successful young people. These assets have the power during critical adolescent years to influence choices young people make and help them become caring, responsible adults.

The following activities refer to what Developmental Asset they are appropriate for. The numbers below refer to the specific Developmental Asset.

 2   Family Communication: Comfortable Conversatoin Starters, Dinner Notes
 4   Caring Neighborhood: Nearly all of the activities in this book
15   Postive Peers: Partner Watch
16   High Expectations: Having My Say, Goals in Motion
17   Creative Athletics: Random Ricochet, Buzz Ring
18   Youth Programs: Nearly all of the activities in this book
25   Reading for Pleasure: Journaling, Reflective Readings, Team Resume
26   Caring: Feeling Cards, Friendship Bracelets
34   Cultural Competence: Metaphor Cards, Multicultural Expressions
36   Conflict Resolution: Fears in a Hat
37   Personal Power: Magical Box, Journaling
38   Self-Esteem: Clothes Line, Dinner Notes
39   Sense of Purpose: Later Letters, Dinner Notes, Clothes Line
40   Positive View: Virtual Slideshow

For more information about Developmental Assets go to www.search-institute.org.

Jim's Favorites

Virtual Slide Show, Processing Cube, Traffic Signs and Worms, Raccoon Circles, Partner Watch, I Would Like to Thank . . . , Chiji Cards, Shuffle Left—Shuffle Right, and A Circle of Kindness

Michelle's Favorites

Body Part Debrief, Buzz Ring, Pocket Processor, Virtual Slide Show, Processing Cube, All My Neighbors Who, Puzzles, Index Card Castles, and Masks.

Jennifer's Favorites

Journaling, Treasure Chest-Mini, Chiji Cards, Group Juggle Metaphor, Concentric Circles, Postcards, Stones, Group Drawing, Body Parts Debrief, and Shuffle Left Shuffle Right.

A Note of Thanks

No doubt you have noticed, as you read through the pages of this book, that we have been the fortunate recipients of great ideas shared by our friends and fellow facilitators. One of the most outstanding features of the experiential education world is the unique and generous sharing that goes on between members of this field. We are grateful to every person who has allowed us to share their unique insights and their wonderful ideas for exploring processing, debriefing, reviewing and reflection.

In every way we could imagine, we have attempted to thoroughly research the origins and creators of the activities in this book. To the best of our ability, we have tried to credit those who deserve recognition for their contributions.

If, after reading this book, you are aware of any activity for which we have not yet given an appropriate reference or credit, it would be our pleasure to correct this situation in the next printing of the book. Please direct any information you have related to appropriate crediting to Michelle Cummings at michelle@training-wheels.com. We also

enjoy hearing from you about your usage of the activities in this book. Please tell us your stories, tales and experiences with the audiences you serve. And, if you happen to create a new debriefing activity that you would like to share with the world, send us a photo and activity description. If we use it in a future publication, we will send you a copy of that book.

Sincerely,
Jim, Michelle and Jen

The best rules to form a young man, are,
to talk little, to hear much,
to reflect alone upon what has passed in company,
to distrust one's own opinions, and value others that deserve it.

Sir W. Temple

Contact the Authors

Individually Jim Cain, Michelle Cummings and Jennifer Stanchfield have three lifetimes worth of experience in facilitation, education and training. Collectively, they can fill an entire conference worth of keynote speaches, pre-conference workshops, hands-on conference sessions, evening programs and more.

For more information about the authors, check out the biography section of this book. For conference appearances, staff development workshops, customized teambuilding programs, educational classes, and especially their unique and outstanding train-the-trainer workshops, please contact them directly at:

Jim Cain
Teamwork & Teamplay
468 Salmon Creek Road
Brockport, NY 14420 USA
Phone (585) 637-0328
jimcain@teamworkandteamplay.com
www.teamworkandteamplay.com

Michelle Cummings
Training Wheels, Inc.
Owner/Trainer/Big Wheel
7095 South Garrison Street
Littleton, CO 80128 USA
888-553-0147 phone
303-979-1708 phone
888-553-0146 fax
michelle@training-wheels.com
michmc3@aol.com

Jennifer Stanchfield
High 5 Adventure Learning Center
130 Austine Drive
Brattleboro, VT 05301 USA
877-356-4445 phone
802-251-7203 fax
j.stanchfield@high5adventure.org

For more information visit www.ateachablemoment.com

The real art of conversation is not only to say the right thing at the right place but to leave unsaid the wrong thing at the tempting moment.

Dorothy Nevill

About the Authors

Jim Cain

Dr. Jim Cain is the author of five adventure-based teambuilding texts, including *Teamwork & Teamplay,* which received the Karl Rohnke Creativity Award presented by the Association for Experiential Education (AEE), *The Book on Raccoon Circles, A Teachable Moment, Teambuilding Puzzles,* and *The Value of Connection—In the Workplace.* He is the owner and creative force behind Teamwork & Teamplay—The Adventure-Based Training Company, Senior Consultant for the Cornell University Corporate Teambuilding Program, and a former Executive Director for the Association for Challenge Course Technology (ACCT). Jim makes his home in Brockport, New York. He holds four engineering degrees, including a Ph.D. in Mechanical Engineering from the University of Rochester. Dr. Cain frequently serves as a visiting professor on subjects ranging from experiential education using adventure-based activities to corporate leadership, recreational dancing and games leadership, and from structural engineering and chaos theory to powder mechanics. In the past five years, he has presented programs and workshops in 38 states and nine countries, and generally has more toys and a library of adventure-based books larger than that of many developing nations. Jim presents nearly 120 programs each

year on a variety of teambuilding, staff training and community building topics, for audiences ranging from summer camp counselors to graduate level coursework to corporate executives. Visit the Teamwork and Teamplay website for more information.

Jim Cain, Ph.D.
Teamwork & Teamplay
468 Salmon Creek Road
Brockport, NY 14420 USA
Phone (585) 637-0328
Email: jimcain@teamworkandteamplay.com
Website: www.teamworkandteamplay.com

Michelle Cummings

Michelle is the Big Wheel and creator of her business, Training Wheels Inc. Training Wheels is a known leader in the portable, adventure equipment industry and prides itself in creating quality, affordable activities, books and training for those seeking experiential resources. Michelle has created a wide variety of facilitation, debriefing and reviewing activities that have collectively changed the way adventure-based educators and trainers work. She has facilitated a wide variety of programs, from therapeutic populations, corporate and school groups, to train-the-trainer programs for professionals. Visit the Training Wheels web site for more information about these programs. Michelle has her Bachelor's degree in Psychology from Kansas State University and her Master's degree in Experiential Education from Minnesota State University at Mankato. Michelle actively seeks and/or creates new processing activities to enhance her processing workshops and to provide new resources

for facilitators. Michelle has authored two books, *A Teachable Moment* and *Bouldering Games for Kids* (an educational guide for traverse walls). Michelle grew up on a farm in Norton, Kansas and currently lives in Littleton, Colorado with her husband, Paul, and two sons, Dawson and Dylan.

Michelle Cummings
Owner/Trainer/Big Wheel
7095 South Garrison Street
Littleton, CO 80128
888-553-0147 phone
303-979-1708 phone
888-553-0146 fax

michelle@training-wheels.com
michmc3@aol.com
www.training-wheels.com

Jennifer Stanchfield

Jennifer Stanchfield of High 5 Adventure Learning Center, a certified recreational therapist and educator, is a leader in the field of challenge course facilitation training. Jen has developed and directed experiential based programming for audiences ranging from elementary school students to corporate executives. She professionally trains challenge course facilitators and develops facilitation skills programs for adventure practitioners in a variety of settings nationally. Jen is known internationally for her work in developing innovative and engaging ways to process adventure experiences. She is

creator of the "Adventures In Learning and Teaching Program," focused on helping school based adventure programs increase their effectiveness, sustainability, and quality through curriculum development and teacher training and support. Jen has a degree in recreational therapy from the University of New Hampshire and a Master's Degree in Experiential Education from Minnesota State University, Mankato.

Jennifer Stanchfield
High 5 Adventure Learning Center
130 Austine Drive
Brattleboro, VT 05301
877-356-4445 phone
802-251-7203 fax

jstanchfield@high5adventure.org

For more information

visit

www.ateachablemoment.com

Index

DATE DUE

5/6/10			
6/17/12			
3/16/13			